First published by the Howard R. Egan Estate, Richmond, Utah, 1917, and has now entered the public domain.

ISBN 13: 978-1-59955-040-4

Published by Council Press, an imprint of Cedar Fort, Inc.
2373 W. 700 S., Springville, UT, 84663
Distributed by Cedar Fort, Inc., www.cedarfort.com

Printed in the United States of America

10 9 8 7 6 5 4 3 2 1

Printed on acid-free paper

PIONEERING
THE WEST
1846 to 1878

MAJOR HOWARD EGAN'S DIARY

ALSO

Thrilling Experiences of Pre-
Frontier Life Among Indians;
Their Traits, Civil and Savage,
and Part of A u t o b i o g r a p h y,
Inter - Related to His Father's,
BY   HOWARD   R.   EGAN

Edited, Compiled, and Connected
In Nearly Chronological Order
BY   .   .   .   Wm.   M.   EGAN

ILLUSTRATED

Published by
HOWARD R. EGAN ESTATE
Richmond, Utah
1917

DEDICATED TO
THE EGAN FAMILY
Their Friends
and All Interested in the Work
of the
Pioneers of the West

Press of
SKELTON PUBLISHING CO.
Salt Lake City, Utah

Major Howard Egan, Author of the Diaries of Pioneering the West, Trail Blazer of the Overland Route, Pony Express and Overland Mail Agent. Captain of 50s with Mormon Exodus, Special Messenger for Mormon Battalion 1846, Capt. 9th Ten of the Original 144 Pioneers, made three trips to Salt Lake from the States, and innumerable trips to California on three or more routes.

*Preface

THERE is always a degree of interest in the pioneering of any locality in which one lives; and as time goes on, more importance and interest is attached to it.

When a great inter-mountain commonwealth grows up and develops in a few short years, the memory of those hardy pioneers, who were the first to make possible such progress, are looked upon with greater interest as the years go by and the records of all who took an important part are sought after.

It was well known by all who were in any way acquainted with Major Egan that his life work, if written, would make a remakably interesting book provided the information could be obtained. Neither himself or family were of a literary turn of mind, and hence much that would be of great interest was never committed to paper. During his life time no thought was ever given to anything of a literary nature.

The family all knew that Father (as Mother and all the family called him) had a private desk packed full of papers, but that any of them had any thing of value more than private correspondence none of the family knew. Even at the time of his death (1878) no attempt was made to exmine his papers and see if there was anything worthy of preservation until Mother died (1905) which took place some twenty seven years after. At the time of her death this writer was on a mission to the Eastern States and was unable to return until after the funeral and the old home had been ransacked ready to be pulled down when he returned.

Howard R. Egan, the principal writer of the latter part of the book looked over Father's desk and took home with him what he judged might be interesting to read over when he got home. The rest were scattered over the floor and later the house was pulled down. In looking over the papers Howard got interested and having plenty of time on his hands, not being able to walk or work much, and he read and re-wrote Father's entire Diary of the Pioneer trip nearly as we have put it in type, also some other trips that were in diary form. This was necessary on account of the difficulty of reading the fine writing, which is shown in fac-simile exact size on page 110.

The interest in the matter began to grow and correspondence with this writer met with sufficient encouragement and help so the manuscript was typewritten ready for the press. Later some incidents that Howard was so familiar with were written and his family was desirous of having them preserved and they were also typewritten. The work having been done by this writer as also the compiling and editing for the press.

The value of this book lies in its strict adherence to truth, and fidelity to fact. First of all it is the story of eye-witnesses and it often touches the story and romance of the mountains. One of its missions will be to preserve the real spirit of Pioneering the Great West, and the commencement of the first enterprises, which were only the forerunner of greater things. Many of the events protrayed in this volume are as fascinating as any in all history. The events had their dangers and some- times ended in tragedy.

Our desire is to awaken an interest with old-timers, and those who have descended from Pioneer stock, as well as all those, who are in any way concerned in the early development of this western and inter-mountain country, to show the hardships, difficulties and the toil that it took to open up the way, and the resolution, determination and untiring efforts put forth by those ''Pilgrim Fathers'' that were driven from their homes by mobs and forced to hunt a new home for themselves and those who followed after.

The Diary, in the First Part, is corroberative of other writers, but it also contains many things not mentioned by any one and not likely to be given any where else. All the writing in Diary form was taken from Major Howard Egan's old Diaries just as he penned them as near as practical, preserving the diction intact. The writing of the compiler and editor are preceeded by a star*. All the rest of the writing except as credit is given not in diary form and not starred were written by H. R. Egan, whose brief preface is as follows:

''Some of my children and brothers have expressed the wish that I write some of my earliest recollections and on up to date. Well, I am now over seventy-five years old and have a good memory. It would take a long time to tell all I can remember, and, if printed would make a good many volumes. So I will necessarily have to be brief on many events as I come to them. I shall not pretend to give these few sketches of Pioneer life in routine or give dates as to when they happened as I am not writing from any memorandum but just as I remember them.''—H. R. Egan.

At first it was intended to print only Father's Diaries, about 200 pages of about 250 words in larger type, but when Howard R got his writings together it was decided to select smaller type. Then we wanted the engravings to come in the proper places so a smooth thin paper was selected. In discussing about this Howard R. wrote as follows:

''The trend of modern times is to utilize and conserve space, which becomes more valuable as time passes. This is the case in all kinds of human endeavor, whether in agriculture or in the mechanical arts, effi- ciency, durability, space and cost are all considered.

But in ''cheap John'' affairs the first two don't count and only the last is reckoned with. As in books, to use very thick paper, very large type and leave great marginal space at each side of pages, besides having the subjects, put in a great number of paragraphs, any thing to eat up space and spread a little over enough thick paper to make the desired thickness, and the number of pages. Then sometimes, to make amends put on a cover that is quite attractive and frequently costing more than the rest of the book—unwise and expensive.

''Multum in Parvo'' suits the intelligent person best, and this is what we cater to. A book of 200 pages of 250 words each, and another of 500 words each is worth one-half more, if the contents are only of the same value. But this again has a great deal to do with the price.

We are offering a book that is not built to catch the eye, but is presentable and durable. We are offering a book that contains valuable information not printed in any other book or form. We are offering a book that contains no fiction, but is the actual experiences and personal views of the writers. We are offering a book that we think should be very interesting to those seeking Pioneer History. We are offering a book that will become more valuable as time passes, for a reminder of frontier life. We are offering a book that takes less space than most books on the market, yet with good readable type. We are offering a book at a lower price, considering the contents, than the price of the same sized book.''

These were the last words of the publisher, H. R. Egan, written just before his death, which occurred in March 1916, but were not found until after the funeral. These words stand for the truth and the book itself supports the statements.

The book is not written from a religious nor scientific standpoint; nor is it written in poise of a hero, ostentation or self praise, but is simple in style and diction. No effort, either, has been made to change it from the original writings. Perusal of the book illustrates how close to the exact fact it adheres, and that no embelishments of story or fiction is introduced, although there is ample opportunity to picture the circumstances in that manner, and still it often runs into startling episodes of the mountains and plains and thrilling experiences which often ended in tragedy. The book is divided into four parts.

The stereotyped form of chapters is avoided, the four parts above referred to being each divided into sections as the classifications could be made and yet preserve their natural and chronological order. Other divisions are made in all about seventy-five articles or headings numbered consecutively, with some few sub-headings.

The conclusion brings the closing incidents down to a recent date and finishes in brief the biography of Major Howard Egan and his son, Howard R. Egan, as well as a brief account of his other sons, his progenitors and the family tree of his descendents.

The statement in the conclusion that four of Mother's children were alive was true when that was written, but was overlooked in the proof although it was stated in a previous paragraph when Howard R. died.

The Appendix deals with genealogy and makes a connecting link, by the aid of an old Irish Chart, from Adam to the stem of the Egan Family.

We now commit to each reader the facts, faith, and experiences that attended the trips of the Pioneers; also thrill'ng experiences of pre-frontier life and stories of the habits, customs and character of Indian life by one who knew their language and was well acquainted with them, and knew how to deal with them. To all it will be a pleasure to know the situations, thoughts and experiences of eye-witnesses and be able to see some things as they were in early days. We are indebted to the Improvement Era for many of the engraving used and we are thankful for the use of same. We continue to find many things that should have been said in this book but its limits has required us to make all statements as brief as possible consistent with proper explanation in order to preserve what has been written by Father and brother Howard R. Egan.

THE COMPILER AND EDITOR.

Contents.

PART 1.

PIONEERING: NAUVOO TO SALT LAKE.

		Page				Page
Introduction		9	8.	Platt River Crossings		62
Sec. I.	Nauvoo to Winter Quarters		9.	Rocky Mountains		91
2.	Mormon Exodus	13	Sec. III.	What was Done		103
3.	Trip to Santa Fe	15	10.	Work at Salt Lake		114
4.	The Pioneers, A Poem	17	11.	Meeting the Trains		134
5.	Original Band of 144	18	Sec. IV.	Second Trip		138
6.	Howard Egan's Diary	21	12.	Winter Quarters		138
Sec. II.	Details of Trip	21	13.	On to Salt Lake		140
7.	Laramie Plains	32	14.	Scenes By The Way		141

PART II.

SALT LAKE: INCIDENTS OF EARLY SETTLEMENT.

Sec. I.	Our Home Life	147	21.	The Indian Portrait	155
15.	The Old Fort	147		Deep Snow—Freezing	155
16.	Our New Home	148	Sec. III.	Stories of Salt Lake	160
17.	Grasshoppers and Crickets	150	22.	The Cold Swim	160
18.	Another Home	151	23.	Setting Gun for Bear	161
19.	Burning of the Barn	152	24.	The Hornets	163
Sec. II.	Relics	155	25.	The Stampede is Stopped	164
20.	Indian Mounds	155	26.	Taby We-Pup	166

PART III.

PIONEERING: SALT LAKE TO CALIFORNIA.

Sec. I.	Route South, and North	169	Sec. III.	Central Route	202
27.	A Diary, 1849 to 1850	169	36.	Getting Rid of an Indian	202
28.	Tecumsee	182	37.	A Run For Life	203
29.	Indian Snake Eating	187	38.	Tracking Stolen Mules	205
30.	The Sleeping Mule	188	39.	Changing Camp After Dark	207
31.	A Fearful Fall	190	40.	My Three Day's Fast	208
Sec. II.	The Central Route	193	41.	Mail Carrier	211
32.	A Ten Day's Trip	193	42.	Father's Indian Doctor	216
33.	Finding the Egan Trail	194	43.	A Trip to Ruby Valley	217
34.	Pony Express—Stations	198	44.	Short Line Cut Off	220
35.	Deep Creek	201	45.	Irrigation	222

PART IV.

THRILLING EXPERIENCES OF PRE-FRONTIER LIFE.

Sec. I.	Indian Practice	226	Sec. IV.	Indian Cruelties	251
46.	A Little Surprise	226	60.	Old Indian Left to Die	251
47.	Lasso Practice	227	61.	How Bill Got His Wife	252
48.	Eating Ants	228	62.	The Cross Indian	254
49.	Indian Cricket Drive	230	63.	The Indian Outbreak	256
50.	Trapping A Coyote	233	64.	Burning of Canyon Station	263
Sec. II.	Hunting, Harvesting	235	65.	Jessie Earl's Death	264
51.	A Rabbit Drive	235	66.	The Indian, No Legs	265
52.	Mountain Rat Food	237	67.	Playful Goats	267
53.	The Antelope Drive	238	68.	Wagon Going No Team	268
54.	Pine-Nut Harvest	241	69.	The Dog Pompy	269
55.	Hunting for Water	242	70.	Wild Pets	272
56.	Squaws Catching Moles	245	71.	The Sand Hill Cranes	274
Sec. III.	Hard Experiences	248	72.	Indian Story of Great Cave	273
57.	Saved by a Rabbit	248	73.	Express Rider's Experience	280
59.	Around a Bush all Night	249	74.	Unpleasant Experiences	280
58.	Lost and Found	248	75.	Conclusion	282

APPENDIX.

Genealogy		285	Howard Egan's Travel in 1849	298
Pedigree of Howard Egan		289	The Egan Family Organization	300
rish Hitsory		297	Articles of Agreement	301

LIST OF ENGRAVINGS

Major Howard Egan........Frontispiece
W. M. Egan 8
Irish Home Birth Place. 10
Howard Ransom Egan 12
S. F. Kimball................................ 16
On the Way.................................. 20
Gathering on the Elk Horn........ 22
Prairie Burned Over................... 34
Buffalo 41
Indians Near Laramie 49
Buffalo Hunt................................ 51
Brigham Young............................ 52
Top O'the Rockies........................ 67
Stream from Tunnel.................... 70
Mountain Lake............................ 71
Ready to Move from Camp........ 82
Corn for Jim Bridger.................. 88
Indian Encampment..................... 93
Aspen Forest................................ 100
Result of Irrigation..................... 105
Heber C. Kimball......................... 106
Facsimile of Diary....................... 110
First House Built in Salt Lake 117
Dave Kimball and Wife............. 137
Chimney Rock............................... 143
Camping at Echo......................... 144
Native and Ensign Peak............ 146

Salt Lake Temple........................ 149
Upper Main Street, 1860........... 153
Gov. Cumming's Recommend...... 156
Amunition from H. Egan............ 157
News and Tithing Offices........... 158
Brigham Young and Brothers..... 165
Growth of Salt Lake City.......... 166
Jebow and Squaw........................ 168
Cactus and Fencing..................... 177
Washikee, Peace Chief.............. 184
Kanosh Pavant Chief.................. 186
First Salt Lake Store.................. 191
Pony Express............................... 199
Deep Creek Ranch....................... 201
Marked Arrows............................ 208
Overland Mail Coach.................. 212
R. E. Egan, Express Rider.......... 214
Log Cabin 225
Pioneer Cottage........................... 234
Bill and Wife............................... 253
H. R. Egan................................... 256
Church Offices etc....................... 284
Family Tree................................. 288
Father and Mother...................... 289
Ira Ernest Egan.......................... 291
Hyrum Wm. Egan....................... 291
Pioneer Monument...................... 303

WM. M. EGAN,
Compiler and Editor of "Pioneering
the West"; Editor and Publisher of
"Our Deseret Home" and "The Utah
Industrialist." Address, No. 3
Gerard avenue, Salt Lake City.

1.—INTRODUCTORY.

*Howard Egan was born in Tullemore, King's County Ireland June 15th, 1815. His father's name was Howard and his mother's maiden name was Ann Meade. His Grand Father's name was Bernard and his Grand Mother's name was Betty. After the death of his Mother, when about eight years of age, 1823, with his father and eight other children, he left Ireland. He was the fourth child and the first son, there being ten in the family. The last two being twins, one of whom was left with an aunt in Ireland.

The family went to Montreal, Canada and settled there. Howard's Father died in Montreal in 1828, leaving six orphan children. Howard went to sea and followed the life of a sailor until grown when he settled in Salem Mass., and worked at rope making. In 1838 he became acquainted with Miss Tamson Parshley, who was born July 27th 1825 at Barnstead, N. H., being the tenth child of Richard Parshley and Mary Caverly. They were married Dec. 1st 1838, he being over 23 years of age and his wife a girl of 14 years and four months.

Their first son Howard R. Egan was born April 12th 1840, also the second son R. Erastus Egan March 29th 1842, in Salem. In Oct. 1841 he was naturalized as an American Citizen, and in 1842 he and his wife were converted to "Mormonism" by Elder Erastus Snow and baptized, moving to Nauvoo the same year. He became one of the Nauvoo Police, and the Prophet Joseph's guard, who has said "he felt safe when Howard Egan was on guard." He was also Major in the Nauvoo Legion.

Sept. 24th 1844 he and his wife each received a Patriarchal blessing under the hands of Hyrum Smith, the Patriarch and brother of the Prophet in which it is stated that he was "of the lineage of David and of the tribe of Judah....and have a right to the priesthood and blessings according to the prophetic visions of his fathers....and shall be numbered with the called and chosen....and also prepetuated by his posterity in the blessing of the priesthood from generation to generation until the latest generation." That his wife should receive these blessings in common with him, that she was the seed of Joseph through the loins of Ephraim. He filled several missions in the states.

After the martyrdom of the Prophet and Patriarch at the time of the return of the Twelve Apostles, when Oliver Cow-

House built by Bernard Egan, where his sons Howard and William and grandson Howard (Major Howard Egan) were born. The man in doorway is the last of William's descendants (a bachelor) The descendants of Bernard through his son Howard and grandson Major Howard Egan are given in the Appendix.

dery was trying to lead the Church, Mother saw Brigham Young look like Joseph and speak in his voice at a meeting held Aug. 8th, 1844 showing conclusively where the authority of leadership laid. H. R. Egan introduced his writings as follows:

EARLY DAYS.

I will start by saying, "I was born in Salem Mass." although I was there I don't recall the event, but I do remember of Mother leading me by the hand up to the Nauvoo Temple and showing me the large baptismal font that was supported on the backs of twelve stone oxen. (When at the age of six years.) There were four on the side where we stood, one at each corner and two between them just as natural as life. I remember the house we lived in. There was two rooms facing the street with a hall between. We lived in the left hand room, another family lived in the right hand room. I don't remember of ever going in there. There was a flight of stairs in the hall that led to two rooms above. I remember the stairs but nothing more about the house but what I have stated.

Father had a rope factory down close to the river where Mother used to go with his dinner and often took me with her, I remember of seeing Father with a big arm-full of hemp backing down the walk as he was spinning out the twine to make ropes of, and at other times he and another man would be throwing hemp over a hatchel, and dragging it back to free it of sticks or dirt and make it ready for spinning. At one time I saw him as he was finishing a large and long rope, there were three strands each composed of many small ones. The three strands were each hooked on one turning hook, and a man far down the walk had the three strands fastened to a hook called a looper. This was in a belt the man wore around his waist, so he could lean back and keep the cords tight and off the ground.

As Father could not stop then to eat his dinner we had to wait till the twisting was done, Father held a conical shaped block of wood that had three grooves in it in his hands. In each groove laid one of the strands, and as they would twist enough to suit him he would back down towards the lower end. I was following him down the walk when he gave me a scare by turning to face the man and putting one hand, side of his mouth, yelled out at the top of his voice, "slack up on that looper." The man was pulling too hard I suppose.

I remember of seeing posts that had arms across the top with pegs sticking up like rake teeth to hold twine separate as twisted. I don't know how far apart these posts were, but it seemed to me they were about two or three rods, and as high as a man could reach. The factory was very long but not enough when Father had to make sea cables, so he had placed a good many posts beyond the lower end of the walk. Some of them were on the sand bar, but as I saw them then, there were a few standing in the river.

One day I was with Mother when she showed me the foundation of a house and said, "They were going to build our home there, then it wouldn't be so far to the factory.

Howard Ransom Egan,
Author of ''Thrilling Experiences,''
Began this Publicat'on 1915.
Died March, 1916.

Pioneering the West.

PART I.

PIONEERING: NAUVOO TO SALT LAKE.

SEC. I.—PIONEERING TO WINTER QUARTERS—1846.

2.—MORMON EXODUS.

I well remember the Mormon Exodus and of sitting in a covered wagon with Mother and brother Erastus, and this is the first I remember of him. (Howard six and Erastus four years old.) The wagon was standing on the bank of the Mississippi river with the front end facing the water. There was another wagon close by. I had seen two wagons on a flat boat leave the shore and go out of sight. Mother said we could go next when the boat came back. I did not see it when it came back for I had gone to sleep, but the next morning when I opened my eyes it was raining, and peeping out of the front end of the wagon I could see that Mother and quite a large crowd of people were standing by a large fire that had been built against a stump just in the edge of the forest. The Mississippi river was just back of us. We had been brought over in the night. The next I remember was of some man unhitching the team from the wagon and putting it ahead of another team on another wagon and going off out of sight. I don't know where this place was and don't believe anyone else does, (probably Sugar Creek, which place they left March 1, 1846), for it was raining all the time and water all over the ground except here and there a small point sticking up above the water. The land must have sunk, and how we got out of it I don't know, but now I think it was there or there abouts that Mother and I got our start of rheumatism.

The next place I think was Garden Grove, a most beautiful place. (East fork of Grand river 145 miles from Nauvoo, ar rived April 24th.) The wagons were all placed in a row side by side with room to pass between them. There was a bowery built along the front and the tongue of each wagon was tied to it, thus making a long shady lane.

I went with some other boys with some men that were getting brush for the top of the bowery, and when we got to the Grove that was on the lower ground, I thought it was the prettiest place I had ever seen. I and the rest of the boys wanted to run into the edge of the timber. There was no under brush and there was a nice grass sod all over, under the trees, making it a boy's paradise play-ground, but the men would not let us go out of their sight, saying there was lots of wild animals in there, and when they had their loads ready made us go to camp with them.

*In addition to what Howard R. has said in the preceeding paragraphs the compiler adds the following: The family moved with the general exodus of the Saints about the 1st of March, 1846, the first campanies crossing the Mississippi river from Nauvoo to Montrose upon the ice, led by Brigham Young, H. C. Kimball and others of the Twelve, it being the start of the emigrating of the Latter-day Saints from the State of Illinois. At that time there was no definite plan as to the future destination of the people. There had been vague ideas afloat of Oregon, Vancouver and Upper California as probable places of refuge. The only guide was the more or less undefined plans of the Prophet Joseph Smith, of migrating to the West in the midst of the Rocky Mountains.

The first camping place was on Sugar Creek, where the Saints were organized by Pesident Young. The roads were almost impassable, and the Saints suffered much from cold and exposure. They reached Garden Grove, on a fork of Grand River, 145 miles from Nauvoo, April 24th, and May 11th went on to Mt. Pisgah, 172 miles from Nauvoo. Here, May 21st, a general council of the camps had under consideration the subject of sending an expedition company to the Rocky Mountains that year, but the call for 500 men by the Government to fight with Mexico, made that impossible. Four companies were raised on the 13th and the fifth a few days later.

They left this place June 5th and arrived on the banks of the Missouri River, (Council Bluffs), on the 14th. The last company of the Mormon Battalion left the camps of the Saints July 22nd and started for Fort Levenworth. A boat was built and some of the Saints crossed the river, but Cutler's Park became the first temporary head-quarters of the camps, which is three miles from the spot where Winter-Quarters was afterwards built. —Dates from Jenson's Church Chronology.

3.—*TRIP TO SANTA FE AND RETURN.

"After Col. Allen died, Aug. 23rd, 1846, at Fort Levenworth, by suggestion of Maj. Horton, Lieut. Pace returned to Council Bluffs, bearing letters from Lieut. Smith and Dr. Sanderson, Gulley and others to Pres. Young. He arrived at Cutler's Creek Aug. 26th, sat in council, answering questions and received letters of special council for the Battalion, which was some 45 miles out beyond Fort Levenworth continuing on their march.

Howard Egan and John Lee accompanied him on his return with a special duty of going on with the Battalion until they received their pay and to return with it, and to act as special messengers returning from the Battalion. On reaching Fort Levenworth, Maj. Horton charged them to keep with one train until they were sure of reaching another the same night. Fresh horses and all the grain the carriage could haul were furnished, also three packages of letters for different commands were sent. They left the Garrison at Fort Levenworth on the 6th of Sept. and overtook the Battalion on the 11th, while crossing the Arkansas River." The above is gleaned from the "History of the Mormon Battalion," and the following is some of the headings of chapters of the same work during the travel to Santa Fe.

"Wagon upset and man injured—Higgins detatchment sent to Peublo—Dissatisfaction—Alva Phelps drugged to death—Suffer from thirst—Forced marches—men salivated. Rations reduced—Bones of mule found—Ancient Ruins—Rush on to Santa Fe—Sick left to follow without a doctor—Arrived at Santa Fe—Partiality shown. Col. Cooke takes command of Battalion. By special arrangemnts and consent the Battallion boys were paid in checks not available at Santa Fe.

"About noon Oct. 19th we tcok leave of Howard Egan and John Lee, who started with our checks for Council Bluffs. They were accompanied by S. L. Gulley, ex-quartermaster and R. Stevens. The Battallion continued on the same day."

The following from the Deseret News copied from the journals kept by some of the boys adds a little more information. "Friday Oct. 16th.—In the afternoon Company B. drew 1½ months pay, $2.60 to each person in money, the rest in check. Oct. 17th.—Bros. Lee and Egan were making preparations to return to the Bluffs. They received about $4000 from the Battallion to take back with them to the Church.

About a month later, Nov. 21st, John Lee and Howard Egan arrived at Winter Quarters, as special messengers from the camps of the Mormon Battalion beyond Santa Fee."

Either before or after this trip he established his family in Winter Quarters. "The settlement consisted of 700 houses of log, turf and other materials; and was laid out with streets, workshops, mills, etc., and a Tabernacle of worship. Winter Quarters was on a pretty plateau overlooking the river, and was built for protection from Indians. There were 22 Wards with a bishop over each, also a High Council; and the population was over 4000." So says Whitney's History.

Howard Egan's log hut was neatly arranged and papered and hung with pictures and otherwise decorated by his wife, which made it very pleasant and habitable. Having given this little prelude of the facts that we are acquainted with we now present the Pioneer trip in the language of Howard Egan as he wrote it from day to day as they proceeded on their journey. We do not try to contract or expand or change diction only to give just what he intended to say.

We first, however, insert the Pioneer poem and the names of the original band of 144 Pioneers called and chosen to lead out in this pioneering work, just as they were written down in his Diary including Ellis Ames, who returned on account of sickness, but the Diary states it was a lack of faith. Also including the three women and two children that went along with them.

S. F. KIMBALL
Born at Winter Quarters. Author
of poem, "The Pioneers."

4.—THE PIONEERS.

By Solomon F Kimball

Faithful, noble men of worth,
Men who came of Pilgrim birth,
Who were sent from courts above, on their mission to the earth;
Sent to plant the family tree,
Near the shores of Salt Lake Sea,
And to build their happy homes and family hearth.

First there came that bitter test,
Martyred Prophets laid to rest;
Then with hearts extremely sad, in God's Temple they were
bless'd;
Then they turned their backs on home,
Faced the land where redmen roam,
And departed on their journey to the west.

O'er mountains they would go,
Through the brush, and through the snow;
Braving dangers night and day, as they faced the savage foe;
Driving o'er the rugged heights,
Standing guard on stormy nights,
Nothing daunted, nothing fearing, weal or woe.

Trailing through the dust and heat,
With but scanty food to eat;
Tramping o'er the rocky hills, with their bruised and bleeding
feet;
Oft they crossed the raging streams,
With their gall'd and jaded teams,
Oft they pushed their way through drenching rain and sleet.

When they reach'd the salted sea,
Loud they shouted, ''Vic-to-ry!''
Then they call'd on God in prayer, with bow'd head and bended
knee;
Then they made the welkin ring,
And his praises they did sing,
the promised land that He had made so free.

5.—ORIGINAL BAND OF 144 PIONEERS
With Three Women and Two Children.

FIRST TEN.

1 Wilford Woodruff (captain).
2 John S. Fowler.
3 Jacob D. Burnham.
4 Orson Pratt.
5 Joseph Egbert.
6 John M. Freeman.
7 Marcus B. Thorpe.
8 George A. Smith.
9 George Wardle.

SECOND TEN.

10 Ezra T. Benson (captain).
11 Thomas B. Grover.
12 Barnabas L. Adams.
13 Roswell Stevens.
14 Amasa M. Lyman.
15 Starling G. Driggs.
16 Albert Carrington.
17 Thomas Bullock.
18 George W. Brown.
19 Willard Richards.
20 Jesse C. Little.

THIRD TEN.

21 Phineas H. Young (captain).
22 John Y. Green.
23 Thomas Tanner.
24 Brigham Young.
25 Addison Everett.
26 Truman O. Angell.
27 Lorenzo D. Young.
28 Bryant Stringham.
29 Joseph S. Scofield.
30 Albert P. Rockwood.

FOURTH TEN.

31 Luke S. Johnson (captain).
32 John G. Holman.
33 Edmund Ellsworth.
34 Alvarus Hanks.
35 George R. Grant.
36 Millen Atwood.
37 Samuel B. Fox.
38 Tunis Rappleyee.
39 Eli Harvey Peirce.
40 William Dykes.
41 Jacob Weiler.

FIFTH TEN.

42 Stephen H. Goddard (captain).
43 Tarlton Lewis.
44 Henry C. Sherwood.
45 Zebedee Coltrin.
46 Sylvester H. Earl.
47 John Dixon.
48 Samuel H. Marble.
49 George Schales.
50 William Henrie.
51 William A. Empey.

SIXTH TEN.

52 Charles Shumway (captain).
53 Andrew P. Shumway.
54 Thos. Woolsey.
55 Chauncey Loveland.
56 Erastus Snow.
57 James Craig.
58 Wm. Wordsworth.
59 Wm. P. Vance.
60 Simeon F. Howd.
61 Seeley Owen.

SEVENTH TEN.

62 James Case
(captain).
63 Artemas Johnson.
64 *Wm. C. A. Smoot.
65 B. F. Dewey.
66 Wm. Carter.
67 Franklin G. Losee.
68 Burr Frost.
69 Datus Ensign.
70 Franklin B. Stewart.
71 Monroe Frink.
72 Eric Glines.
73. Ozro Eastman.

EIGHTH TEN.

74 Seth Taft
(captain).
75 Horace Thornton.
76 Stephen Kelsey.
77 John S. Eldredge.
78 Charles D. Barnum.
79 Alma M. Williams.
80 Rufus Allen.
81 Robt. T. Thomas.
82 Jas. W. Stewart.
83 Elijah Newman.
84 Levi N. Kendall.
85 Francis Boggs.
86 David Grant.

NINTH TEN.

88 Howard Egan
(captain).
87 Heber C. Kimball.
89 William A. King.
90 Thomas P. Cloward.
91 Hosea Cushing.
92 Robt. Biard.
93 George V. Billings.
94 Edson Whipple.
95 Philo Johnson.
06 Wm. Clayton.

TENTH TEN.

97 Appleton M. Harmon
(captain).
98 Carlos Murray.
99 Horace K. Whitney.
100 Orson K. Whitney.
101 Orrin P. Rockwell.
102 Nathaniel T. Brown.
103 R. Jackson Redding.
104 John Pack.
105 Francis Pomeroy.
106 Aaron F. Farr.
107 Nathaniel Fairbanks.

ELEVENTH TEN.

108 John S. Higbee
(captain).
109 John Wheeler.
110 Solomon Chamberlain.
111 Conrad Kleinman.
112 Joseph Rooker.
113 Perry Fitzgerald.
114 John H. Tippetts.
115 James Davenport.
116 Henson Walker.
117 Benjamin Rolfe.

TWELFTH TEN.

118 Norton Jacobs
(captain).
119 Charles A. Harper.
120 George Woodard.
121 Stephen Markham.
122 Lewis Barney.
123 George Mills.
124 Andrew Gibbons.
125 Joseph Hancock.
126 John W. Norton.

THIRTEENTH TEN.

131 John Brown
(captain).
127 Shadrach Roundy.
129 Levi Jackman.

130 Lyman Curtis.
128 Hans C. Hansen.
132 Matthew Ivory.
133 David Powers.
134 Hark Lay (colored).
135 Oscar Crosby (colored).

FOURTEENTH TEN.

136 Joseph Matthews
    (captain).
137 Gilroid Summe.
138 John Gleason.

139 Charles Burke.
140 Alexander P. Chessley.
141 Rodney Badger.
142 Norman Taylor.
143 Green Flake (colored).
144 Ellis Ames (returned).
  1 Harriet   Page   Wheeler
       Young.
  2 Clara Decker Young.
  3 Ellen Sanders Kimball.
   *Isaac Perry Decker.
   *Lorenzo Sobieski Young
Survivores are designated *.

On the Way.

6.---A DIARY KEPT BY HOWARD EGAN,
one of the Pioneers of 1847.

FROM WINTER QUARTERS (FLORENCE. NEBRASKA) TO GREAT
SALT LAKE VALLEY AND RETURN TO SWEETWATER.

SEC. II.   DETAILS OF TRIP TO SALT LAKE.

Thursday, April 8th, 1847.—We started for the west to find a home for the Latter-day Saints, and went out as far as the Haystacks, about three miles, where the rest of the boys had already preceded us. Brigham Young's camp was about four miles ahead. Soon after we arrived, Porter Rockwell came up on horseback and informed us that P. P. Pratt had just arrived at Winter Quarters from England, and that O. Hyde and John Taylor were soon expected. We went back home in the carriage to pass the night, in company with Heber, Bishop Whitney, Sister Kimball and Horace.

Friday, April 9th.—It was fine weather for traveling, and we went back to where we left our wagons and continued our journey. Wm. Kimball went with us and intends going as far as the "Elkhorn." We went about four miles and came to Brigham Young's camp, but did not stop, going on three miles further and encamped for the night, having made ten miles. .

Saturday, April 10th.—It was a fine day, as usual, and we traveled fifteen miles and encamped on the prairie near a ravine, which supplied us with water, for the night, we being now six miles from the "Horn" river.

Sunday, April 11th.—There was fine weather, and we started in good season and arrived at the "Horn" about 2 o'clock p. m. There were 72 wagons crossed the river on a raft drawn by cattle with ropes on either side. Brother Bullock, Dr. Richards' clerk, took down the number of the wagons as they passed. We went down the river about a mile, after crossing, and encamped for the night. Father (*H. C. Kimball) told the brethren of his company that he hoped that they would not go hunting or fishing today, for if they did they would not prosper, as this was a day set apart for the service of the Lord and not for trivial amusements.

Monday, April 12th.—It was fair weather, and Pres. Brigham Young, Father (*Heber C. Kimball), Bishop Whitney and a number of others went back to Winter Quarters, the rest of us going on, by counsel, in order to cross an extensive bottom of twelve miles before the water should rise and the roads get muddy. Accordingly we went on and encamped on the banks of the Platte river, the width of which much surprised me, it being larger than I had anticipated. Here we intend to remain until the Twelve Apostles return. The brethren were called together this evening by S. Markham, who stated to them that it was the wish of the Twelve that some men familiar with the route should go ahead and survey the track. Accordingly, Father (James) Case, J. Redding and two others will start tomorrow for that purpose.

Gathering on the Elk Horn River.

Tuesday, April 13th.—This morning was warm and pleasant, the wind being west. The blacksmiths put up their forges, three in number, Brothers Devenport, Frost and Tanner, and commenced setting tires and shoeing horses. With the assistance of the boys I propped up my wagon box and took out the running gears, and Brother Harper went to work and put in two new axeltrees. Those who went to hunt out the road returned this evening and reported unfavorable, as there was a low, flat bottom that could not be crossed in wet weather. It has the appearance of rain this evening. The wind shifted to the east and it looked cloudy. Brother S. Markham called the brethren together and gave some general instruction and placed the guard.

Wednesday, April 14th.—This morning it was raining, but about 10 a. m. it cleared off, there being high winds and somewhat cloudy. J. Higby, J. Redding and four or five others went up the river with the seine to hunt a place to fish, and returned in the evening with about two dozen fish. My horses strayed away and I took Brother Redding's horse and went across towards the "Horn" and found them, one of which I succeeded in catching; the other I could not, but had to return without her to the camp.

Thursday, April 15th.—This morning was cool and pleasant. Brother King and myself started early in search of my horse and found her ten miles from the camp. Some of the brethren went across to the "Horn" to fish. About 3 p. m. the Twelve, Brother Clayton, Brother Whitney, Brother Little, from New Hampshire, Brother Bullock, Wm. Kimball and others returned to the camp and we commenced forthwith to rig up our wagons.

About sundown President Young called the brethren together and instructed them to have a care of their teams, and cease all music, dancing and lightmindedness; and instructed them, exhorted them to prayer and faithfulness. He also stated that the traders and missionaries were stirring up the Indians to plunder us of our horses and goods. He said that if we were faithful and obeyed counsel the Lord would bless us and we should pass through safe.

Tuesday, April 16th.—This morning the wind was north and it was cloudy. Brothers Little, Rockwood and Redding went to Winter Quarters to bring on Brother Little's things. At 7:30 the brethren were called together in order to organize them. The meeting was opened by prayer by President Young, after which G. A. Smith made some remarks; also H. C. Kimball, N. K. Whitney and others. The camp was divided into two divisions, 72 in each division; A. P. Rockwood captain of the First and S. Markham of the Second Division. Night guard was started and on the 17th the camp was organized under regiment. On the 18th the Council of Captains made laws regulating the camp as follows:

LAWS OR RULES.

1.—After this date the horn or bugle shall be blown every morning at 5 a. m., when every man is expected to arise and pray; then attend to his team, get breakfast and have everything finished so that the camp may start by 7 o'clock.

2.—Each extra man is to travel on the off side of the team with his gun on his shoulder, loaded, and each driver have his gun so placed that he can lay hold of it at a moment's warning.

Every man must have a piece of leather over the nipple of his gun, or if it is a flintlock, in the pan, having caps and powder-flask ready.

3.—The brethren will halt for an hour about noon, and they must have their dinner ready cooked so as not to detain the camp for cooking.

4.—When the camp halts for the night, wagons are to be drawn in a circle, and the horses to be all secured inside the circle when necessary.

5.—The horn will blow at 8:30 p. m., when every man must return to his wagon and pray, except the night guard, and be in bed by 9 o'clock, at which time all fires must be put out.

6.—The camp is to travel in close order, and no man to leave the camp twenty rods without orders from the Captain.

7.—Every man is to put as much interest in taking care of his brother's cattle, in preserving them, as he would his own, and no man will be indulged in idleness.

8.—Every man is to have his gun and pistol in perfect order.

9.—Let all start and keep together, and let the cannon bring up the rear, and the company guard to attend it, traveling along with the gun, and see that nothing is left behind at each stopping place.

INVENTORY.

The number of oxen in the camp 66, horses 89, mules 52, cows 19, dogs 17. Teams belonging to H. C. Kimball: Horses 5, mules 7, oxen 6, cows 2, dogs 2, wagons 6. List of provisions: Flour 1228 lbs., meat 865 lbs., sea biscuit 125 lbs., beans 296 lbs., bacon 241 lbs., corn for teams 2869 lbs., buckwheat 300 lbs., dried beef 25 lbs., groceries 290¾ lbs., sole leather 15 lbs., oats 10 bus., rape 40 lbs., seeds 71 lbs., cross-cut saw 1, axes 6, scythe 1, hoes 3, log chains 5, spade 1, crowbar 1, tent 1, keg of powder 25 lbs., lead 20 lbs., codfish 40 lbs., garden seeds 50 lbs., plows 2, bran 3½ bus., 1 side of harness leather, whip saw 1, iron 16 lbs., nails 16 lbs., 1 sack of salt 200 lbs., saddles 2, tool chest worth $75, 6 pair of double harness worth about $200, total amount of breadstuff 2507 lbs. at $55.40, 241 lbs. of bacon at 6c, $14.46; 2869 lbs. feed corn $28.69; 300 lbs. seeds $3.00, 300 lbs. buckwheat $6.00, 25 lbs. dried beef $3.12½, groceries $35, sole leather $4, oats $4, rape $10. seeds $10, hoes $2, axes $8, keg of powder $10, lead $2, codfish $2, 200 lbs. salt $8, tool chest $75, cross-cut saw $5, whip saw $5, scythe $2, hoes $1.50, 5 log chains $20, spade $2, crowbar $3, 2 plows $24, side of harness leather $4. 16 lbs. iron $2, 16 lbs. nails $2. tent $10, harness $20, 5 horses $360, 7 mules $350, 6 wagons $600, 2 saddles $30, bran $1, 3 yoke of cattle $120, 2 cows $24. Total $1592.87½.

After the organization we prepared for traveling. Brother Whitney, Wm. Kimball and Lyman Whitney prepared to return home. Father Kimball took William into the wagon and blessed him. William was very much affected. About 3 p. m. we moved off and traveled three miles and encamped for the night. About dark the wind blew up from the north very cold. We took our horses and cattle down in the timber and cut down trees and made a fence to put our horses in, and placed a guard around them, selected for that purpose, aside from the regular camp guard.

Saturday, April 17th.—This morning was cold and the wind northwest. At 9 o'clock we started on our journey, the wind blowing very strong, which made it very disagreeable, as it was a sandy road. We came seven miles and encamped near a beautiful grove of cottonwood. This evening a trader from the Pawnee village encamped near us. He had one wagon loaded with buffalo robes. At sundown the bugle sounded for the brethren to come together. President Young said it was necessary to have a military organization before we left this place. It was moved and carried that the two divisions be formed into one regiment, under Colonel Markham. There were also two majors appointed, John Pack and Shadrack Roundy, and Thomas Tanner to take command of the camp. Each captain was to command his own ten in case of an attack from the Indians.

Father (*Heber C.) Kimball has taken Brother William Clayton into his mess. Sister Ellen Sanders and myself, with others, make up the mess, and I thank the Lord for the privilege of being one of the number and enjoying the society of my father Heber. Ellis Ames returned from this place in consequence of sickness, so he said, but I think he is weak in the faith.

Sunday, April 18th.—This morning there was high winds from the south and very cold. Today, being the day set apart by the Almighty God for His people to rest, we do not intend to travel. Three wagons loaded with furs passed this morning; also four or five pack mules, a short time afterward, going to the settlements. H. C. Kimball wrote a letter to his companion this morning and sent it by Brother Ames, the contents of which I heard read and it done my heart good. It portrayed the feelings of his heart and his affection for his family, in the most simple and beautiful language that would touch the soul and cause the heart to rejoice.

The wind continued to blow so hard, and it was so cold, it was thought wisdom not to call the brethren together to have meeting. The Twelve retired back in the woods to council one with the other. About sundown President Young called the Captains together and gave them the following instructions: At 8:30 p. m. the bugle would sound and all should retire to their wagons and bow before the Lord and offer up their supplications before going to bed, and all fires should be put out; also the bugle would sound at 5 a. m., when all would arise and offer up their thanks to the Lord, and at 7 o'clock be ready to start. All the spare hands were to walk by the off side of their wagons with their rifles loaded. The weather continues very cold.

Monday, April 19th.—This morning the weather was fair, calm and pleasant. At 5 a. m. the bugle sounded for all hands to turn out and return thanks to the Lord. At 7:30 the camp was in motion with orders to travel in double file. We passed over a beautiful level prairie in sight of the Platte river, and passed a number of small lakes between us and the river. The brethren shot a number of ducks as we passed along. At 1:30 p. m. we stopped to feed near a bend in the river, after traveling thirteen miles. While there O. P. Rockwell, J. Redding, Brother Little and Thomas Brown arrived from Winter Quarters and brought a number of letters for the brethren. I received one from Brother Jacob Feryier, who has my thanks for his kindness. I also heard that my family was all well, which I thank the Lord for. At 2:40 p. m. we started on our journey and came eight miles and encamped in a circle, in order to have our horses and cattle in the center to secure them from the Indians, with the guard placed outside of the wagons. This evening looks cloudy and the wind blows fresh from the north. Brother John Rigby and several others went down the river two miles with the boat and seine to seek a place to fish, and after being gone about two hours returned with only two fish. I had the pleasure this evening of sitting in Brother Horace Whitney's wagon to write. Brother Harper gave Father (*Heber C.) Kimball two ducks he shot today. Brother Kimball gave one of them to President Young. Brother Hanson also let him have two snipes.

Tuesday, April 20th.—This morning I arose at 4:30 a. m. and took my horses out to feed and then commenced getting breakfast at 6:30. We made a first-rate breakfast of our wild fowls. At 7:30 we started, it being clear weather but very high winds from the southwest. We traveled about six miles and crossed a small stream called Shell creek, about two miles from the Platte river, then went on about four miles and stopped to feed, which made ten miles this forenoon. Three deer ran past our camp within a half mile. Brothers Porter and Brown ran them with their horses, but could not get within gunshot of them. J. Higby, L. Johnson and S. Markham and some others started a half hour ahead this morning, with the boat and seine and three wagons with them, to fish. President Young and H. C. Kimball went ahead this afternoon to pick out a camping place. About 4:30 p. m. we arrived at the spot, after traveling ten miles. It is a beautiful place near the banks of the river.

We took our horses across a small branch of the river, where there was plenty of cottonwood for them, and then put our oxen and cows inside of the circle. Those who went fishing returned with a large quantity of fish that they caught in a small lake one mile above where we are encamped. I cooked one for supper, a large buffalo fish. President Young came into our wagon and ate supper with Father (*Heber C.) Kimball. This evening the wind blows fresh from the northwest. Father Kimball sits close by me writing a letter to his companion. It is about 10 p. m.; Dr. Richards has just come to our wagon to inquire for Brother Markham. They thought, as the Pawnees were encamped only eight miles from us, it was necessary to have a patrol guard out tonight.

Wednesday, April 21st.—It is cloudy weather and has the appearance of rain, with wind from the northeast. At 7 a. m. the bugle sounded for the ox teams to start, and at 7:30 we started. The horse teams started about two hours after we started. We met five or six Pawnee Indians. We traveled about eight miles and came in sight of the Pawnee village. Two of the chiefs and a number of the Indians came to our camp. Father Kimball gave them some tobacco and salt. President Young gave them some powder and lead and other things. They manifested some dissatisfaction because they did not receive more presents, and told us we must go back. We paid no attention to them. At 2 p. m. we continued our journey and traveled ten miles. About twenty minutes after we started we had a severe thunderstorm and rain fell in torrents, which lasted about thirty minutes, and it blew a gale all the afternoon from the northwest. At 5 p. m. we encamped near the Loop Fork, which is a large stream that empties into the Platte. About sundown the bugle sounded for all the brethren to come together. Colonel Markham called off 100 men to stand guard, 50 the first part of the night and 50 the latter part. Porter Rockwell took charge of ten men as picket guard. I stood guard until 10 p. m. It was a bitter cold night.

Thursday, April 22d.—It continues cold with wind northeast. We traveled two miles and crossed a small stream called

the Looking Glass creek. We went on eight miles and stopped
to feed near a stream called Bear creek, making ten miles this
forenoon. At 2 o'clock we hitched up and started. We were
under the necessity of having men on the opposite side of the
creek we were crossing, with a rope to help our wagons up, as
the bank was so steep we could not get up without help.

This afternoon we traveled through a beautiful country,
with the Loop Fork on one side and a ridge on the other and
groups of trees that resembled orchards in an old settled country. We came seven miles and stopped at the old Missionary
station that was vacated last summer. The Sioux Indians drove
them off. There is quite a large farm fenced in and some very
good buildings on it. We had plenty of corn fodder and hay
for our teams. It is the prettiest location that I have seen this
side of the Mississippi river. In the latter part of the day the
wind moderated and this evening it is warm and pleasant. Captain Tanner exercised his men at the cannon. President Young
called the brethren together and forbid them taking anything
off of the premises. Twenty men was thought sufficient tonight
to guard the camp.

Friday, April 23d.—This morning was warm and pleasant.
Brigham, Heber and others started on at 7:45 a. m. to look out
a fording place to cross the Loop Fork. While they were gone
Sister Ellen and myself took the opportunity to wash. They
returned at 11:45 a. m. and reported that we could go about four
miles and build a raft. Tarlton Lewis was appointed to build
it. About 1 o'clock the wagons started and we crossed a small
creek, soon after, called Plum creek. We traveled about two
miles and crossed another stream. I could not find out the
name. Father Kimball said to call it Looking Glass creek, because it was very clear.

At 3 p. m. we arrived at the fording place and found that
a raft could be of no use and concluded to ford it. Luke Johnson was the first that crossed the river. He took the boat off
and crossed with an empty wagon. Brother Orson Pratt took
out part of his load and got about half way across and could
not get any further. Four or five of us waded out to his assistance. The water in some places was waist deep. Brigham
came as near as he could with the boat and we took the valuable
part of his load and put it on board and went on a little farther, when one of his horses fell down. It was with difficulty
we saved them. We loosened them from the wagon and hauled
it over by hand. Brothers Pack and Woodruff crossed safe.
President Young ordered them to stop crossing wagons today.

We went about a half mile up the river and encamped till morning, which was at 5:30 p. m. The day was very hot.

A little after dark President Young called the captains together to council which was the best way to cross the river. Brother Rockwood motioned to build three rafts to take across the goods, and the empty wagons to ford the river. Brother Kimball motioned to build one first and try it before there was any more built, as it was doubtful whether there could be any used. Brothers Lewis and Woolsey were appointed to take charge of building the raft. Brother Markham was to go and pick out the best fording place and stake it out, and drive all the loose cattle over. The leaders informed us that the sand would pack down and make better traveling.

Saturday, April 24th.—This morning one of President Young's horses was found dead. He was chained near a large hole and fell in and choked himself. The morning was very pleasant. H. C. Kimball and Lorenzo Young went up the river about a mile to see if they could find a better fording place. I was requested to go along with them. Brother Woodard and myself went across the river, but found some places very difficult for crossing. On our return we found they had commenced crossing wagons, about 8 a. m. We took half the load out of some of our wagons and doubled our teams and crossed without any difficulty. Brother Kimball marched in the water with the rest of us. At 3 p. m. all the wagons were over on the sandbar safe, and at 4 o'clock all were over safe. We started on again and traveled about three miles southwest, up the river. It was a sandy bottom and more bare of grass than on the other side. We encamped on the west side of a small lake, near the river. There was plenty of sunfish in it. Brother Clayton caught a mess for us and they were first-rate. All hands were tired working, crossing over the river. I thank the Lord the morrow is a day of rest.

Sunday, April 25th.—This morning we had fair weather with wind south. We took all our teams out to feed and left some hands to watch them. At 5 p. m. a meeting was called at the wagon of President Young. Remarks were made by several and instructions given by President Young, chiefly in reference to the folly of conforming to Gentile customs on an expedition of this nature. There were eight men selected to hunt on horses, also to hunt on foot.

Monday, April 26th.—This morning about 3:30 an alarm was given. The guard on the northwest corner of the camp discovered some Indians crawling up to the wagons. They fired at them, when six Indians jumped up and ran. All hands were up and prepared for action in a few minutes, under their respective captains. Nothing more was seen of the Indians. At 8 a. m. the camp started. There is no road here, consequently President Young, Kimball and some others went ahead on horseback to hunt out the best track. We traveled about seven miles and stopped at 11:30, near some holes of water, to feed our teams. At 1:45 all the wagons were on the way. At 6:15 we encamped near a small creek, having come seven miles, which makes fourteen miles today.

About 3 o'clock Brother Matthews was out hunting his horses and saw a horse at a distance, supposing it to be Brother Little's, went toward him. Before he got near him the horse put off at full speed toward the river. He then supposed there was an Indian on him. He returned to the camp and gave the alarm, when five or six men jumped on their horses and followed in the direction, but could not see or hear anything of the Indian. When they returned President Young and Kimball with some others went out on horseback in search of him and traveled till 11 o'clock, but could not see anything of him and returned. Dr. Richard's horse is gone.

Tuesday, April 27th.—At 8:30 a. m. the wagons commenced moving off. We traveled twelve miles and stopped about 2:15 p. m., coming nearly a south course. O. P. Rockwell and others went back to look for the horses that were lost. We stopped at noon near a ravine, where feed was very good but no water. We dug about four feet and got a little water for our horses. At 3:15 the teams started again. Brother Woodruff and two others shot an antelope. President Young and Kimball are still ahead. We traveled four miles and encamped at 5:30 for the night. Soon after we arrived it began to thunder and lightning, and gave us a light shower with very heavy wind. Those who went to hunt the horses returned. They reported that they went back near where we were encamped April 26th, and saw fifteen Indians well armed. They endeavored to get near enough to get hold of the horses by pretending friendship, but the brethren would not let them come near. One of the brethren cocked his pistol and pointed it at one of them, when they all ran. After they got off a little distance they turned and fired a shot at the brethren. They did not see the lost horses and the shot did not take effect. About the time the brethren returned, a rifle accidentally went off, which was in Brother Brown's wagon, and broke the right fore leg of a horse. That makes four of the best horses in the camp lost in the last four days.

Wednesday, April 28th.—This morning was fine and pleasant, and we commenced crossing a small creek about 9 a. m. The last wagon got over at 10 o'clock. President Young and Kimball went ahead to point out the track. While we were crossing the creek Luke Johnson shot the horse that had its leg broken. We traveled about a south course about eleven miles and stopped to feed near the main Platte river about 2:30. At 4 p. m. we started again and traveled four miles and encamped about 6 o'clock, having traveled fifteen miles today. The evening was cool and cloudy.

Thursday, April 29th.—The morning was cool, and we started to find better feed for our horses, traveling three miles, and stopped at 6:30 to breakfast. At 8:20 we started and traveled about two miles and crossed a very pretty stream of water. We stopped at 1 p. m. near a lake to feed, having traveled about ten miles. At 2:30 we started again and traveled about eight miles, when we stopped at 6 o'clock. The wind was southwest and cold.

Friday, April 30th.—The morning was cool and pleasant. At 8:20 a. m. we again started, stopping at 12 noon to feed, near a small creek, having traveled eight miles. At 1:20 p. m. we started again, the wind blowing tremendously strong from the north and very cold. We traveled about eight miles and stopped about 5 p. m. and encamped about two miles from the river near a bluff, with neither wood nor water. We picked up some dry buffalo dung, which made a very good fire, and we dug a well and found plenty of water.

7.—LARAMIE PLAINS, MAY, 1847.

Saturday, May 1st, 1847.—This morning was very cold and, as feed was very poor, it was now thought best to start before breakfast, which was done at 5:20 a. m., stopping at 8:15 to feed, having come six miles. Soon after we started this morning we saw three buffaloes about two miles off on the bluffs. Three of the brethren went in chase of them on horseback. We could see a large herd of buffaloes a few miles ahead. At 10:15 we again started. Those who started after the buffalo early this morning returned, but they did not kill any. There were seven or eight hunters picked out to charge on the large herd, some being footmen scattered out. Before the brethren got to them they got started by one of our dogs that ran an antelope near them. H. C. Kimball now started across and headed them off and killed the first one, and helped to kill two others. Soon after, H. C. Kimball, S. Rockwood and others returned, and one of our teams that George Billings drove, was sent out with two others to bring in the buffalo meat. There was one bull, three cows and six calves killed.

Brother Joseph Hancock went off early this morning on foot and has not been seen or heard from up to this evening. During the afternoon we traveled eight miles, and encamped about 6:30 near a small lake about a mile above the head of Grand island. This day we traveled about eighteen miles.

Sunday, May 2d.—This morning is cold but clear weather, and the ice is about an inch thick. A buffalo calf came within a short distance of the camp last night and one of the guards shot it in the thigh and brought it into the camp alive. Just before breakfast Brother Hancock came into camp and reported that he had shot a buffalo yesterday afternoon and got lost. He was about four miles from the camp, built a fire and cooked supper; returning on horseback, he shot an antelope on the way. This morning we cut up a quarter of a buffalo cow and salted it down.

I started in company with President Young, Fairbanks and others ahead to hunt a camping ground where we could have better feed. We returned a little after 2 o'clock p. m. and ate dinner. At 3:15 we started, and traveled two miles over a prairie dog town. A little after 4 o'clock we encamped near a long lake of clear water. President Young and Kimball with some others went ahead three or four miles to view the country. All hands were employed putting up racks to dry the buffalo meat.

Monday, May 3d.—This morning was cold, and there was ice in the water buckets. The hunters are going out this morning on foot. Brothers Tanner and Davenport put their forges up to repair some of the wagons. We had some of the tires set on Brother Cushing's wagon. There was a small party sent on horseback to hunt the route. At 2:30 p. m. the horsemen returned and reported that Brother Empey had discovered a large war party of Indians in a hollow twelve miles from the camp. There were orders given for a company of horsemen to start, to call the hunters back to the camp. About 6 o'clock the last of them got in safe, bringing two antelope and two calves. The cannon was taken out in front of the wagons and prepared for action. There was a round fired about 9 p. m.

Tuesday, May 4th.—This morning was fine but cool, wind being about southwest. About 7:30 a. m. the camp was called together and instruction was given by President Young in regard to leaving the wagons, and scattering off hunting, without council. A company of ten men was added to the guard. About 9 o'clock the wagons commenced to cross the lake, near the river. The wagons were placed four abreast with the cannon in the rear, and traveled so for about half a day, in order to be prepared if attacked by the Indians. Soon after we started we discovered three wagons on the opposite bank of the river. They were traders going to Council Bluffs. There were nine men in the company and were from Fort Laramie. One of the men came across to see us. He agreed to carry letters for us to the settlements. Brother Brown and two others went across the river to carry the letters to his wagon. The river is about two miles wide at this place but is good fording. I finished writing the letter I commenced some time since, before they went, and sent it to my wife. We gave the man some bread and bacon to last him to the settlements. He said he had not eaten any bread for a long time.

About 1:20 p. m. we again started and at 3:30 we stopped to feed, having traveled six miles. While our cattle were feeding the company was called out to drill. We again started and traveled about three miles and encamped near a creek of good water. The prairie burned nearly all over. Some few spots were left that the fire had not touched. The wind was south and very dusty.

Wednesday, May 5th.—This morning was fine and very pleasant. At 7:30 a. m. we started and traveled over a low, soft

Prairie Burned Nearly All Over. Indians Watching the Result.

prairie, and at 11:30 we stopped to feed. We had come about
nine miles in a west course, a very strong wind from the south
blowing. At 1 p. m. we continued our journey. Between 3 and

4 o'clock President Young and Kimball, who had been ahead, returned and ordered the teams to go back about half a mile to a small island and encamp for the night, in consequence of the prairie being on fire ahead. This day there was one cow and six buffalo calves killed.

Thursday, May 6th.—This morning it was thought best to start before breakfast and go to where we could find better feed, and at 6:30 we started. Last night the Lord sent a light shower, which put the fire out and made it perfectly safe to travel. We came about two miles and stopped to feed. At 8:45 we again started, President Young and Kimball still going ahead on horseback. We traveled about six miles and found a little more grass. The feed is very scarce, as the numerous herds of buffalo eat it close to the ground.

There were orders given that no more game should be killed, as there was sufficient meat in the camp. While we were stopping for noon some of our cows took after the buffalo. President Young and Kimball rode after them and drove them back. At 1:30 p. m. we started on and traveled about two miles and found a lake of pure water. President Young returned to look for his spyglass he had lost. We encamped at 6:30 near an island in the river, having come about fifteen miles.

Friday, May 7th.—This morning the wind was northwest and very cold. The camp was called together and measures taken to raise some horses to haul the cannon, as some of the horses and cattle had given out. President Young scolded E. Snow for not taking better care of the cows yesterday. O. P. Rockwell went back this morning to hunt President Young's spyglass. About 10 o'clock the camp started. We traveled about eight miles and encamped about 2.30 near several islands in the river. About 4 p. m. Porter returned. He found the spyglass. At 6:30 the company was called out to drill.

Saturday, May 8th.—The morning was cold but fine, and we started at 9 o'clock. We came seven and a half miles and stopped at 1 p. m. to feed. The prairie on both sides of the river is literally covered with buffalo. This evening we encamped near the river. We took some of our horses on a small island in the river. Feed is very scarce and very little wood. We have to use buffalo chips to cook with. The bluffs ahead appear to run down to the river.

Sunday, May 9th.—This morning is very cold and the wind southeast. At 7:50 we proceeded on and traveled three and a half miles, going a little around some of the bluffs, and turned down again towards the river on a low sandy bottom. We en-

camped near some islands and have plenty of wood, but poor
feed. We took our horses on the island and cut down cottonwood for them. I went to the south end of the island and
washed myself and changed my clothes. At 3 p. m. the bugle
sounded for the brethren to come together for meeting. Prayer
was offered by Brother Lyman. Brothers Woodruff, Pratt,
Benson and Stevens spoke, and they gave us some very good
instructions. Soon after meeting President Young, Kimball and
some others went a few miles west to view the country.

The evening was cold, with strong wind from the northwest. President Young ate supper with H. C. Kimball. Ellen
tried to bake some bread, but could not. the wind blew so. I
have to sleep on a chest in the front part of the wagon, crossways, and cannot stretch myself nor keep the clothes over me.
It was so cold tonight, and the wind blowing in the wagon, so
I went to bed with Brothers King and Cushing.

Monday, May 10th.—This morning was cool and calm. I
got up this morning at 4 a. m. I had the best night's rest I
have had for some time. I made a fire and put the bread down
to bake, then went to Brother Johnson's wagon to write up my
journal, as I have not much time to do it during the day or
evening. I have to catch most of the time after taking care
of my horses. When the weather gets warmer, I hope I shall
be able to write some early in the mornings. I have so little
time, it accounts for my not writing much. Brother Clayton
has kindly let me have his journal to take minutes from until
I can get time to keep it up every day, which I am very thankful for.

Dr. Richards has deposited a letter in a board prepared
for that purpose, nailed to a long pole, with the distance marked
on it of 316 miles from Winter Quarters. He was assisted by
President Young and others. At 9:05 a. m. the camp proceeded
onward. After traveling about two miles we crossed a small
creek, which Brother Kimball named Skunk creek. About this
time we discovered a stray horse coming toward us. The brethren tried to catch it, but he was so wild they could not get near
him. We traveled until 11:55 and found a little better feed,
then stopped for dinner, having come about six miles. The
prairie is low and soft, which makes very heavy traveling.
Some of the brethren shot a buffalo today. At 2 p. m. we continued our journey, and after traveling a half mile we crossed
a very bad slough. About 4 p. m. President Young's team gave
out, and many others also. H. C. Kimball rode up to us and
told Brother H. Cushing to take off two of his mules and go
back to help President Young up. At 4:50 we encamped near

an island where we had plenty of cottonwood for our horses. The feed is a little better this evening, for which we thank the Lord. This day we traveled about ten miles. Some of the hunters killed a deer. The evening is warm and pleasant, and the wind light from the northwest.

Tuesday, May 11th.—The morning is cold with east wind. It appears to me that vast herds of buffalo have wintered around this place, but have mostly left and gone eastward some time ago, as we have the full growth of this year's grass, which is very short. This morning we overhauled our wagon, and took part of our load and placed it in Brother Cushing's wagon. At 9:30 a. m. we again started, President Young and Kimball going a half hour ahead of us. Our Ten took the lead today, which brought my wagon first. We traveled five miles and stopped at 12:20 for a half hour to water and take some dinner. We traveled on three miles further and crossed over a creek of clear water. We traveled on a half mile and stopped, the feed being pretty good, making eight and one-half miles today. The water being a half mile off, the brethren dug two wells about four feet deep and found plenty of good water. This evening I felt quite sick, having a very bad cold.

Wednesday, May 12th.—The morning was very cool, and we started at 9:10 a. m. and traveled eight miles, and stopped at 1:12 p. m. to feed. The roads are pretty good and the feed is a little better. There is a strong wind blowing from the southeast. H. C. Kimball informed me today that we had passed the junction of the forks of the river two days ago. The hunters report that they have seen many dead buffalo between here and the bluffs with the hides off and the tongues taken out, which proves that Indians have been here recently, as the flesh looks fresh as if lately killed. The range of bluffs on each side of the river extends much farther apart, and near the foot of the south range can be seen scattering timber, which is an evidence that the south fork runs along there in the distance. At 3:30 we again started and traveled four miles, and encamped again at 5:45 near a group of small islands. This evening is cloudy and it looks like rain. Brother Clayton thinks we are about fourteen miles above the junction of the north and south forks of the Platte river. Some of the hunters killed a buffalo this evening and the remnants were sent out after.

Thursday, May 13th.—This morning is very cold and cloudy with wind northwest. I went out early to take care of my horses, and went in sight of an Indian camp ground. There appeared to be two or three hundred wickiups and, from the

appearance of things, I supposed that they had not been gone
long from there. At 9 a. m. we started and traveled four miles,
nearly a west course, and stopped at 11 a. m. to feed our teams.
The grass continues to get better. The buffalo are not so plenty
here, which accounts for the feed getting better. The wind is
blowing very strong from the north and northeast. At 12:30
we again moved onward and traveled ten and a quarter miles
and stopped on the west side of a large stream about six rods
wide, which runs from the northeast and empties into the North
fork of the Platte river. The bottom is quicksand and difficult
to cross unless it is crossed over quick. It is about two feet
deep.

We are encamped within a quarter of a mile of the Platte,
and the feed is better here than any we have had since we left
Winter Quarters. I feel much better today, and I thank the
Lord for it. This stream is not laid down on the map. President Young and Kimball traveled ahead as usual, and they reported that the bluffs run down to the river, but they discovered that we could go around the bluffs by going a mile around.
*We are about twenty-five and a quarter miles above the junc-
tion of the North and South forks, and 361 miles from Winter
Quarters, according to Wm. Clayton's account.

Friday, May 14th.—The morning is cloudy and very cold,
and streaks of lightning can be seen occasionally in the west.
About 8 o'clock it commenced to rain very heavy, accompanied
with thunder and lightning. Just before it commenced raining
the bugle sounded to gather up our horses. After the storm
ceased we started onward at 10:15, and after traveling a mile
we passed between the high bluffs, our course being north for
some time. After traveling about six and a quarter miles we
stopped to feed at 1:40 p. m. within three-quarters of a mile
the river. We are on the large low bottoms again, and not more
than three miles from where we started this morning. President Young and Kimball went ahead to look out the route.

Brother Higby killed an antelope and a badger. We had a
shower just before we stopped, and now the weather is some
warmer. At 3 p. m. we proceeded on our journey. We went
two and a half miles and stopped at 4:30. President Young
and Kimball returned and thought it was best to encamp, as
there were high ranges of bluffs west of us that extended down
to the river. We made about eight and three-quarters miles
today. The revenue cutter has been dispatched after two buffaloes and two antelope that have been killed by the hunters.
There was an alarm given by the guard last night a little before
12 o'clock, and one of them fired at an object he thought to be

an Indian, and those who had horses outside of the circle were called up to bring them in. It is my opinion that the guard was mistaken, as we could not see any sign of Indians, neither could we see any tracks in the sand the next morning.

Brother Wm. Clayton has invented a machine, and attached it to the wagon that Brother Johnson drives, to tell the distance we travel. It is simple yet is ingenious. He got Brother Appleton Harmon to do the work. I have understood that Brother Harmon claims to be the inventor, too, which I know to be a positive falsehood. He, Brother Harmon, knew nothing about the first principles of it, neither did he know how to do the work only as Brother Clayton told him from time to time. It shows the weakness of human nature. I will give a description of it hereafter. The camp are all well.

Saturday, May 15th.—This morning is cloudy and very cold and feels like a morning in January, the wind blowing strong from the north. The brethren who killed the buffalo did not bring it to the camp last night. They put it in the boat and left it until morning. It was with difficulty that they found their way to camp, as it was so dark. They brought it in about 7:30 this morning and divided it to the Captains of Ten. At 8 o'clock it commenced raining, but cleared off a little before 9, when we started. After traveling about three-quarters of a mile we began ascending the sandy bluffs and it commenced raining again, making it very cold and disagreeable. The road was much of a zigzag one over the bluffs. We traveled about a mile, the sand being very deep and heavy pulling for the horses, and when we ascended a sand bluff we discovered the bottoms just below. We traveled on the bottoms a little way, when it was considered best to turn out our teams and not travel in the rain. It was 10:30 when we stopped.

My wagon being heavily loaded, Brother Kimball told me to take the mules Brother Johnson worked ahead of his cattle and put them before my horses. We traveled about two and a half miles. About noon it cleared off again and the signal was given to gather up our teams, and at 12:30 we proceeded on our journey and traveled until 2:45, the distance being four and a half miles. About three miles ahead the bluffs appear to run down to the river. The feed is good, but wood is very scarce and the buffalo chips are not a very good substitute for wood when they are wet. This morning I baked some bread and fried some antelope meat, made some coffee and had a very good breakfast, all cooked with wet buffalo chips.

Sunday, May 16th.—The morning was cold and the wind was still blowing from the north. The buffalo that was killed yesterday evening was divided this morning to the Captains of Tens. This forenoon my time was principally occupied baking bread and drying beef. President Young and Kimball with several others went ahead on horseback to explore the country, and returned this afternoon, reporting that we pass over the bluffs by going about four miles.

The bugle sounded this afternoon for the brethren to come together for meeting. Brothers H. C. Kimball, Dr. Richards, Markham and Rockwood spoke. The principal part of the time was occupied in exhorting the brethren to faithfulness, and also to obey the council of those whom God had placed in the Church to lead and direct the affairs of His Kingdom. Brother Kimball spoke in his usual and interesting and impressive manner, exhorting the brethren to adhere to council and to be humble and prayerful, and the Lord would continue to bless us, and we should be healthy, and not one of us should fall by the way. He also stated that he had traveled much, but never witnessed so much union as there was in the camp. He advised the brethren not to hunt on the Sabbath day, when there was plenty of meat in the camp, but said he had no fault to find. He believed that everybody was trying to do the best they could. He said that if we were faithful the angel of the Lord would go before us and be around about us to ward off the harm of the destroyer. He knew the Lord was with us, that our teams were gaining strength and the prayers of the Saints were answered. He had prayed that the Indians would turn to the right and to the left that we might pursue our journey in peace, and asked the brethren if they could get sight of an Indian near? Their answer was, No. He also cautioned them not to use profane language, as the angel of the Lord would turn away from a man that would swear and take the name of the Lord in vain. The Lord loves a faithful man as a father loves a faithful son. The Spirit of the Lord rested upon him and he spoke with power, which cheered my soul.

A number of buffalo herds are in sight, and some of them are making down the bluffs toward our horses. Brother Eric Glines went out to stop them, but they still kept on, when he fired three shots at them, all the shots taking effect on one, which ran a little way and then fell. Francis (*Boggs) came with an antelope. The revenue cutter went out and brought the buffalo in, and it was divided among the camp. I have the pleasure this evening of writing by the light of a candle made by Brother Edson Whipple out of buffalo tallow, and it burns beautifully. The evening was calm and pleasant, and the rules and regulations for the camp (of April the 18th) were read by

Buffalo on Platte River Near Bluffs.

Brother Bullock. President Young and Kimball took a walk to the bluffs about dark, and returned and went to President Young's wagon and remained in council until after 10 p. m.

Monday, May 17th.—The morning was cold and chilly and the wind was northwest. Dr. Richards left another letter on the camp ground for the benefit of the next company, putting it up the same as the others. About 8:13, after traveling about a mile and a half, we arrived at the range of bluffs, which extended to the river, came about a quarter of a mile and crossed a stream of fresh spring water about three feet wide. When we first ascended the bluffs our course was north for a short distance, but we then turned westward and passed over a number of sand bluffs. After traveling two and a half miles beyond the above mentioned stream we arrived at the west side of the bluffs, the last part of the road being very sandy with several very steep pitches to go down. The teams got over without any difficulty. The grass is very good west of the bluffs, and about a mile from the bluffs we passed three streams of spring water. The whole of the bottoms seem to be full of springs. We have to keep near the bluffs, the bottoms are so soft and wet. About 11:45 we stopped to feed, having traveled about six and three-quarter miles; we encamped about half a mile west of a stream of spring water, which we crossed. Brother Redding and myself went back to get some water. We went to the head of the stream and found five boiling springs, boiling up several inches. One of Brother Phineas Young's horses got mired in a swamp where he went in to feed. The brethren hauled him out with ropes.

This forenoon is warm and pleasant, the first warm day we have had for some time. At 2 p. m. we proceeded on our journey and traveled about half a mile, when we came to a stream of pure water about thirty feet wide and very shallow, and there was no difficulty in crossing it. We passed over same safe, some hills a quarter of a mile further, and then came to level prairie again, which is low and soft. We crossed a number of small streams which rise from springs near the bluffs. About 3 o'clock word came that there was a buffalo killed by the hunters about a mile from the camp and two men were sent out to dress it. About the same time the revenue cutter arrived with two buffaloes and an antelope. The meat was taken out of the boat, and a fresh team put on and sent after the other buffalo. At 4:30 the wagons moved onward and traveled until 6 o'clock, when we encamped on the wide bottom plain. We have traveled today about twelve and three-quarters miles in about a west course. We are about a half mile from the river. Brother Harris and myself went down to the river and brought up a keg of water. The brethren dug several wells. Soon after we arrived the boat came in with the other buffalo. The meat was divided equally among the companies. We are in latitude 41 degrees 12 minutes 50 seconds.

Tuesday, May 18th.—The morning was fine and pleasant and at 7 o'clock President Young called the Captains of Tens together and gave them instructions not to let their men kill any more game, as we had more on hand now than we could take care of, and for them not to take life merely to gratify their propensities. He also stated that life was as dear to the animal, according to their understanding, as it was to us. That if the horsemen hunters would go ahead and hunt out the road they would be of more utility to the camp than pursuing every band of antelope that passed the camp; that there were men among us in responsible positions who cared no more for the interest of the camp than the horses that they rode; that the spirit of the hunter as was now manifested would lead them to kill all the game within a thousand miles as inconsistently as the butcher would apply the knife to the throat of a bullock. President Young, after some other remarks, dismissed the captains, telling them that they must lead their men by their own good example, for the men would do well if the captains would set them the proper pattern.

Soon after meeting was dismissed the bugle sounded to collect our teams. At 8:15 a. m. we proceeded on our journey, Brigham, Heber and some others going on ahead on horseback. After traveling three and three-quarters miles a west course we arrived at a stream twenty or twenty-five feet wide and about eighteen inches deep, with a very strong current. We gave it the name of Rat Bank creek. From this stream we traveled near the bank of the river, about a northwest course. At 11:10 a. m. we stopped to feed, having traveled about six and a half miles. This afternoon has been very hot. We saw several spots of small cedar trees growing in the sandy crevices of the rocks opposite here, the head of Cedar bluffs, as named by Fremont, is three miles west of where we were encamped last night. We continued our journey, our route lying near the banks of the river. This forenoon we crossed a number of small streams. We had a little rain this afternoon, accompanied with lightning and distant thunder. This afternoon we traveled nine and a half miles, and during the day fifteen and three-quarters miles. The feed is not very good here.

This evening Colonel Markham called the camp together to remind them of their duty in regard to traveling and getting up their teams. After some other instructions the meeting was dismissed. The wind changed to the north and blew up cold and cloudy.

Wednesday, May 19th.—This morning was cloudy and it rained considerable last night. About 10 o'clock I got up to put the harness under the wagons, H. C. Kimball's saddle and other things which would get damaged by rain, when I discovered Brother Jackson Redding, who was captain of the guard, going around with some of his men picking up the harness and other things and putting them under cover. Captain Redding is a faithful, praiseworthy man, and a man who works for the good of the camp.

As the feed is not good here it was thought best to move on a few miles before breakfast and find better feed. We started out about 5:05 and crossed two small streams, traveling three and three-quarters miles and stopped to eat breakfast. Some of the teams are a quarter of a mile ahead of the main body of the camp. H. C. Kimball and Brother Woolsey went ahead to hunt a place where the feed was good. As they neared the bluffs they discovered that the feed was not so good, and Brother Kimball sent Brother Woolsey back to tell the brethren to stop, while he went on to look out the road through the bluffs. He returned just before we started. After traveling about ten miles alone, he saw a number of wolves, some of them being very large. He tried to scare them, but they would not move out of their tracks, and he had no firearms with him. If he had been afoot I presume they would have attacked him. Brother Kimball has rode so much ahead to look out the way for the camp he has almost broke himself down and is pretty near sick, but his ambition and the care he has for the camp keeps him up.

At 8:40 we again started, came about three miles and began to ascend the bluffs, which are very steep and sandy. Just before we came to the bluffs we crossed a stream about twenty feet wide. We traveled a winding course of about three-quarters of a mile through the bluffs, came 200 yards from the west side and crossed another small stream. It has rained heavy all the time since we started after breakfast. About 10:30 the camp halted, having traveled six miles. About 2:30 the weather looked a little more favorable, and we started at 2:55. Soon after we started it commenced raining again very heavy. We traveled two miles and encamped for the night on the banks of the river, having come eight miles today. The small stream that we crossed west of the bluffs we named Wolf creek. The evening was cold and cloudy, but it cleared off about 6 o'clock.

Thursday, May 20th.—The morning was cloudy with light winds from the northwest and cold. We started about 7:45, and soon after passed Brother Clayton's wagon. He and Brother Harmon were repairing the roadometer, which had suffered by the rain and broke one of the teeth out of the small wheel. Three-fourths of a mile from where we started we crossed a stream eight feet wide and two and a half feet deep. About 11:15 we halted to feed, having traveled seven and three-quarters miles, the latter part of the road being very good. The bluffs on the south side of the river project near to its banks. They appear rocky, and several beautiful groves of cedar are growing on them. Brothers O. Pratt, L. Johnson, A. Lyman and J. Brown went across the river in the boat and discovered we were opposite Ash Hollow, where the Oregon road crosses to the North fork of the Platte. Brother Brown found the grave where he helped to bury an emigrant last summer when he was going west. The boat returned and we again moved onward. Some of the brethren killed a large rattlesnake. This afternoon about three and a half miles from where we stopped for noon we crossed a stream six or eight rods wide and two and a half feet deep, the bottom being quicksand and the current swift. At 5:30 we encamped, having come eight miles, which makes fifteen and three-quarters miles during the day. The road has been very good this afternoon, and the feed is pretty good. We had a light shower this afternoon, but the evening is pleasant.

Friday, May 21st.—The morning was very calm and pleasant, but tolerably cool. At 7:35 we proceeded on our journey. Brother Clayton put up a guide board this morning with the following inscription on it: "From Winter Quarters, 409 miles; from the junction of the North and South forks of the Platte, 93¼ miles; Cedar Bluffs on east side of the river, and Ash Hollow 8 miles; Camp of Pioneers, May 21st, 1847. According to Fremont, this place is 132 miles from Laramie. N. B.— The bluffs on the opposite side are named Castle Bluffs."

We found the prairie very wet and many ponds of water standing, which must have been caused by the heavy falls of rain. At 11:15 we stopped for dinner, having traveled seven and three-quarters miles in a north-northwest course, it being warm and calm.

President Young and Kimball rode ahead to pick out the road. Near this place they saw a nest of wolves. They killed two of them and three others escaped to their holes. Brother Kimball caught one of them by the tail and killed him. At 1:30 we proceeded on our journey, and found the prairie very wet and high grass of last year's growth. Brother Clayton saw a very large rattlesnake. At 5 o'clock Brother Kimball stopped the forward teams to let the rear teams get up, saying that he saw Indians come down from the bluffs. When the last wagons got up we traveled on a quarter of a mile and encamped in a circle, the wagons close together. We have come seven and three-quarters miles this afternoon, which makes fifteen and a half miles during the day.

While we were forming our camp an Indian and his squaw came near the camp. They were Sioux. They made signs that there was a party of them on the bluff north of us, not far distant. President Young ordered them not to bring them into the camp. The Indian was well dressed. Their horses appear to be work horses, which I presume they had stolen from some travelers. The day has been quite warm and some of our teams lagged a little. Brother Cushing drove my team this afternoon, while I rode in Brother King's wagon and drove some for him. The feed is not so good here, there being considerable old grass. This evening is very pleasant. The latitude at noon was 41 degrees 24 minutes 5 seconds.

Saturday, May 22d.—This morning is calm and pleasant; all is peace and quietness in camp. At 8 o'clock we started on our journey, and having to bend to the banks of the river made our road much more crooked than usual. The prairie was soft and uneven. We traveled about five and a half miles and crossed a very slow stream about twenty feet wide. The bluffs are about a mile from the river, and on the south side about two miles. At 11:30 we stopped to feed, having come about seven and a quarter miles, the latter part of the road being much better. Our course was west-northwest, and a light breeze from the east was blowing. Brother Kimball and others go ahead as usual to look out the road. The stream last crossed was named Crab creek, as some of the brethren had seen a very large crab in it.

While we were stopped Brother Clayton went up on the bluffs, which were very high and romantic in their appearance. He said he could see Chimney Rock with the naked eye very plain. He judged it to be about twenty miles distant. We started again at 1:30 p. m. and crossed a number of dry creeks today from one rod wide to six, all appearing to have been very rapid streams some seasons of the year. We found the prairie so much broken between the bluffs and the river that it was impassable with wagons. We traveled a winding course between the bluffs of about two and a quarter miles, and again emerged on the bottoms. Between 4 and 5 o'clock this afternoon the clouds gathered very black from the west, streaks of lightning can be seen and the distant rumbling of thunder can be heard. It has the appearance of a tremendous storm. About 5 p. m. the wind blew up strong from the northwest and the storm passed to the northeast of us. At 5:45 we encamped in a circle within a quarter of a mile of the river, having come eight and a quarter miles this afternoon, which makes fifteen and a half during the day. I saw a very large rattlesnake this afternoon.

Wood is very scarce. We find a few sticks along the bank of the river, which has been drifted there by high water. We have not seen any buffalo for a number of days, and very little game of any kind. Some of the brethren brought a young eagle into camp, which they took out of its nest on the top of one of the high bluffs. It measured forty-six inches from tip to tip of its wings when stretched out. The bluffs and peaks have a very remarkable appearance, the tops being like the ruins of some ancient city with its castles, towers and fortifications. I had no time to examine them. Brother Clayton has given a full description of them, which is very interesting. This evening is very pleasant and all is peace and harmony. The feed is not very good. The inside of our circle is a solid bed of sand, and there were four rattlesnakes killed in the camp.

Sunday, May 23d.—This morning is very fine and pleasant. I went down to the river before sunrise and made a fire and washed some clothes. President Young, Kimball and others walked up to the bluffs to view them, and returned about 11:30. Brother Clayton saw an adder about eighteen inches long. Brother Nathaniel Fairbanks came into camp, having been bit on the leg with a rattlesnake. He had been up on the bluffs, and he said he felt the effects of it all over his body. Three minutes after he was bit he felt a pricking in his lungs. They gave him a dose of Lobelia and some alcohol and water. He is suffering much from pain.

Brother O. Pratt said the highest bluff was 235 feet above the surface of the river. At 12 o'clock the horses were all tied up and the brethren called together for meeting. After singing and prayer, Brother E. Snow made some remarks, followed by President Young. We had a first-rate meeting. Brother Young gave us some glorious instructions, which done my soul good. He said he was perfectly well satisfied with the conduct of the camp and the spirit which they manifested toward him and toward one another and all things were going right. Brother George A. Smith and others made some remarks. Brother Young notified the four Bishops present to prepare to administer the sacrament on next Sunday at 11 o'clock. Soon after the meeting the wind blew up very cold from the

northwest, thick black clouds gathered all around us, and about
7 o'clock rain began to pour down, accompanied with thunder
and lightning and hail for a short time. We feared for some
time that our wagon tops should blow off. The rain ceased
about 10 p. m. and the wind continued to blow nearly all night.
We found all things safe in the morning, not sustaining any
damage whatever.

Monday, May 24th.—The morning was very cold, the wind
continuing northwest. At 8:35 a. m. we started and traveled
over a level prairie somewhat sandy. At 10:45 we stopped to
feed, having come ten miles. About noon the weather moderated a little. Two Indians came across the bluffs to our camp
on foot. They made signs that we should give them something
to eat and they would go away. Some of the brethren gave
them some bread. They started up the river a little way and
crossed over. At 3 p. m. we proceeded on our journey and
traveled until 6 o'clock, six and a half miles. This afternoon
several of the horse teams gave out. Just before we stopped,
a party of Indians was discovered on the opposite side of the
river. After we camped, which was a quarter of a mile from
the river, we discovered the Indians had a flag flying, which
is their mode of finding out whether they would be admitted
in the camp or not. President Young sent a man up the river
with a white flag, when they all crossed the river on their
ponies, some of them singing. They were thirty-five in number. Some of them were women. They were all well dressed
and behaved themselves better than any Indians I have ever
seen before. Four of their chiefs came down to the camp.
Colonels Markham and Sherwood showed them around the camp.
They took some provisions to those who were encamped up
the river, and gave the chiefs their supper at the camp. The
brethren put up a tent for the head chief and his squaw to
sleep in. The evening was pleasant, and we left our horses out
until 11 o'clock to feed, with a guard to watch them. H. C.
Kimball's health is very poor and he is unable to ride ahead,
but is confined to his wagon most of the time.

Tuesday, May 25th.—The morning was fine and pleasant.
All the Indians, both men and women, came into camp this
morning. Some of the brethren traded horses with them and
bought moccasins from them. At 8:20 we proceeded on our
journey. Soon after we started the Indians left us. They appeared to be well satisfied. They crossed the river and went
in the direction they came from. After traveling one mile we
ascended a sandy ridge, traveled about three-quarters of a mile
over very deep sand and came on the bottoms again. We came

two and a half miles and stopped to feed at 11:15, several small ponds of water being there. We continued our journey at 1:30

Indians Seen Near Laramie.

p. m., having come four and three-quarters miles over a low, soft prairie bottom. By the appearance of it there must have been very heavy rains ahead of us. The traveling was very heavy for our teams, but at 3 p. m. we started on again and traveled until 5:45, having come four and three-quarters miles, and twelve miles during the day. We encamped about two miles from the river. The brethren dug a number of wells and found very good water. Our camp ground is very low and wet, which makes it very disagreeable. The evening was very pleasant and the brethren were in good spirits.

Wednesday, May 26th.—This morning was calm and pleasant, and at 8 a. m. we proceeded on our journey. After traveling between four and five miles we came to a point directly opposite Chimney Rock. We had traveled forty-one and a half miles since it was first seen with the naked eye. At 12 o'clock we stopped to feed, having come seven and a quarter miles in a north-northwest course. This forenoon the roads were good. Brother Kimball rode ahead to look out the way. The hunters brought in four antelope to camp today.

Brother Pratt ascertained Chimney Rock to be 260 feet high. It is in about latitude 41 degrees 42 minutes 58 seconds. At 2:25 we again started and traveled near the river. We came five miles and encamped on the bank of the river about 5 p. m., having come twelve and a quarter miles during the day. The feed is better than we have had for a number of days, but wood was very scarce. Soon after we encamped, a heavy black cloud arose in the west, which had the appearance of a heavy storm The wind blew up very strong from the northwest, accompanied with a few drops of rain. About 6 o'clock it cleared off and we had a beautiful evening. Some of the brethren were moving Brother George Billings' wagon and run the wheel over the young eagle and killed it. Brother Billings discovered that the end of an axeltree was broke, and Brother Harper went to work on it.

Thursday, May 27th.—This morning was very fine and the scenery was beautiful. The bluffs north of us are about three miles from the river, the prairie is level and the feed very good. At 7:50 a. m. we proceeded on our journey along the bank of the river and stopped to feed at 11:45, having come eight miles. O. P. Rockwell killed two antelope and brought them into camp and they were divided. There are some heavy thunder clouds in the south and west. At 2 p. m. we again moved westward, the prairie being level and the road very good. We passed Scott's bluffs, which is nineteen and three-quarters miles from Chimney Rock, between 3 and 4 o'clock. At 4:45 we encamped a short distance from the river, having come five and three-quarters miles, which makes thirteen and three-quarters miles during the day. Brother Pratt measured the North fork of the Platte river with his sextant and found it to be 792 yards wide. The north peak of Scott's bluffs is in latitude 41 degrees 50 minutes 52 seconds.

Buffalo Hunt Near Scott's Bluffs.

Friday, May 28th.—The morning was cool and damp, cloudy weather, and some rain with wind northeast. At 8 a. m. the brethren were called together and the question proposed, whether we should go on or wait for fair weather. All agreed to wait for fair weather. About 11 o'clock it cleared off, and we gathered up our teams and started.

Before we started Brother Luke Johnson and myself went up the river about three miles with the cutter in search of wood. We came to a beautiful clear stream of water about eight feet wide, and saw large numbers of small fish in it. It is not very deep, has a gravel bottom and the water tastes very good. It is about three miles long, rises from springs and runs in a line with the river for some distance, then takes a turn to the south and empties into the river.

Part of the road today was sandy. At 4:45 we encamped near the river, having come eleven and a half miles. The feed is not so good here, but driftwood is tolerably plenty. The evening was cold and the weather dull and cloudy, with wind northeast. O. P. Rockwell and Thomas Brown went out hunting north of the bluff. The latter saw five or six Indians and the signs of a large company.

Saturday, May 29th.—This morning was cold, wet and cloudy, with wind northeast, but about 10 a. m. it cleared off. At 10:30 the bugle sounded to get up our teams. After we got all ready to start there was notice given for the brethren to come together to the boat in the center of the ring. President Young, taking his station in the boat, ordered the Captains of

Tens to call out their respective companies and see if all their men were present. He then ordered the clerk to call all the names to see if they were all present. Joseph Hancock and Andrew Gibbons were reported to be absent hunting. President Young arose and addressed the meeting as follows: (Reported by Brother Wm. Clayton, who has kindly permitted me to copy it from the journal.)

Pioneer Sermon by President Young.

"I remarked last Sunday that I had not felt much like preaching to the brethren on this mission. This morning I feel

Brigham Young Before Pioneer Days.

like preaching a little, and shall take for my text, that 'As to pursuing our journey with the company, with the spirit they possess, I am about to revolt against it.' This is the text I feel like preaching on this morning, consequently I am in no hurry. In the first place, before we left Winter Quarters it was told the brethren, and many knew it by experience, that we had to leave our homes, our houses and lands, our all, because we believed in the Gospel as revealed to the Saints in these last days. The rise of the persecution against the Church was in consequence of the doctrine of Eternal Truth taught by

Joseph. Many knew this by experience. Some lost their husbands, some lost their wives, and some their children through persecution. And yet we have not been disposed to forsake the Truth and mingle with the Gentiles, except a few, who have turned aside and gone away from us. And we have learned in a measure the difference between a professor of religion and a possessor of religion, before we left Winter Quarters.

"It was told the brethren that we were going to look out a home for the Saints, where they could be free from persecution by the Gentiles, where we could dwell in peace and serve God according to the Holy Priesthood, where we could build up the Kingdom so that the nations would begin to flock to our standard. I have said many things to the brethren about the strictness of their walk and conduct, when we left the Gentiles; and told them we would have to walk uprightly or the law would be put in force, and many have turned aside through fear.

"The Gospel does not bind a good man down, and deprive him of his rights and privileges; it does not deprive him of enjoying the fruits of his labors; it does not rob him of blessings; it does not stop his increase; it does not diminish his kingdom; but is calculated to enlarge his kingdom as well as to enlarge his heart; it is calculated to give to him privileges, and power, and honor, and exaltation, and everything which heart can desire in righteousness all the days of his life. And then, when he gets exalted in the eternal worlds, he can still turn around and say: 'It hath not entered into the heart of man to conceive the glory, and honor, and blessings, which God hath in store for those who love and serve him.'

"I want the brethren to understand and comprehend the principles of Eternal Life, and watch the Spirit, be wide awake, and not be overcome by the adversary. You can see the fruits of the Spirit, but you cannot see the Spirit itself. With the natural eye you behold it not. You can see the result of yielding to the evil spirits and what it will lead you to, but you do not see the spirit itself, nor its operations only by the spirit that is in you.

"Nobody has told me what was going on in this camp, but I have known it all the while. I have been watching its movements, its influence, its effects; and I know the result of it, if it is not put a stop to. I want you to understand that, inasmuch as we are beyond the power of the Gentiles, where the devils have tabernacles in the priests and all the people; but we are beyond their reach, we are beyond their power, we are beyond their grasp; and, what has the Devil now to work upon? Upon the spirits of the men in this camp. And if you don't open your hearts so that the Spirit of God can enter your hearts and teach you the right way, I know that you are a ruined people, I know that you will be destroyed and that without remedy. And, unless there is a change and a different course of conduct, a different spirit to that which there is now in this camp, I go no further. I am in no hurry.

"Give me the man of prayer; give me the man of faith; give me the man of discretion; a sober-minded man, and I would rather go among the savages with six or eight such men, than to trust myself with the whole of this camp with the spirit they now possess. Here is an opportunity for every man to prove himself, to know whether he will pray, and remember his God, without being asked to do it every day. To know whether they will have confidence enough to ask of God that they may receive, without my telling them to do it. If this camp was composed of men who had newly received the Gospel; men who had not received Priesthood; men who had not been through the ordinances in the Temple; and who had not had years of experience, enough to have learned the influence of the spirits, and the difference between a good and an evil spirit, I should feel like preaching to them and watching over them and teaching them all the time, day by day. But here are the Elders of Israel, men who have had years of experience, men who have had the Priesthood for years; and have they got faith enough to rise up and stop a mean, low, groveling, contentious, quarrelsome spirit? No. They have n₁ t, nor would they try to do it, unless I rise up in the power of God and put it down . I don't mean to bow down to the spirit there is in this camp, and which is rankling in the bosoms of the brethren, which shall lead to knockdown, and perhaps to use the knife to cut each other's throats, if it is not put a stop to. I don't mean to bow down to the spirit which causes the brethren to quarrel—and when I wake up in the morning, the first thing I hear is some of the brethren jawing each other and quarreling because a horse has got loose in the night.

"I have let the brethren dance and fiddle and act the nigger, night after night, to see what they would do, and what extremes they would go to, if suffered to go as far as they would; but I don't love to see it. The brethren say they want a little exercise to pass the time evenings; but if you can't tire yourselves enough with a day's journey, without dancing every night, carry your guns on your shoulders and walk, and carry your wood to camp, instead of lounging and sleeping in your wagons, increasing the loads until your teams are tired to death and ready to drop to the earth. Help your teams over mudholes and bad places, instead of lounging in your wagons, and that will give you exercise enough without dancing.

"Well, they will play cards; they will play checkers; they will play dominoes; and, if they had the privileges, and were where they could get whisky, they would be drunk half of their time, and in one week they would quarrel, get to high words, and draw their knives to kill each other. That is what such a course of things would tend to. Don't you know it? Yes. Well, then, why don't you try to put it down? I have played cards once in my life, since I became a 'Mormon,' to see what kind of a spirit would attend it, and I was so well satisfied that I would rather see the dirtiest thing in your hands that you could find on the earth, than to see a pack of cards in your hands. You never read of gambling, playing cards, checkers, dominoes, etc., in the Scriptures. But you do hear of men praising the Lord in the dance, but who ever heard of praising the Lord in a game of cards? If any man had sense enough to play a game of cards, or dance a little, without wanting to keep it up all the time; but exercise a little and then quit it, and think no more of it, it would be well enough. But you want to keep it up till midnight, and every night, and all the time. You don't know how to control yourselves.

"Last winter when we had our season of recreation in the Council House, I went forth in the dance frequently; but did my mind run on it? No. To be sure, when I was dancing my mind was on the dance, but the moment I stopped in the middle or the end of a time, my mind was engaged in prayer and praise to my Heavenly Father; and whatever I engage in, my mind is on it while engaged in it, but the moment I am done with it, my mind is drawn up to my God.

"The devils which inhabit the Gentile priests are here. Their tabernacles are not here. We are out of their power. We are beyond their grasp. We are beyond the reach of their persecutions. But the devils are here and the first we shall know, if you don't open your eyes and your hearts, they will cause division in our camp, and perhaps war, as they did the former Saints, as you read in the 'Book of Mormon.'

"We suppose that we are going to look out a home for the Saints, a resting place, a place of peace, where we can build up the Kingdom and bid the nations welcome, without a low, mean, dirty, trifling, covetous, wicked spirit dwelling in our bosoms. It is vain, vain!

"Some of you are very fond of passing jokes, and will carry your joke very far, but will you take a joke? If you don't want to take a joke, don't give a joke to your brethren.

Joking nonsense, profane language, don't belong to us. Suppose the Angels were witnessing the hoedown the other evening, and listening to the haw-haws, would they not be ashamed of it? I have not given a joke to any man on the journey, nor felt like it. Neither have I insulted any man's feelings, but I have bellowed pretty loud, and spoke sharp to the brethren, when I have seen their awkwardness at coming into camp.

"The revelations in the Bible, in the 'Book of Mormon,' and Doctrine and Covenants teaches us to be sober. And let me ask you Elders that have been through the ordinances in the Temple, what were your covenants there? I want that you should remember them. When I laugh I see my folly and nothingness, and weakness, and am ashamed of myself. I think meaner and worse of myself than any can think of me. But I delight in God, and in His commandments, and delight to meditate on Him, and to serve Him; and I mean that everything in me shall be subject to Him, and I delight in serving Him.

"Now let every man repent of his weakness, of his follies, of his meanness, and every kind of wickedness—and stop your swearing, and your profane language—for it is in this camp. I know it and have known it. I have said nothing about it; but I tell you, if you don't stop it, you shall be cursed by the Almighty, and shall dwindle away and be damned. Such things shall not be suffered in this camp. You shall honor God and confess His name, or else you shall suffer the penalty.

"Most of this camp belong to the Church, nearly all, and I would say to you brethren, and to the Elders of Israel, if you are faithful you will yet be sent to preach the Gospel to the nations of the earth, and bid all welcome, whether they believe in the Gospel or not. And this Kingdom will reign over many who do not belong to the Church; over thousands who do not believe in the Gospel. By and by every knee shall bow, and every tongue confess, and acknowledge, and reverence, and honor the name of God and His Priesthood, and observe the laws of the Kingdom, whether they belong to the Church and obey the Gospel, or not. And I mean that every man in this camp shall do it. This is what the Scriptures mean by 'Every knee shall bow,' etc., and you cannot make anything else out of it.

I understand that there are several in this camp, who do not belong to the Church. I am a man who will stand up for them, and protect them in all their rights: and they shall not trample on the rights of others, nor on the Priesthood. They reverence and acknowledge the name of God, and His Priesthood, and, if they set up their heads and seek to introduce iniquity into this camp, and to trample on the Priesthood, I swear to them they shall never go back to tell the tale. I will leave them where they will be safe. If they want to return they can now have the privilege; and any man, who chooses to go back, rather than abide the laws of God, can now have the privilege of doing so before we go further.

"Here are the Elders of Israel who have got the Priesthood, who have to preach the Gospel, who have to gather the nations of the earth, who have to build up the Kingdom so that the nations can come to it. They will stoop to dance like nigers. I don't mean this as debasing the nigers by any means. They will hoedown, all turn summersets, dance on their knees, and haw-haw out loud. They will play cards, and they will play checkers and dominoes. They will use profane language. They will swear.

"Suppose when you go to preach, the people ask you what you did, when you went up on this mission to seek out a location for the whole Church? What was your course of conduct? Did you dance? Yes. Did you play cards? Yes. Did you play checkers? Yes. Did you use profane language? Yes. Did you swear? Yes. Did you gamble with each other and threaten each other? Yes. How would you feel? What would you say for yourselves? Would you not want to go and hide up? Your mouth would be stopped, and you would want to creep away in disgrace.

"I am one of the last to ask my brethren to enter into a solemn covenant, but, if they will not enter into a solemn covenant to put away their iniquity, and turn to the Lord, and serve Him, and asknowledge and honor His name, I want them to take their wagons and return back, FOR I SHALL NOT GO ANY FARTHER under this state of things. If we don't repent and quit our wickedness, we will have more hinderances than we have had and worse storms to encounter. I want the brethren to be ready for meeting tomorrow at the appointed time, instead of rambling off and hiding in their wagons to play cards, etc. I think it will be good for us to have a fast meeting tomorrow, and a prayer meeting, and humble ourselves and turn to the Lord, and He will forgive us.''

He then called upon all the High Priests to step out in a line in front of the wagon; and then the Bishops to step out in front of the High Priests. He then counted them and ascertained their numbers to be four Bishops and fifteen High Priests. He then called for all the Seventies to form a line in the rear. There was seventy-eight in number. The Elders were then called out in line. Their number was eight. There was also eight of the Twelve.

He then asked the brethren of the Twelve, if they were willing to covenant to turn to the Lord with all their hearts, to repent of all their follies, to cease from all their evils, and serve God according to His laws? If they were willing, to manifest it by holding up their right hands. Every man raised his hand. He then put the question to the High Priests, and Bishops, to the Seventies and Elders, and last to the other brethren. All covenanted with uplifted hands, without a dissenting voice. He then addressed those who were not members of the Church and told them they should be protected in their rights and privileges, while they would conduct themselves well and not seek to trample on the Priesthood, nor blaspheme the name of God, etc.

He then referred to the conduct of Benjamin Rolfe's two younger brothers in joining with the Higby's and John C. Bennett in sowing discontent and strife among the Saints in Nauvoo, and remarked that, ''There will be no more Bennett scrapes suffered here. He spoke highly of Benjamin Rolfe's conduct, although not a member of the Church, and also referred to the esteem in which his father and mother were held by the Saints generally. He then very tenderly blessed the brethren and prayed that God would enable them to fulfill their covenants, and withdrew to give a chance to others to speak, if they felt like it.

Brother Heber C. Kimball arose and said: that he agreed to all that President Young had said. He received it as the word of God to himself, and it was the word of the Lord to this camp, if they would receive it. He had been watching the motions of things and the conduct of the brethren for some time, and had seen what it would lead to. He had said little but had thought a good deal. It had made him shudder, when he had seen the Elders of Israel descend to the lowest and dirtiest things imaginable—the last end of everything. But what had passed this morning would be an everlasting blessing to the brethren, if they would repent and be faithful and keep their covenants. He could never rest satisfied until his family were liberated from the Gentiles and their corruptions, and established in a land where they could plant and eat the fruit of their labors. He had never had the privilege of eating the fruits of his labors yet, neither had his family, but when this was done he could sleep in peace, but not until then.

He said: ''If we will serve the Lord and remember His name to call upon Him, we shall not one of us be left under the sod, but shall be permitted to return and meet our families in peace, and enjoy their society again. But, if this camp continues the course of conduct they have done, the judgment of God will overtake us. I hope the brethren will take heed to what President Young has said, and let it sink deep into their hearts.''

Brother Kimball made some very feeling remarks, with some instructions, that have not been written. He blessed the brethren in the name of the Lord, and he appeared to be very much affected and very humble.

Elder Orson Pratt wanted to add a word to what had been said. ''Much good advice has been given to teach us how we may spend our time profitably—by prayer, meditation, etc. —but there is another idea which I want to add: There are many good books in the camp and worlds of knowledge before us, which we have not attained, and, if the brethren would devote all their leisure time to seeking after knowledge, they would never need to say, they had nothing to pass away their time. If we could spend twenty-three hours of the twenty-four in gaining knowledge, and only sleep one hour, all the days of our lives, there would be worlds of knowledge in store yet for us to learn.

''I know it is difficult to bring our minds to dilligent and constant study, in pursuit of knowledge all at once, but by steady practice and perseverance we shall become habitual to it, and it will become a pleasure to us. I would recommend to the brethren, besides prayer and obedience, to seek after knowledge continually, and it will help us to overcome our follies and nonsense. We shall have no time for it.''

Elder Woodruff said: ''He remembered the time Zion's camp went up to Missouri to redeem Zion, when Brother Joseph Smith stood upon a wagon wheel and told the brethren that the decree had passed and could not be revoked; that: the destroying angel would visit the camp; and the brethren began to feel what Brother Joseph had said. We buried eighteen in a very short time, and a more sorrowful time I never saw before. There are nine men here that were in that camp, and they all recollect the circumstances well, and will never forget it. I was thinking while the President was speaking; that, if I was one who had played cards or checkers, I would take every pack of cards. and checker board and burn them up, so that they would not be in the way to tempt us.''

Colonel Markham acknowledged that he had done wrong, in many things. He had always indulged himself before he came into the Church, with everything he desired and he knew he had done wrong on this journey. He knew his mind had become darkened since he left Winter Quarters. He hoped the brethren would forgive him, and he would pray to God to forgive him, and he would try to do better. While he was speaking, he was very much affected indeed, and wept like a child.

Many of the brethren were very much affected, and all seemed to realize for the first time, the spirit to which they had yielded, and the awful consequences of such things, if persisted in. Many were in tears and felt humble. President Young returned to the boat as Brother Markham closed his remarks, and said in reply:

"That he knew that the brethren would forgive him, and the Lord will forgive us all, if we turn to Him with all our hearts and cease to do evil. The meeting was then dismissed, each man returned to his wagon.

At 1:30 p. m. we again pursued our journey in peace, all reflecting on what had been said today, and many expressing their gratitude for the instructions they had received. It seemed as if we were just starting on this important mission, and all began to realize the responsibility resting upon us, to conduct ourselves in such a manner, that this mission may prove an everlasting blessing to us, instead of an everlasting disgrace. No loud laughter was heard, nor swearing, no profane language, no hard speeches to man or beast; and it seemed as if the cloud had broke and we had emerged into a new element, and a new atmosphere, and a new socity.

We traveled six miles about a north-northwest course, and then arrived at the foot of the low bluffs, which extended within ten rods of the river, the latter forming a large bend, northward at this point. At the foot of the bluffs the road was sandy and very heavy on our teams. Like all other sandy places, it is entirely barren, there being only a tuft of grass here and there. After passing over the sand, we changed our course to a little north of west, not, however, leaving the bluffs very far. The river tends again to the south, where we then found the ground hard and good to travel over, but perfectly bare of grass for about a mile.

At 5 o'clock it commenced raining very hard, accompanied with lightning and thunder and a strong northeast wind. It also changed to considerable colder again. At 5:30 we found our encampment, near the highest bench of the prairie. The feed is not very good on the bottoms, and here there is none at all. We have passed a small grove of tolerable sized trees, all green, growing on an island in the river. There is no timber on this side of the river. We picked up driftwood enough to do our cooking. The distance we have traveled today is eight and one-half miles, and during the week seventy-four and one-half miles, making us 514½ miles from Winter Quarters. There is a creek of clear water about 200 yards to the south of us from which we obtain our water.

Sunday, May 30th.—The morning was fair and pleasant, and about 9 a. m. the brethren met together a little south of the camp, and had a prayer meeting. Many of the brethren expressed their feelings warmly, and confessed their faults one to another. Between 11 and 12 o'clock the meeting was dismissed, and the brethren gathered up their horses and tied them, and met again about 12 o'clock, and partook of the Sacrament. The Twelve with some others went north of the bluffs and had a meeting. All conducted themselves peaceably and quiet today. They seem to have profited by the instructions we got on Saturday. We had some rain this afternoon, but the evening is pleasant.

Monday, May 31st.—This morning was cool but pleasant, and at 8:15 we proceeded on our journey over a good hard road. At 12:30 we stopped to feed, having come nine and one-half miles. At 3 p. m. we again started, coming seven and one-quarter miles and stopped at 6:45 and encamped near a stream about a rod wide, the feed being very poor. We came sixteen and three-quarters miles today. This afternoon we passed some timber on this side of the river, the first we had seen since the 10th inst. (being a distance of 215 miles), except a little driftwood the brethren have picked up. The road has been very sandy. Some of the brethren killed a deer this afternoon, and wounded two others. Last Sunday President Young and Kimball saw the Black Hills. The camp are all well and in good spirits.

8.—PLATTE RIVER CROSSINGS, JUNE, 1847.

Tuesday, June 1st, 1847.—The morning was very fine,
warm and pleasant, and at 9 o'clock we proceeded on our
journey. At 11:30 we halted to feed, having come about four
and one-half miles. At 1:30 we started on again and continued until 4:15, and came in sight of Fort Laramie, about four
miles southwest of us. At 5:45 the wagons formed an encampment in the form of a V, having traveled seven and one-
half miles.

Six wagons, which are a part of the Mississippi Company,
that wintered at Pueblo, are here. They have been here two
weeks, and they report that the remainder of their company
were coming on with a detachment of the "Mormon Battalion,"
who expected to be paid off and start for this point about the
first of June. Two of the brethren came across the river to
see us, and they report that nothing has been heard from the
main body of the Battalion and that there has been three or
four deaths at Pueblo. They said that three traders from the
mountains arrived here six days ago, having come from the
Sweet Water in six days and nights, traveling day and night
with horses and mules to prevent them from starving to
death. Two of their oxen had died for want of feed. The
snow was two feet deep at the Sweet Water. It is evident
that we are early enough for the feed.

I make the distance from Winter Quarters to Laramie
541¼ miles, which is two miles less than Brother Clayton, and
we have traveled it in seven weeks, lacking half a day, and
have not traveled but a few miles on Sundays. We have come
this far without accidents, except the loss of two horses stolen
by the Indians, and two killed. The Lord has blessed and
prospered us on our journey, and the camp enjoys better health
than they did when they left Winter Quarters. The country
begins to have a more hilly and mountainous appearance, and
some of the Black Hills show very plainly from here. The
timber is mostly ash and cottonwood on the low bottoms on
the river, but there are some cedar groves on the bluffs.
There is an Indian baby wrapped around with skins, deposited
in the branches of a large ash tree, which is in the center of
our camp. It is said that this is the mode of burying their

dead. The bark is peeled off of the tree to prevent the wolves climbing up.

Wednesday, June 2nd.—The morning was pleasant, and about 9 o'clock the Twelve and some others went across the river to view the fort, and inquire something concerning our route. Brother Pratt measured the distance across the river and found it to be 108 yards. The water is deep in the channel, and the current runs about three and one-half miles an hour. There is an old fort near the bank of the river on the other side, and the outside walls are still standing, but the inside is ruins, having been burned. The walls are built of Spanish brick, which is large pieces of tempered clay dried in the sun, and laid up like brick with mortar. The dimensions of this fort, outside, from east to west, is 144 feet, and from north to south 103 feet. There is a large door fronting the south, which led to the dwellings, fourteen in number when burned.

Fort Laramie is about two miles from the Platt, situated on the bank of a stream, called by the same name, which is forty-one yards wide with a very swift current, but not very deep. The brethren, who went to the fort, were informed that we could not travel more than four miles further on the north side of the Platte, the bluffs being impassable with wagons; also that the first year corn was planted there it done very well, but none could be raised since for want of rain as it had not rained for two years there until a few days ago. They, at the fort, have a very good flat boat, and will let us have it for $15, or ferry us over for $18, or 25c per wagon. The trade of this place is principally with the Sioux Indians. The Crow Indians came here a few weeks ago and stole twenty-five horses, which were within 300 yards of the fort and a guard around them. The lattitude of this place is 42 degrees 12 minutes and 13 seconds.

When the brethren returned they brought the boat with them. Some of the brethren went fishing this afternoon with the seine, in the Laramie Fork, and caught sixty or seventy small fish. The Twelve have decided that Brother Amasa Lyman should go with R. Stevens, John Tippets and T. Woolsey to Pueblo.

Thursday, June 3rd.—This morning was cold with a strong southeast wind, and the first division commenced crossing their wagons early. The wind blowing strong up the river, made it easier crossing. They ferried a wagon over in fifteen minuets. The blacksmiths got their forges up, and went to work repairing wagons and shoeing horses. At 11:15 the brethren started for Pueblo on horseback. President Young, Kimball, Richards and Pratt accompanied them to the Laramie Fork and there held a council, kneeled down and dedicated them to the Lord and blessed them. At 1:40 p. m. it commenced raining, accompanied by hail and lightning with very loud thunder, which lasted until 3:30. During the storm the horses were secured in the old fort, and the ferry ceased running. About 5 o'clock the first division was over. The boat was then manned by the second division, lead by John S. Higby. They averaged a wagon across in eleven minutes.

About 7 o'clock it commenced raining again with wind southeast, which stopped the ferry, leaving three companies of about fifteen wagons on the other side. Four men have arrived from St. Joseph, Mo., who report that twenty wagons are three miles below and 600 or 700 were passed on the road. They think that there will be about 2000 wagons leave the states this season for Oregon and California. The Crow Indians stole four of their horses.

Friday, June 4th.—The morning was very fine, and Laramie Peak shows very plain. The brethren commenced ferrying at 4:30, and at 8 o'clock President Young, Kimball and others went up to Fort Laramie, returning about 11 o'clock. They heard very favorable reports from the traders about Bear River valley, being well timbered and plenty of grass, light winters and very little snow; also fish in abundance in the streams. About 11:30 Brother Crow's company came and joined the second division.

At 12 o'clock we again started on our journey, following the wagon road, and at 1:20 we halted to feed, having come three miles. The bluffs are very high and come near the river. At 2:30 we continued our journey and found the road very uneven and sandy. About seven and three-quarters miles from Laramie we descended a very steep pitch, or hill, and had to lock our wheels for the first time for six weeks. At 5:30 we encamped, having come eight and one-quarter miles during the day. About the time we encamped we had a very heavy thunder shower.

I will give the names of Brother Crow's company. They are as follows: Robert Crow, Elizabeth Crow, Benjamin Crow, Harriet Crow, John McHenry Crow, Walter H. Crow, William Parker Crow, Isa Venda Exene Crow, Ira Minda Almerene Crow, George W. Therlkill, Matilda Jane Therlkill, James William Therlkill, Milton Howard Therlkill, Archibald Little, James Chesney and Lewis B. Myers, seventeen in number, making 161 souls in the Pioneer company, deducting the four that have gone to Pueblo. J. B. Myers is represented as knowing the country to the mountains, having traveled it before. They have five wagons, one cart, eleven horses, twenty-four oxen, twenty-two cows, three bulls and seven calves. The number of animals in the camp are ninety-six horses, fifty-one mules, ninety oxen, forty-three cows, nine calves, three bulls, sixteen chickens, sixteen dogs, seventy-nine wagons and one cart.

Brother Clayton put up a signboard at the ferry: Inscription, "Winter Quarters, 561¼ miles." Brother O. Pratt took the altitude of Fort Laramie and found it to be 4090 feet above the level of the sea. Fremont makes it 4470, a difference of 380 feet. The longitude of Fort Laramie is 104 degrees 11 minutes 53 seconds.

Saturday, June 5th.—The morning was pleasant though somewhat cloudy, and the bugle sounded early to start, but we were detained until 8:30 on account of several oxen being missing. After traveling a little over four miles we ascended a steep bluff, where the road runs on top of it for a short distance in a winding direction. The surface in some places is very rough, and many places are covered with ledges of rocks, which shakes our wagons very much. In descending there is a short turn near the bottom, where Brother Crow's cart turned over, though there was no damage done. After winding our way around and through sand and over rocks we came to a very large spring, the water of which was warm and soft.

At 11:35 we stopped to feed, the grass being very short. We had come six and one-half miles. About a quarter of a mile ahead we discovered a company of eleven wagons bound westward. They came on to our road from a south direction, where the road forks. One runs to Fort John (*Laramie) and the other that we came on runs by the old fort. They say the road they came on is ten miles to the spring, and the one we came on is fourteen and one-quarter miles. While we were stopped we had a fine shower. At 1:40 we proceeded on our journey. The latitude of the warm spring is 42 degrees 15 minutes 06 seconds.

After traveling a mile we turned in a narrow pass to the northwest between two high bluffs, and after traveling half a mile further we came to where the road rises a very high, steep bluff, at the foot of which is a short sudden pitch, and then a rugged ascent of a quarter of a mile. When we arrived at the top, we found the road tolerably good, but still rises for a quarter of a mile. After traveling five and one-quarter miles we descended the bluff, the road being sandy though pretty good. At 6:30 we encamped on the west bank of a small stream and near a spring of very good water, having come ten and one-half miles.

Brother Clayton put up a guide board every ten miles. The feed is very good here and there is plenty of wood. The Oregon company is encamped about a quarter of a mile back. Brother Kimball has traveled ahead this afternoon and picked out this camp ground, which is the best we have had for a long time. About dark it rained, accompanied with thunder and lightning. Tomorrow is set apart as last Sunday was for prayer and fasting. It is reported that there are three or four companies between here and Fort John (*Laramie), which was formerly called Laramie. The camp are all well and in good spirits and the Lord continues to bless us.

Sunday, June 6th.—This morning is cool and cloudy and looks like rain. At 8 a. m. the eleven wagons that camped back a little ways passed us again. At 9 o'clock the brethren assembled for prayer meeting, and we had a very good meeting. Brothers E. Snow, Little and others occupied the time. The meeting was dismissed a little before 11 a. m. Three or four men came to camp on horseback and reported that their company was a short distance back. They had encamped at the warm springs last night.

At 11:40 the brethren assembled for preaching, when it commenced raining very heavy, accompanied with lightning and thunder. While it was raining the Oregon company came up, and they had nineteen wagons and two carriages. They have a guide, who says he shall find water six miles ahead and no more for fifteen miles. Between 12 and 1 o'clock the weather cleared off, and it was thought best to travel six miles this afternoon, in order to shorten our day's travel tomorrow, and at 2:30 we moved forward, crossing the stream three-quarters of a mile ahead. Brother Young, Kimball and Woodruff went ahead to look for a camp ground. We came a little over four miles to where the company of seventeen wagons were encamped, south of the road, and at 5:30 we encamped, having come five miles. The feed is very good and a stream of water is running near the camp and there is wood in plenty. The company of eleven wagons are encamped a short distance ahead of us, but, notwithstanding, we have much the best camping ground. Brother Frost put up his forge and done some blacksmithing. There is a strong wind blowing from the west.

Monday, June 7th.—The morning was fine and we took our horses out early, about half a mile east, where the feed was very good. At 6:30 the Oregon company passed us and at 7:10 we again commenced our journey. At 11 o'clock we halted to feed on the west bank of a small stream, the grass being short. We had come seven and three-quarters miles in a course north northwest, and the road was even and good traveling. Soon after we halted another Oregon company of thirteen wagons passed us. They say they are from Andrew County, Missouri. At 12:40 we proceeded onward and after traveling a short distance we came to a hill, which was a quarter of a mile from the bottom to the top, the ascent being gradual.

Top o' the Rockies Just Below the Sky.

From the top of this hill, we had a very pleasant view of the surrounding country, the scenery being truly romantic. The country is very much broken, with a forest of pine covering the surface. From this hill we have a fine view of Limavama Peak, and there appears to be snow on the top of it. At 3:30 we arrived at Horse Shoe Creek and formed our encampment in the center of a grove of ash and cottonwood, having traveled five and one-quarter miles over a crooked road, and during the day thirteen miles. We have the best feed we have had since we left Winter Quarters, and the most pleasant camp ground. There is a beautiful large spring of cold water here also.

Brother Kimball picked out this camp ground and found the spring and called it Heber's Spring. The creek is also clear and is said to have trout in it. There is an abundance of wild mint and sage growing here. Just before we stopped a very heavy thunder shower blew up, and while we were forming our encampment the rain poured down in torrents, accompanied with thunder and lightning, which lasted a little over an hour. The hunters killed a deer and an antelope this afternoon. The evening is very cool.

Tuesday, June 8th.—The morning was fine, though it continues cool. At 7:30 a. m. we started on our journey, crossing the creek, which is about a rod wide, and we traveled two and one-half miles winding around the high bluffs and then began to ascend them. This is the worst bluff we have had to ascend since we started. It is nearly a half mile, and three very steep pitches to go up, and most of the teams had to double. From the top of this hill we saw a buffalo south of us, which is the first we have seen since the 21st of May. Two and a half miles from the foot of this bluff we passed over a small creek, nearly dry, and then ascended another high bluff.

At 11:45 we halted for noon near a small creek, with very little water in it. We came six and three-quarters miles this forenoon. One of Brother Crow's daughters got run over by one of their wagons, the wheel passing over the leg, but there was no bones broken. At 1:40 we proceeded on our journey and after traveling a mile and a half we crossed a small creek, and again ascended a high bluff. This afternoon there was a strong wind from the west, and it was very cold. The country is very much broken and our road is very crooked and tending to the north. After traveling five miles we began to descend gradually, and at 6:10 we crossed a stream about forty feet wide and about two feet deep, the current being very swift. It is called on Fremont's map Fabant river. We traveled this afternoon eight and three-quarters miles, and during the day fifteen and one-half miles. The evening is cold and has the appearance of rain.

The hunters killed a deer and an antelope. O. P. Rockwell says he has been to the Platte river, and it is about four miles from here. Soon after we stopped three traders came into the camp. They were part of the company that lost their cattle in the snowstorm on the Sweet Water.

Wednesday, June 9th.—The morning was very pleasant, and the feed being scarce, it was thought best to start before breakfast, and at 4:45 we moved onward. At 5:45 we halted for breakfast near the traders' camp, having come one and one-quarter miles. It was thought best to send a small company ahead to build a raft, as the traders say it is about seventy miles to where we cross the Platte. They left some hides at the crossing, that they used on a wagon box, which answered for a ferry boat. They told Brother Crow that he might have them, if he could get there before the Oregon company.

There was nineteen of the best teams with about forty-nine men sent ahead; five wagons from the first division and fourteen from the second. They started about half an hour before we did. About 7:45 we proceeded onward, and soon after we started we came to a gully, which was very difficult to cross. Four men on their work horses and mules passed us. They said they were from Pueblo and were going to Green River. We came three and one-quarter miles and crossed a stream about ten feet wide, the banks of which, on either side, were very steep. Some of the teams required help.

This forenoon the soil we have passed over looked red as far as the eye could reach, and most of the rocks and bluffs were of the same color. President Young and Kimball saw a large toad about a quarter of a mile from the camp that had a tail and horns, though it did not jump like a toad, but crawled like a mouse. At 12:40 we halted for noon, having come ten miles since breakfast. Feed is scarce and there is very little water. Our road has been crooked, and hilly, and mostly rocky. The ground is literally covered with large crickets. At 2:30 we were on the move again. The road has been much better this afternoon. At 6:15 we encamped on a stream about a rod wide, two feet deep, with a very swift current. We have traveled eight miles this afternoon, and during the day nineteen and on-quarter miles. The feed is good. A number of antelope have been killed today. The evening was fine and pleasant.

Thursday, June 10th.—The morning was calm and very pleasant. At 7:30 we moved on and came four and one-half miles and crossed a small stream, passed on a little farther and crossed another creek some larger. At 11:20 we halted for noon on the east side of a stream about thirty feet wide and tolerably deep with a rapid current, having come eight and three-quarter miles. We had several long steep bluffs to ascend and descend, and it was very difficult to cross some of the creeks without help. We saw one of the Oregon companies a few miles ahead of us. Our road has been crooked and mostly winding northward. The creek where we camped last night is called La Pine. About a mile from where the road crossed it, it runs through a tunnel from ten to twenty rods under the high bluffs. The tunnel is high enough for a man to stand upright in it, and the light can be seen through from the other side.

At 1:45 we continued our journey, with more even ground and good traveling. This afternoon we came in sight of the Platte river. We left it last Saturday and since then we have

Stream After Leaving the Tunnel.

been winding through valleys and over bluffs all the way to here. As we near the river the road is more level, but sandy. At 5:45 we crossed a stream about thirty feet wide and two feet deep, the current being swift and the water clear, with plenty of timber on its banks, and the feed very good. We encamped on its west bank, near a grove of large timber. We traveled nine miles this afternoon, and during the day seventeen and three-quarters miles.

In this stream there is plenty of fish. Brother Clayton caught twenty-four with a hook and line, that would weigh sixteen pounds, all herring. Some of the brethren caught a few catfish. Some of the camp found a bed of stone coal about a quarter of a mile up stream. The hunters killed a number of antelope this afternoon. The evening was warm and pleasant. I noticed that Brother Ellsworth brought an antelope into camp this evening and it was cut up and divided among their own Ten by Brother Rockwood. A few days since Brother Rockwood gave Brother Crow a lecture for not dividing an antelope among the camp, when Brother Crow's companions are short of provisions, and only have five ounces to a person per day. If this is consistency I don't know what consistency is.

Friday, June 11th.—The morning was very pleasant. I stood guard the later part of the night, in the place of some of the brethren that have gone ahead. About 3 o'clock this morning I commenced cleaning the fish Brother Clayton caught. I fried them and we had a firstrate breakfast. This is the first place I have seen since we left Winter Quarters, where I should like to live. The land is good and plenty of timber and the warbling of the birds make it very pleasant. At 7:35 we proceeded on our journey, along the bank of the river, which appears wider here than at Laramie. We came four and one-half miles and Brother Clayton put up a guideboard, "100 miles from Laramie," which we came in a week lacking two and one-quarter hours. At 11:50 we halted for noon in a grove, where the feed is very good.

The road this forenoon was generally level and sandy, but there was very little grass. We have traveled nine and one-half miles this forenoon. At 2 o'clock we started again, and after traveling one mile we crossed a very crooked, muddy stream about twelve feet wide and one foot deep, came five and three-quarters miles and crossed another creek. At 5:30 we came to a halt, and we saw a number of wagons encamped about a mile ahead. After waiting about half an hour, Brother Kimball, who was ahead, returned and reported that there was no feed ahead for three miles.

The company ahead is one of the Oregon camps. They are making a raft to cross here. They say the regular crossing place is twelve miles ahead. We turned off to the river about a half mile from the road near a grove, the feed being tolerably good. We encamped about 6 o'clock, having come six and three-quarters miles, and seventeen during the day. Brother Kimball reports that he and some of the brethren tried to find a fording place to cross the river, but were unable to do so. Some places the water was deep enough to swim their horses. The brethren killed three antelope today.

Saturday, June 12th.—The morning was very fine with a light breeze from the east. Brother Markham has learned, this morning, that Obediah Jennings was the principal in killing Bowman in Missouri. Bowman was one of the guard of Joseph and Hyrum Smith and the others that got away when prisoners in Missouri. The mob suspected him, and they rode him on a bar of iron until they killed him.

At 8:15 we started on our journey and came one and one-half miles, where we crossed a deep ravine with a steep bank that was very difficult to ascend. We came one and three-quarters miles and crossed a creek about two feet wide on a bridge, which the brethren had made. One mile from this we crossed another creek about five feet wide and one and one-half feet deep. At 11:45 we halted for noon, having come seven and one-quarter miles, over a sandy, barren prairie. Here the brethren tried to find a fording place. They succeeded in riding across the river, but it was considered unsafe to cross with our wagons, as the current runs very swift. The brethren turned out this noon to dig down the banks of a deep ravine, and made it passable for wagons in a short time.

At 2:30 we again started, came about three and one-quarter miles and crossed a creek about five feet wide. At 4:30 we encamped on the bank of the river, having traveled about six miles this afternoon, and during the day eleven and one-quarter miles. Our camp is about half a mile below the camp of the brethren who went ahead. They arrived here yesterday about noon, and two of the Missouri companies arrived soon after. The brethren made a contract with them to ferry our wagons over for $1.50 each, and take their pay in flour at $2.50 per hundred. They crossed the last of them this evening. The bill amounted to $34. They received their pay mostly in flour, but some little in meal and bacon. Brother Badger traded a wagon with one of them. He got a horse and 100 pounds of flour, twenty-eight pounds of bacon, and some crackers to boot. The horse and provisions were worth as much as his wagon.

Since the brethren arrived here, they have killed three buffalos, one grizzly bear, three cubs and two antelope. The buffalos are very fat and the brethren say they are very plenty back of the hills. Brother J. Redding made H. C. Kimball a present of a large cake of tallow, and dried some beef for the benefit of the camp. Tunis Rappleyee and Artemus Johnson are missing this evening. A company was sent out in search of them. Brother Rappleyee returned about 11 o'clock at night. He said that he started to go up to the mountains to get some snow, about 5 o'clock, thinking he would be back before dark, but he found the hills to be eight or ten miles off. Johnson was found by the company. He went out hunting and got lost. They returned still later.

Sunday, June 13th.—The morning was fine and pleasant. At 9 o'clock the brethren assembled for meeting. Some of the brethren freed their minds, and Brother Kimball arose and addressed them, exhorting them to be watchful and humble, and remember their covenants, and above all things to avoid everything that would tend to a division. He gave some very good instruction and council. Brother Pratt made some remarks, followed by Brother B. Young and others. The captains or Tens were notified to meet at Brother Young's wagon. It was agreed to take the wagons over on rafts and the provisions in the cutter.

I went across the river with five or six men and built a raft, while some of the brethren went up to the mountain to get some poles. The day has been very warm and more like a summer day than any we have had since we left. The ground here is covered with crickets.

Monday, June 14th.—The morning was cloudy and cool. The first division commenced ferrying their provisions over the river in the cutter, and the second division with the raft, but the current was so strong it was not safe to take provisions over on the raft, and we only took two loads. The second division then stretched a rope across the river at the narrowest place, and lashed two wagons together, and made the rope fast to them to float them across. When the wheels struck the sand on the other side, the current being so strong, it rolled them one over the other, and breaking the bows, and loosening the irons, etc., to the amount of $30, belonging to Brother John Pack. We next lashed four together, abreast and dragged them over as before, with poles each side of the wagon, and then long poles to reach across endways. They all got over safe. One of the poles broke and let the upper one turn on its side, but there was no damage done.

Not having poles or rope enough to lash them, we thought we would try one wagon alone. Some of the brethren thought that if some person would get in the wagon and ride on the upper side, it would prevent it from turning over. I volunteered to go across in it. Soon after we pushed off, Brother Gibbons jumped in the river and caught hold of the end of the wagon. When we got out about the middle of the river, the wagon began to fill with water, and roll from one side to the other, and then turn over on the side. I got on the upper-side and hung on for a short time, when it rolled over leaving me off. I saw that I was in danger of being caught in the wheels or the bows, and I swam off, but one of the wheels struck my leg and bruised it some. I struck out for the shore with my cap in one hand. The wagon rolled over a number of times and was hauled ashore. It received no damage, except the bows were broken. We then thought it the safest way to take the wagons over on a raft, notwithstanding it is very slow, and will take three or four days.

The wind blows very strong from the southwest, which is very nearly down stream. We have cattle on the other side to tow the raft up. The current and the wind being against us, we have to tow our raft up about one mile above, where we load the wagons. At 3:30 we had a very heavy thunder storm, the rain pouring down in torrents, accompanied with hail, and the wind blew a perfect gale. After the storm was over we continued ferrying the wagons over. The river is rising very fast. After toiling all day nearly up to our armpits in the water, we got over eleven wagons in the afternoon, making twenty-three during the day.

Tuesday, June 15th.—The morning was fine but very windy, and we continued ferrying over our wagons. We took Brother George Billing's wagon over this morning. The brethren have built two more rafts. The wind continues to blow down stream, which makes it very hard work to cross with the rafts. This afternoon Brother Crow's company commenced swimming their horses over. They forgot to take the rope off of one of the horses, and after he got out in the middle of the river, they discovered that it was drowning. They pulled to him with the cutter and dragged him ashore, but he was dead. They supposed that he got the rope around his legs and could not swim. It was concluded today to leave about ten of the brethren here, to build a boat and keep a ferry, until the next company comes up. Brother Kimball told me to have a wagon and six mules ready to start early in the morning after a log to make a canoe. The wind continued to blow nearly all day. We succeeded in getting twenty wagons over today.

Wednesday, June 16th.—This morning was fine, with a strong wind from the west. I got Brother Coltrin's wagon and Brother Gleason's mules, and a pair of mules belonging to Brother Flake, drove by a colored man, and a pair that Brother Billings drives, and delivered them to those who were going after the timber for the boat. The first division sent a wagon. There was about twenty men went, principally those who had their wagons across the river. I understand there is a contract made to ferry over a company of wagons at the same rate the others were crossed.

Two men came up from a small company below, who they say belong to a company ahead. They stopped at Ash Hollow in consequence of some of them being sick. They also wished to be ferried over. There was a small company sent up the river this afternoon to get out timber for the boat. I crossed the river this forenoon and eat dinner with Brother Whipple. My health is not very good, having worked in the water for two days, and in the course of it I caught cold, and have pains in my bowels. The wind blows very strong this afternoon from the west. The brethren that went down the river, returned this evening, and brought two canoes twenty-five feet long and partly finished.

Thursday, June 17th.—The morning was windy and cold, and all hands were engaged ferrying. We hauled our three wagons down to the river and unloaded Brother King's wagon and lashed the wagons, and took the loading over in the cutter. We took a part of the loading out of Brother Kimball's wagon, and took it over on the large raft, Brother Hansen and myself pulling it over. The wind blowing very strong down stream made it very difficult to cross. President Young also crossed his wagon this forenoon.

Early this morning we tried to swim our horses across, but the water being so rough we could not get them in. Soon after noon we got the last of our wagons over. Two of the Oregon companies arrived, and the brethren made preparations to cross them at $1.50 per wagon. The brethren suffered much working in the water, for it is very cold. Our wagons formed in a circle, this afternoon, near the ferry. We got our horses up this afternoon to swim them across, but Brothers Young and Kimball thought it was too cold, and the wind blowed too strong, and they told us to leave them until morning. A company of men are working at the canoes.

Friday, June 18th.—This morning was calm but very cold.

The brethren had worked all night and ferried over one company of ten wagons and part of another. They paid the brethren $5.00 extra for working in the night. We went across the river early, and swam our horses over. The camp concluded not to start today, but stop and help to finish the boat, and wait for the pay we were to get for ferrying the companies over. Brother Clayton crossed the river this afternoon and went back to the last creek we crossed, about one and one-half miles, and caught sixty fish that would weight about half a pound apiece.

The new canoe was launched this afternoon, and the brethren commenced ferrying over the company of Missourians. The boat would carry a common sized wagon and its load, and it works very well considering the wood is green. There has been a small company of the brethren appointed to remain at this place until the next company of Saints comes up, and then to come on with them. They are to take charge of the boat and cross all wagons they can until the brethren arrive, at $1.50 per wagon. About dark this evening the Twelve and those who were appointed to remain, went off a little ways from the camp to council. The names of those who were to stop were read over as follows:

Thomas Grover, John S. Higbee, Luke S. Johnson, Appleton M. Harmon, Edmund Ellsworth, Francis M. Pomeroy, William Empey, James Davenport and Benjamin F. Stewart. Thomas Grover was appointed their captain. The President then referred to Eric Glines, who wanted to stay, but the President said he had no council for him to stay, but he might do as he pleased. Some explanation followed by Glines, but the unanimous feelings of the brethren were for Glines to go on. The President preached a short sermon for the benefit of the young Elders. He represented them as eternally grasping after something ahead of them, which belonged to others, instead of seeking to bring up those who were behind them. He said the way for the young Elders to enlarge their dominions and to get power, is to go to the world and preach the gospel, and then they can get a train and bring it up to the house of the Lord with them, etc.

The letter of instructions was then read and approved by the brethren. The council was then dismissed. This evening Brother Rockwood divided some of the provisions which was realized for ferrying, among some of the Tens. Brother Kimball let the brethren have a coil of rope to use on the boat, worth about $15. He got 263 pounds of flour, 100 pounds of meal and twenty-seven pounds of soap toward the pay. There has been provisions enough received for ferrying to last this camp for about twenty-three days, which is a great blessing, which we should all be thankful to the Lord for. At the rate they sell provisions at Fort Laramie, what we received would cost about $400, which was earned in about a week, besides ferrying our own wagons over.

Saturday, June 19th.—The morning was fine but cool, and at 7:50 a. m. we proceeded on our journey, all enjoying good health. The first six miles we traveled about a west course, over several high bluffs, where the road turns to the south and rises a high bluff about a mile long. The whole face of the country as far as the eye can extend, appears to be barren and very much broken. The descent on the south side of the bluff was crooked and uneven. At 1 o'clock we halted for noon on a spot of good grass, about a quarter of a mile from a good spring, which is the first water we have come to since we left the ferry, which is about eleven and one-quarter miles. There is no timber nearer than the bluffs, which is about two miles. The Red Buttes are nearly opposite this place in a southeast direction.

After stopping about an hour it was thought best to move on to the spring. We found it to be a small stream of water rising out of the quick sand. About twelve miles from the ferry there is a lake, supposed to be supplied by the spring. We could see the water boiling out of the mud in several places. The grass on the banks of this lake is very good. After watering our teams we proceeded on our journey, at 2:50 p. m., bearing a southwest course over a rolling prairie. About eight miles from the spring there is a steep descent from a bluff, and at the foot there is a ridge of sharp-pointed rocks, running parallel with the road for nearly a quarter of a mile, leaving only a narrow space for the wagons to pass and the road is very rough.

At 7:40 we encamped on a small spot, surrounded by high bluffs, having traveled ten and one-quarter miles and during the day twenty-one and one-half miles. Our camp ground this evening is the poorest we have had for some time; very little grass and no wood and bad water. The country is sandy and barren, very little vegetation growing here. There is plenty of wild sage, and several low marshes near our camp ground, where our cattle get mired. O. P. Rockwell came into camp and reported that he had a fat buffalo about two miles from the camp. A team was sent out to bring it in, which did not return for some time after dark. Myers killed two buffaloes and took the tallow and tongues, and left the meat to rot on the prairie. J. Norton and A. Gibbons left the camp at the springs and went out hunting, expecting that we would remain there until

Mountain Lake Supplied by Spring.

Monday. Gibbons has not been heard from since. Norton has returned and reported that he had killed a buffalo back near the springs.

Sunday, June 20th.—The morning was fine. We found two oxen almost buried in the mud. At 5:15 we left this miserable place. The first mile was very bad traveling, there being several steep pitches to pass over. A number of the brethren went ahead with picks and spades to improve the road. We traveled three and three-quarters miles and halted at 7 a. m. for breakfast near a small stream of clear spring water. The feed is good but there is no wood. Brother Kimball and Benson state that, when they were riding ahead last evening to find a camp ground, they saw six men suddenly spring up out of the grass, with blankets, that looked like Indians. They turned their horses and rode in a parallel direction to the road. The brethren also kept on their course. After going a short distance one of the supposed Indians left the rest and rode toward the brethren and motioned with his hand for them to go back. They went on and paid no regard to him. When he discovered that he could not bluff them off, he turned his horse and run for the others, and all put spurs to their horses and galloped off. They soon descended a ridge and were soon out of sight. Brothers Kimball and Benson run their horses to the top of the ridge and discovered a camp about a mile off. The brethren were satisfied that those Indians were Missourians, and that they had taken this plan to keep us back from this camp ground. It is considered an old Missouri trick and an insult to our camp, and if they undertake to play Indian games, they might meet with Indian treatment.

Their camp left here a little before we arrived this morning. It is President Young's intention to press on a little faster, and crowd them up, to see how they will.like it. We have learned from one of the emigrants in the rear that Andrew Gibbons staid with them last night, and that when he arrived at the springs he found a Missouri company there and us gone. He told them where the buffalo was and they went and got it. At 9:15 we proceeded on our journey, and after traveling three miles we arrived at the Willow Springs and halted a little while to water. The spring is about two feet wide and the water about ten inches deep; clear, and as cold as ice. The grass is very good here and it is a very good camp ground. About a quarter of a mile beyond the spring we ascend a hill. which is about one mile from the foot to the top of it, and the ascent very steep.

From the top of the hill snow can be seen on the top of

the mountains a long distance off. The Red Buttes appear only a few miles distant. Three-quarters of a mile further we found good feed, but no wood or water. We traveled one and one-quarter miles and came to a heavy slough. About a mile from this place we ascended a very steep bluff, and at 2:45 we stopped to feed in a ravine, where the grass is very good and a good stream of water about a quarter of a mile south of the road, but there is no wood. We have traveled nine miles this forenoon over a barren, sandy country, there being no feed only in spots as above mentioned. At 5 o'clock we proceeded on our journey, and after traveling two and one-half miles we descended to the bottom land again, and saw a small stream a little to the left of the road, where there is plenty of feed.

We crossed a stream one and three-quarters miles further, of clear water about six feet wide and one foot deep, but there is neither grass nor timber on its banks. After traveling seven miles this afternoon we turned off of the road to the left, and at 8:20 we found our camp ground, as selected by Brother Kimball, on a ridge near the above mentioned creek, about a quarter of a mile from the road. Our travel this afternoon was seven and one-quarter miles, exclusive of turning off from the road, and during the day twenty miles. There is no wood and we have to use the sage roots for cooking, as it grows wild in abundance in this region. Brothers Woodruff and J. Brown went ahead this morning and have not been seen or heard of since.

Monday, June 21st.—The morning was very fine and warm, and at 8:35 a. m. we proceeded on our journey. After traveling three and one-quarter miles we came to a bed of saleratus, which was a quarter of a mile across, and on which were several lakes of salt water. This place looks swampy and smells bad. Lorenzo Young gathered a pailful in a short time, and tested its qualities, which he considers very good. It is reported by travelers that there is poison springs in this region, but we have not yet seen any. It is probably the brakish water, which tastes some of saleratus, that make them call it poison springs. We passed along a little further and saw two more lakes of the same nature, with the banks mostly white with saleratus. At 12 o'clock we arrived on the bank of the Sweet Water, having come nine and one-half miles over a very sandy road, destitute of wood, water and feed. The distance from the upper ferry on the Platte is forty-nine miles. There has formerly been a ford here, but lately it has been crossed about a mile higher up. The river is probably about seven or eight rods wide and about three feet deep at the fording place, but much deeper in other places. The current runs very swift and the water tastes good, but is some muddy.

On the river there is plenty of good grass, but no wood. There is plenty of wild sage, which answers for fuel. Brother G. Billings and Baird went back about a half mile and got a bucket of the saleratus. Brother Kimball was ahead looking out a camp ground and he and Brother Richards were close to Independence Rock, about a half mile ahead, when they waved their hats for us to come on there, but we did not see them. The day has been very hot and no wind, which makes it very unpleasant traveling. Here Brothers Woodruff and Brown passed the camp. They had passed the night with one of the Oregon companies.

There are many huge hills or ridges and masses of granite rock in this neighborhood, all destitute of vegetation, and presenting a very wild and desolate as well as romantic appearance. The brethren killed two snakes here. Some of the brthren went ahead to view Independence Rock, which is about a half mile west of where we are encamped. The river runs within about three rods of the rock and runs about a west course, while the rock runs a northwest direction. It is a barren mass of bare granite, more so than any others in this region, and is probably 400 yards long and 80 yards wide, and about 100 yards perpendicular height, as near as Brother Clayton could judge. The ascent is very difficult all around, but the southwest corner appears to be the easiest to ascend. There are hundreds of persons who have visited it and painted their names there with different colored paint, both male and female.

At 3 p. m. we proceeded on our journey. Brother Clayton put up a guide board opposite the rock with the following inscription: "To Fort John, 175¾ miles. Pioneers, July 21st, 1847, W. R." Dr. Richards requests that his brand be put on all the signboards that the Saints might know them, as his brand is generally known by the Church. After traveling one mile beyond the rock we crossed the river, all the wagons crossing without difficulty. We then continued a southwest course and traveled four and one-half miles when we were opposite to the Devil's Gate, which is a little west of the road. We traveled a quarter of a mile further, where the road passes between two high ridges of granite rocks, leaving a surface of about two rods of level ground on each side of the road. The road then bends to the west, and a quarter of a mile further we passed over a small creek about two feet wide, but very bad to cross, it being deep and muddy.

We proceeded on a short distance and found our encamp-

ment at 6:35 on the banks of the river, having traveled seven
and three-quarters miles this afternoon and during the day fifteen and one-quarter miles. The feed is very good here, but woo;
is scarc. I went to view the Devil's Gate, and while ascending
the rocks I fell in with some of the brethren, and we went up in
company. Where we arrived at the top of the east rock we
found it perpendicular. The river runs between two high rocky
ridges, which were measured by Brother Pratt and found to be

Ready to Move From Camp on Platte River.

399 feet 6½ inches high and about 200 yards long. The river
has a channel of about three rods in width through the pass,
which increases its swiftness, and it dashes furiously against the
huge fragments of rocks, which has fell from the mountains,
and the roaring can be heard a long distance. It has truly a
romantic appearance, and the view over the surrounding country
is very sublime. The Sweet Water mountains show high and
appear spotted with snow. Mountains can be seen from twenty
to thirty miles distant. West of us, covered with snow, the
high barren rocky ridges on the north side of the river, seem
to continue for many miles.

Tuesday, June 22nd.—The morning was fine, and at 7:20
we continued our journey, and when about 200 yards from where
we camped we crossed a very crooked creek, about six feet
wide, descending from the southwest. After traveling about
three miles over a very heavy sandy road, we crossed another

creek, about two feet wide. Brother Lorenzo Young broke an axletree, which detained him for some time. One of the Oregon company came up, and one of them took Brother Young's load into his wagon, and spliced his axletree, which enabled him to follow the camp. At 11:55 we halted on the bank of the river to feed, having traveled ten miles over a very sandy, barren land, there being no grass only on the banks of the creeks and the banks of the river. During the halt Brother Pratt took an observation and found the latitude to be 42 degrees 28 minutes 24 seconds.

The Oregon company passed us while we were getting up our teams. At 2:25 we started again, the road leaving the river, and traveled about a half mile, passing a large lake on our left. After traveling five and three-quarters miles we crossed a creek about six feet wide and a foot deep, the banks on either side being steep and sandy. The banks of the creek are lined with wild sage, which is very large and thick, instead of with grass. Brother Kimball named it Sage Creek. After passing the creek one and three-quarters miles we again arrived at the banks of the river, and continued to travel near to it, and on three and three-quarters miles we crossed a stream three feet wide, but not to be depended on for water. At 7:50 we encamped at the foot of a very high gravely hill and near the river, having traveled this afternoon ten and three-quarters miles, and during the day twenty and three-quarters miles, mostly over a sandy road. The feed is very good here, and is well worth traveling a few miles further for. Brothers Barney and Hancock have each killed an antelope today, but there appears to be no buffalo in the neighborhood. The camp is all well and we continue to be prospered on our journey.

Wednesday, June 23rd.—The morning was pleasant and warm, and we proceeded on our journey soon after 6 o'clock and traveled one and one-half miles, where we crossed a very shallow stream of clear cold water, about five feet wide. There is but little grass here, but there is a number of bitter cottonwood trees growing on its banks. There being no name on the map for this creek, it is called Bitter Cottonwood Creek. It is probable that this stream is caused by the melting snow on the mountains, and, if so, it should not be depended upon for a camp ground in the dryer summer.

After traveling five miles beyond the last mentioned stream, we again descended to the banks of the river, where there would be a very good camp ground. We traveled until 11:05 on the bank of the river, and then halted for noon, as the road and the river separated at this point and the road was very sandy. Our course has been about south. The day has been very warm with a high south breeze. At 1:10 we continued our journey, and after traveling six and three-quarters miles we came to the banks of the river, and at 6:20 we encamped, having made eight and one-half miles this afternoon and seventeen miles during the day. There is plenty of grass on the river banks, but no wood. There is two Oregon companies about a mile ahead of us. Brother Frost set up his forge after we stopped and done some work for the Missourians. The Sweet Water Mountains appear very plain from here, and all of the mountains that are in sight are all covered with snow.

Thursday, June 24th.—This morning was fine but cool. We proceeded on our journey at 6:15, and after traveling a little over five miles we came to a swampy place, where there is some water standing, and there is a hole here called the Ice Spring, the ice in it being about four inches thick, and the water tastes good. A short distance further we passed two lakes on our left, the water of which tastes soft and is not fit for use. After traveling ten and one-quarter miles from the Ice Spring, over a very uneven road, we descended a very steep bluff, close in the rear of an Oregon company. The other company halted a few miles back and we passed them.

At 3:30 we turned a little south from the road and found a camp ground, and formed a line so as to close a bend of the river. We came seventeen and three-quarters miles without stopping. The feed is good here, and there are plenty of willows, which answers for fuel. The river is about three rods wide, and the water clear and cool. A little before dark, when the brethren were driving up their teams, one of President Young's best horses got shot. While driving him up he tried to run back, when John Holman reached out his gun to stop him. The cock caught in his clothes and it went off, the load entering the horse's body. The horse walked to camp, but it is thought by many it cannot live. The ball entered a little forward of his right hind leg, and he appears to be in much pain.

Friday, June 25th.—The morning was fine but cool. The President's horse is dead. At 6:40 we started on our journey, and forded the river a quarter of a mile below where we camped, the water being about three feet deep and the current very swift. We traveled about a half mile and came to a stream about a rod wide and a foot deep. It appears to come from the north and empty into the river. About a half mile beyond this stream we turned to the northwest and began to ascend a very high bluff, it being over one and one-half miles to the top of it. I was informed, while crossing the river, that Brother Whipple could not find a yoke of his oxen. I went up to the top of the bluff and looked back to the north and discovered two oxen lying down in a ravine near the river. I went back and, while preparing to ford the river, I discovered Brother George Billings hunting for them, and called to him to come and get them.

I remained at the river until he drove them up, the camp being about three miles ahead. I staid with them for about four and one-quarter miles from where we encamped. We came to the river, and traveled a little further, ascending a very steep, sandy ridge, and after leaving the west foot of the ridge we came to a stream about twenty-five feet wide, and a quarter of a mile further we crossed the same, which was only six feet wide. The last crossing the banks were very soft. About 12 o'clock we caught up with the camp, they having halted for noon, having come eight and three-quarters miles. The wind was blowing very strong from the northwest, making it cold and unpleasant traveling. Brother Pratt took an observation at this place and found the latitude to be 42 degrees 28 minutes 36 seconds.

At 1:20 we proceeded on our journey, the road running on the river bank for about two miles, when we began to ascend hill after hill for three miles. After traveling seven and three-quarters miles over a very uneven road we came to a low, swampy place which was very difficult to cross. About one and one-third miles beyond the swamp a creek, about a foot wide, was crossed and another a quarter of a mile further about two feet wide. At 6:45 we formed our encampment on the north side of a creek about five feet wide, having come this afternoon eleven and one-half miles and during the day twenty and one-quarter miles. This is a good camp ground, with wood, water and grass in plenty.

Saturday, June 26th.—The morning was very cold and we had a severe frost last night. At 7:40 we crossed the creek and proceeded on our journey, and after traveling one mile we passed a small creek south of the road and two and one-half miles beyond we crossed a branch of the Sweet Water about two rods wide and two feet deep, with willows growing on the banks, making it a very good camp ground. After crossing the last stream, we crossed another high range of hills, from which we had a good view of Table Rock to the southwest, and the high broken chain of mountains of the Wind River on the north. At 12:40 we halted for noon on the main branch of the Sweet Water, having traveled eleven miles.

The river here is about three rods wide and three feet deep and the current is very swift, the water being very clear and cold. The snow lays on its banks in some places six and eight feet deep. This is a lovely place for a camp ground. Some of the younger folks amused themselves snowballing each other on a large bank of snow. Eric Glines came into camp soon after we halted, having left the brethren at the upper ferry on the Platte River. At 2:20 we proceeded on our journey, ascending a high hill, and found the road pretty good —latitude 42 degrees 22 minutes 62 seconds. After traveling seven miles we arrived on a level spot of low land, where we found some grass and halted, while President Young and some others went over the ridge to look out a camp ground. Brother Young sent back word for the camp to come on. Leaving the road and traveling a northwest course we found our camp ground, at 6:45, on the banks of the Sweet Water about a quarter of a mile from the road, having come this afternoon seven and three-quarters miles, and during the day eighteen and three-quarters miles. This is a good camp ground, there being plenty of grass and willows.

Brothers Kimball, Pratt and some others went ahead and about dark Brother Young told me I had better get up a horse, as there was a small company going in search of them, and he wanted me to go along with them. We got about a mile from the camp and met Brother Kimball traveling on foot, who informed us that Brother Pratt and the others were encamped about six miles ahead, with a small party of mountaineers, who were going to the states. The word came to Brother Kimball that there was no prospect of finding water without traveling some distance ahead. He was to go ahead and find a camp ground, and if the teams were tired they could stop and feed, and then go on again, but finding a good camp ground over the bluffs to the right, it was thought best to stop for the night. Brother Kimball not seeing the camp coming up, started back alone with any fire arms and traveled six miles after dark.

The brethren made a fire on the ridge south of the camp, which he saw some distance off. When he got to camp he was about tired out, as he had traveled on foot about fifteen miles in the afternoon, which blistered his feet very bad. It is ascertained that we are about two miles from the descending ridge of the South Pass by the road. This ridge divides the headwaters of the Atlantic from those of the Pacific, and, although not the highest land we have traveled over, may with propriety, be said to be the summit of the South Pass.

Sunday, June 27th.—The morning was fine, but cold. The ox teams started at 7:55 and the horse teams soon after. The camp passed the eight men that were going back. They had twenty horses and mules, mostly laden with packs, and some of the brethren sent letters back by them. We went two and three-quarters miles and arrived at the dividing ridge. Brother Pratt took a barometrical observation and found the altitude to be ..... This spot is 278½ miles from Fort John (*Laramie) and is supposed to divide the Oregon and Indian Territories by a line running north and south. Between two and three miles further we arrived at the place where Brother Pratt and company camped last night, at the head waters of Green River, and, although the streams are small, we have the satisfaction of seeing the currents run west instead of east.

There is good grass here, but no wood. One of the mountaineers is traveling with us today. He wants to pilot some of the companies to Oregon. He has two pack mules loaded with skins to trade. His name is Harris. He gives a very discouraging account of Bear River Valley and the surrounding country. He said: "It is destitute of timber or vegetation, and the country is sandy, nothing growing there but wild sage." We crossed the stream, which is about three feet wide, and stopped on its bank to feed about 12 o'clock, having come six and three-quarters miles. The latitude of this place is 42 deg. 18 min. 58 sec. At 2:25 we started on again, the roads being pretty good. At 7:20 we encamped on the west bank of the Dry Sandy, having traveled nine miles, and during the day fifteen and a quarter miles. There is no wood here and but little water, and the feed is poor.

Monday, June 28th.—The morning was fair, and many of the brethren are trading with Mr. Harris for buckskins. I tried to trade with him, but I considered them too high. He sold them from $1.50 to $2.00, and made into pants $3.00 and $4.00. At 7:30 we proceeded on our journey, Mr. Harris waiting for the Oregon company to come up. After traveling about six miles the road forked, one continuing a west course and the other taking a southwest course. We took the left hand road to California. The junction of the road is 297½ miles from Fort John (*Laramie).

About 1:40 we arrived at the Little Sandy and stopped on its east bank to feed, having traveled fourteen and a quarter miles without seeing wood or water or feed for our teams. This stream is about twenty feet wide on an average, but at the fording place it is over three rods wide and two and a half feet deep, the water being muddy and the current swift. At 5:15 we commenced fording the river, and at 5:45 all the wagons were over safe, with no other loss than two tar buckets. After traveling a short distance we were met by Mr. Bridger, the principal man of the fort which bears his name, on his way to Fort John, accompanied by two men.

Corn for Jim Bridger at $1,000 an Ear.

As we wished to make some inquiries about the country, he said if we would encamp he would stay with us all night. We turned off the road a quarter of a mile and encamped near the Sandy at 6 o'clock, having come a mile and three-quarters, and during the day fifteen and a quarter miles. We found the feed pretty good. Soon after we encamped the Twelve and some others went to Mr. Bridger to make some inquiries about the country. I understand that it was impossible to form a correct idea from the very imperfect and irregular way in which he gave the description. My health has been very poor for the last two days. I have been afflicted with a very severe headache, but feel a little better this evening. As I had not washed my clothing for some time, I was under the necessity of washing this evening, and did not get through until after dark. After I ate supper I went down to where Mr. Bridger was encamped, and from his appearance and conversation, I should not take him to be a man of truth. In his description of Bear River Valley and the surrounding country, which was very good, he crossed himself a number of times. He said that Harris knew nothing about that part of the country. He says there is plenty of timber there; that he had made sugar for the last twenty years where Harris said there was no timber of any kind. But it is my opinion that, he spoke not knowing about the place, that we can depend on until we see for ourselves. Brother King is sick and there are many in the camp complaining. Brother Kimball does all in his power for the comfort of those that are sick around him.

Tuesday, June 29th.—The morning was very pleasant, and we started at 7:40 a. m., traveling over a very good road, though a barren land. At 10:45 we halted for noon, near the banks of the Big Sandy, having traveled six and three-quarters miles. Most of the second division stopped on the other side of the river, the first division stopping on the north side. The stream appears to be about seven rods wide at this place and two feet deep in the channel. There is some timber on its banks and pretty good feed.

At 1:30 we again proceded on our journey, the road being tolerably good. After traveling nine and a half miles Brother Young, who has been ahead, rode back and told the camp that they would have to travel at least six miles before they could find feed. It was then 6:15, but at 9:05 we found ourselves again on the low lands near the banks of the river. We traveled since noon seventeen miles, and during the day twenty-three and three-quarters miles. The feed is very good here. The brethren found some willows about a mile from the camp, which answered for cooking.

Wednesday, June 30th.—The morning was hot, but at 8:15 we proceeded on our journey. Several of the brethren were reported sick, and not able to drive their teams. The brethren are all taken alike, with violent pains in the head and back and a very hot fever. Some think it is caused by using the salaratus that was picked up on the lakes. At 11:30 we arrived on the banks of the Green River, having traveled eight miles. It is about as wide as the Platte, and the current is swift. After dinner the second divsion was called together, and twelve men selected to build a raft. The first division also went to work to build a raft.

There were men picked out to guard the cattle and some to burn charcoal. Brothers George Billings and Whipple are very sick. Brother Kimball told me to baptize Brother Billings, as he had a very high fever. He got relief immediately.

This afternoon Brother Samuel Brannon arrived from the Bay of San Francisco and had two men with him. One of them I have seen in Nauvoo. His name is Smith. Brother Brannon sailed with a company from New York. He reported them all doing well. There has been some few deaths among them. He gives a very favorable account of the country. About dark the brethren completed the rafts.

Native Belles.

9.—ROCKY MOUNTAINS, JULY, 1847.

Thursday, July 1st, 1847.—This morning was pleasant, and the brethren commenced crossing wagons. The raft made by the second division did not work well, the logs being water soaked. They went to work to make another raft. The wind blew high today and we only got fourteen wagons across. Brother Clayton was taken very sick this morning.

Friday, July 2nd.—The morning was calm and pleasant. I crossed the river early this morning, and helped the brethren finish the raft, and about 9 o'clock we commenced crossing the wagons. The Twelve had a council and decided to send three or four men back to pilot the next company up.

Saturday, July 3rd.—The morning was pleasant, and about noon we got the last wagon over. We hauled one of the rafts up on the east side of the river for the next company. Brothers Young and Kimball went ahead to look out a camp ground. The brethren returned soon after noon and gave orders for us to harness our teams, and at 3:15 we again proceeded on our journey, coming three miles and encamping on the river. The feed was good. The brethren were called together this evening and volunteers called for to go back to meet the companies, when the following persons offered their services: Phineas Young, Aaron Farr, Eric Glines, Rodney Badger and George Woodard. As there were not spare horses enough in the camp for each man to ride, President Young let them have a light wagon to carry their provisions.

Sunday, July 4th.—The morning was fine and pleasant, and the five brethren started back to meet the camps. President Young and Kimball and others went back to the ferry with them. While they were absent some of the brethren assembled in the circle for meeting. At 2:30 the brethren returned from the ferry, accompanied by twelve of the brethren from Pueblo, who belonged to the army. They report the remainder of the company about eight days' travel behind. One of Brother Crow's oxen was found dead this afternoon. My health is very poor, for I have taken cold from working in the water, which has brought on the mountain fever again. It is a distressing complaint, and I took a lobelia emetic this evening, and H. C. Kimball administered to me, which relieved me some.

Monday, July 5th.—At 8 o'clock we proceeded on our journey, though there are many of the brethren sick. I spent a very sick night. We traveled three and a half miles on the banks of the river, at which point the road leaves the river and bends to the westward. At 4:45 we arrived at Black's Fork and encamped, having come twenty miles, sixteen and a half of it without water. This stream is about six rods wide and the current is very swift. There is a place where we might have saved a mile by digging down a bank. We have passed over several steep places today.

Tuesday, July 6th.—The morning was very pleasant, and at 7:50 we started on our journey. We traveled four and three-quarters miles and crossed Haw's Fork, a rapid stream about three rods wide and two feet deep. It would be a good camp ground, as the feed is good. We came a mile and a half further and crossed Black's Fork, a stream about eight rods wide and two and a half feet deep. There is but little grass on its banks. After traveling eleven miles beyond the last stream we crossed a small creek about two feet wide. At 4 o'clock we crossed Black's Fork again, and encamped on its banks, having come eighteen and one-quarter miles.

Wednesday, July 7th.—We proceeded on our journey at 7:45 a. m., and after traveling two and one-half miles we crossed Black's Fork again. There is an abundance of good feed here, and a large quantity of wild flax, also beautiful flowers growing. We traveled two and three-quarter miles further and crossed a stream about two rods wide and two feet deep, the current being very swift. At 12 o'clock we halted for noon on the banks of the last stream, having traveled nine miles over a very rough road. The wind blows strong, which makes it dusty and disagreeable traveling.

At 1:40 we started again, and after traveling seven and a half miles we came in sight of a number of Indian lodges on the south side of the road. The most of them are occupied by half-breed traders. There are also American traders here. One of them, Mr. Goodall, was one who passed us at the Platte River. We continued on and crossed four streams that would average about a rod wide, the current being very swift, when we arrived at Fort Bridger, which is 397 miles from Fort John. We came about half a mile past the fort and encamped, after crossing three more creeks. This afternoon we traveled eight and three-quarters miles, and during the day seventeen and three-quarters miles. Grass is much higher at this place than we have generally seen it. The whole region seems to be filled with rapid streams,

all bending their way to the principal fork. They all, doubtless, originate from the melting snows in the mountains.

Indian Encampment.

Bridger's Fort is composed of two log houses, about forty
feet long each, and joined by a pen for horses, about ten feet
high, and constructed by placing poles upright in the ground
close together. There are several Indian lodges close by, and
a full crop of young children, playing around the doors. The
Indians are said to be the Snake tribe. The latitude of Fort
Bridger is 41 deg. 19 min. 13 sec., and its height above the level
of the sea, according to Elder Pratt's observation, is 6665 feet.

Thursday, July 8th.—The morning was fine, but the wind
was high. It was thought best to stop here today to set some
wagon tires, and let the brethren have an opportunity to trade.
I traded off two rifles, one belonging to Brother Whipple and
one to Brother G. Billings, for nineteen buck skins and three
elk skins and some other articles for making moccasins. A council met and settled some difficulty between George Mills and
Andrew Gibbons. It was decided that Thomas Williams and S.
Brannon should return from here and meet Captain Brown's
company from Pueblo.

Friday, July 9th.—We started at 8 o'clock on our journey
westward, the road being rough. We traveled six and a half
miles and arrived at the Springs, where we halted to rest our
teams. We then proceeded on three and a quarter miles and
began to ascend a long, steep hill, near the top of which Brother
Pratt took observations and found the latitude to be 41 deg. 16
min. 11 sec. It is eight miles from Fort Bridger. The descent
from the top of this hill is the steepest and most dificult we
have ever met with, it being long and almost perpendicular. At

3 o'clock we crossed the Muddy Fork, a stream about twelve feet wide, and encamped on its banks, having traveled six and three-quarters miles, and during the day thirteen miles. There is plenty of tall bunch grass here. The day has been warm and dusty.

Saturday, July 10th.—At 8 o'clock we proceeded on our journey, and after traveling three and a half miles we passed a small copperas spring at the foot of a mountain, a little to the left of the road; and two and a half miles from this spring we found a very steep and rough place to descend, and found it necessary to stop halfway down and repair the road. About twenty miles from Fort Bridger we passed another spring, came a short distance further and arrived at the bottom, where the grass was very plentiful. At 1:45 we halted for noon, having come nine miles, which is in latitude 41 deg. 14 min. 21 sec. In about an hour and a half we again proceeded on our journey, and traveled three and a half miles, where we began to ascend the dividing ridge between the waters of the Colorado and the Great Basin. This mountain is very high, and the ascent is very steep.

The descent was very steep, and we had to lock our wheels for about a half mile, where we traveled on the bottom a few miles between high, rugged mountains. After rising another high ridge, we crossed a small creek about ten feet wide. At 7:45 we encamped on its banks, having traveled this afternoon nine miles, and during the day eighteen miles, over the most mountainous road we have yet seen. Soon after we encamped Mr. Miles Goodier came into our camp. He is the man who is settled near the Salt Lake. He thinks it is about seventy-five miles from here to his place. He gives a favorable report of the country. There is a beautiful spring of water 100 yards southwest of our camp.

Sunday, July 11th.—The morning was very cool, and we found ice in our water pails. During the day some of the brethren found an oil spring, about one mile south of the camp. It resembled tar and is very oily. Porter Rockwell and Brother Little and some others went with Mr. Goodier to look out the road. After dark the brethren were called together to decide which road they would take, as there are two roads. They decided to take the right hand road.

Monday, July 12th.—The morning was cloudy and cool, and we proceeded on our journey at 7:30, traveled one and one-quarter miles and ascended a very steep hill, and a half mile further we crossed Bear river, a very rapid stream about six rods wide and two feet deep, the banks of which were lined with willows and a little timber. About half a mile from the ford we passed over another high ridge, and descended into a narrow bottom, which appeared fertile, there being plenty of grass, but no timber. Beyond Bear river three-quarters of a mile we passed a spring of clear, cold water, and at 11:50 we halted for noon, having come nine and three-quarters miles.

President Young was taken sick this forenoon. After resting two hours all the camp, except eight wagons, proceeded on their journey. President Young not being able to go on, Brother Kimball's three wagons remained behind. Brother Rockwood is also very sick.

Tuesday, July 13th.—This morning was pleasant. Brother Brown and Brother Mathews returned and reported that the camp was six and three-quarters miles ahead. Brother Kimball and myself returned with the brethren to the camp. Brother Young and Brother Rockwood remained very sick today. When Brother Kimball arrived at the camp, he called a meeting and proposed that a company go ahead with Elder Pratt to hunt out the road. Soon after dinner a company of twenty wagons, with Brother Pratt at their head, prepared to go ahead. About a half mile west from the camp there is a cave in the rocks about forty feet long and fifteen feet wide and about five feet high. At 3 o'clock we returned back to the camp, accompanied by George A. Smith.

The following is a list of the names of those who have gone ahead: Orson Pratt (commander of the company), Stephen Markham (aid), O. P. Rockwell, J. Redding, Nathaniel Fairbanks, James Egbert, John S. Freeman, Marcus B. Thorpe, Robert Crow, Benjamin B. Crow, John Crow, Walter H. Crow, George W. Thirlkill, James Chesney, Lewis B. Myers, John Brown, Shadrack Roundy, H. C. Hansen, Levi Jackman, Lyman Curtis, David Powers, Oscar Crosby, Hark Lay, Joseph Mathews, Gilbert Sumner, Gilbroid Sumne, Green Flake, John S. Gleason, Charles Burke, Norman Taylor, A. P. Chesley, Seth Taft, Horace Thornton, Stephen Kelsey, David Grant, James W. Stewart, Robert Thomas, C. D. Barnum, John S. Eldredge, Elijah Newman, Francis Boggs, Levi N. Kendall.

First division	7 wagons	15 men
Second division	16 wagons	27 men
Total	23 wagons	42 men

Wednesday, July 14th.—The morning was pleasant. Elder Woodruff and Adams came from the other camp to see the sick, who were getting better. Brothers Woodruff and Adams ate supper with Brother Kimball. Brother Woodruff is going to bring his carriage in the morning for Brothers Young and

Rockwood to ride in, as they think they will be able to go
ahead in the morning. I went on the top of a high mountain
with Brothers Kimball, Benson, and L. Young and offered our
prayers to the Almighty God in behalf of the sick and for
our dear families.

Thursday, July 15th.—The morning was cloudy. About
8 o'clock Elder Woodruff arrived with his carriage, and we
started soon after, and at 12 o'clock we arrived at the camp
ahead, when orders were given for the brethren to gather up
their teams, and at 1:40 we proceeded on our journey. Just
before we started we had a refreshing shower. After traveling
two miles we passed a cool spring of water at the foot of a
hill to the right of the road. At 3:30 we encamped near the
foot of a high red bluff, having traveled four and a half miles.
We had two more beautiful showers this afternoon. The feed
is good here, and a good spring of water to the left of the
road.

Friday, July 16th.—This morning we had two pleasant
showers, accompanied with loud thunder. At 8:45 we proceeded on our journey, and traveled through a narrow ravine
(Echo canyon), between very high mountains. After traveling
one and one-half miles we passed a steep ravine, where most
of the teams had to double to get up. A half mile further we
crossed the creek and found the crossing very bad. Harvey
Peirce broke his wagon reach and bolster. While they were
repairing the wagon, the brethren found a better place to cross
the creek. At 12:30 we halted to feed, having traveled six
and three-fourths miles.

O. P. Rockwell returned from Brother Pratt's company,
and reported that it is about twenty-five or thirty miles to
the canyon, they have found, that leads to the cut-off over the
mountains. They expect to arrive at the top of the mountains
today. At 2:20 we proceeded on our journey. The road winds
through a narrow bottom, bounded by high mountains on each
side, towering some hundreds of feet above our heads, our road
sometimes running over small hills, and through dense thickets
of willows. At 6 p. m. we encamped, having traveled nine and
one-fourth miles, and during the day sixteen and three-fourths
miles. A short distance ahead can be seen Weber fork.

Saturday, July 17.—It was a bright and beautiful morning,
and we started about 8:30 a. m. The ten to which Father
Chamberlain belongs (eleventh ten), remained behind until his
wagon was repaired. We descended a sloping hill, and came
to the Weber fork, and turned short to the right, came a mile
and a half and encamped on its banks, about 10 a. m., having

traveled about two and one-half miles. The reason of our stopping so soon was in consequence of President Young being suddenly taken quite ill, and could not endure to travel any farther today.

The river is bounded in places by high banks, being lined on either side with dry and green cottonwood trees. The grass is very good on the bottom. I went in company with Elders Kimball, G. A. Smith, Dr. Richards, Brother Benson and others, nine in all, to the top of a very high mountain, and clothed ourselves to pray for President Young and others that were sick, and for our families, etc., etc. We had a glorious time, and I thank the Lord for the privilege. About 6 o'clock Brother Kimball requested me to ride ahead with him and three or four others to see the canyon, which we supposed to be about seven miles from the camp, but when we arrived there it was dark and we could not see much. The evening turned very cold and we started for the camp and arrived about 10:30 p. m.

Sunday, July 18th.—It was a pleasant morning, and the camp was called together before breakfast, at Dr. Richard's wagon, when Brother Kimball addressed them. He told them that President Young was very sick, and it was his mind that the brethren should stay in the camp and not go out hunting or fishing, but have a meeting, and offer up our prayers in behalf of President Young and others who were sick and afflicted. It was motioned that the brethren meet at 10 a. m., the meeting to be conducted by the bishops. We had a very good meeting. It was decided that the camp move on in the morning, except a few wagons to remain with Brother Young; and the first good place they could find they were to put in seeds, such as potatoes, in order to save the seed—buckwheat and all kinds that would grow this season of the year. After an hour's intermission the brethren came together again and partook of the Sacrament. Brother Kimball gave us some good instructions, which done my soul good, and we had a very good meeting.

Monday, July 19th.—The morning was pleasant, and the portion of the camp that were going ahead, forty-one wagons, started at 7:45, leaving fifteen wagons to remain. Three of Brother Kimball's wagons remained behind and three went ahead. Dr. Richards lost one of his steers, and had to remain behind until we started, which was about 9:30. We traveled about a mile and a half and encamped. Soon after we stopped I rode ahead, with Elder Kimball, George A. Smith, Benson and Woodruff, to view the country. About two miles ahead we caught up with Dr. Richards' teams, and one mile further we found Brother E. Snow with his wagon broke down. We traveled about four miles further and came up with the camp, about 1 p. m. near the top of the mountain. We saw two springs on our way up, and crossed a small stream a number of times.

We descended the hill about two miles and then turned off to the right, and ascended a hill to see what direction the road ran. About two miles from the summit of the mountain, the road turned suddenly to the westward. Here Brother G. A. Smith left us and went on with the camp, and we returned to our camp. We found the flies very troublesome to our horses as we returned. We reached the camp about 4:30, having traveled about twenty miles. Brothers Cushing, Murray and some others rode ahead to see the canyon. The brethren have caught a number of trout. President Young is some better this evening. Elder Kimball's health is pretty good, but he is generally reduced, and fatigued by anxiety and riding and looking out roads, etc. All the sick are recovering. The evening is pleasant. In the canyon is a stream of water confined, flowing between rocks.

Tuesday, July 20th.—This morning was pleasant. President Young's health continues to improve, and it was thought best to travel in the cool of the morning, so we started at 5:30, came about one mile and crossed Weber river, which is about five or six rods wide and about two feet deep, and is a beautiful clear stream. We traveled about three-fourths of a mile and came to a guide board, put up by William Clayton, with the following inscription on it: ''Pratt's Pass, to avoid the canyon; 74¼ miles from Fort Bridger.'' Here the road turns to the southwest. We traveled about two miles further and stopped to get breakfast, near a cool, clear stream of water. The feed is pretty good here, and there is some little wood, and it is a pretty good camp ground.

After one and one-half hours' stop, we again proceeded on our journey. I went ahead with four or five others to repair the road. We traveled about six miles, and encamped in a valley that is bounded in on all sides by mountains. There is plenty of feed and water here, and some willows and sage roots that answers for fuel. Elder Kimball and Benson went ahead to see if they could not travel much farther. The brethren returned about 3:30 and reported that they found a good camp ground about three and one-half miles ahead, where there was three wagons encamped, Brother Goddard, Father

Case and William Smoot, who remained behind in consequence of sickness.

We started about 4:30 and traveled about a quarter of a mile and began to ascend a long winding hill, the road bending to the south; we then descended a hill which was very rough. We passed over a number of steep pitches, the road bending to the west for a short distance, and then to the south again. We then came to a beautiful stream, about two rods wide and eighteen inches deep, which we crossed twice in traveling about one-fourth of a mile, and encamped on its banks. The feed is good here, and the banks of the stream are lined with willows. It is reported that Brother Pratt's company is about eight miles ahead, and Brother G. A. Smith's wagon is broke down. For about five miles, it is said, the road is very bad. We traveled today twelve and one-half miles.

Wednesday, July 21st.—The morning was warm and pleasant. Brother Young was not able to travel today, being much fatigued by yesterday's travel. Brothers Kimball, Benson and L. Young rode out to survey the country, and returned this afternoon. They had been to the canyon, which is about seven and one-half miles from here. The stream that we are encamped on, I understand, is Ogden's fork (*East Canyon creek). Its course here is about north, but a short distance below, it turns suddenly to the west, and runs between two mountains, for a half mile it is very narrow. The brethren went down it about half way on foot and could not go any further. The water rushes between the rocks, and some places under them, and is six or eight feet deep in places. President Young is much better this evening, and will probably be able to travel tomorrow. Father Sherwood and the other brethren that are sick are much better. I spent part of this afternoon washing clothes. Brother Biard and myself stood guard the better part of the night, last night.

Thursday, July 22nd.—The morning was cloudy. President Young is some better, and Father Sherwood is doing well. About 7:30 we again proceeded on our journey, about a south course, and traveled about two miles when Father Case rode up and reported that one of his wagon wheels had broken down. About a mile further we stopped. I went back in company with Brothers Kimball and Benson to help Father Case up. Brother Kimball cut a pole and we lashed it under the axletree, and put Brother Benson's horse ahead of the others and hauled him up. We had a light shower this forenoon. The brethren took out most of Father Case's load and we proceeded on our journey, having crossed Ogden's fork four times this forenoon. The road is stoney and rough. This afternoon we crossed the stream seven times, the road winding through a long narrow ravine, and over hills, and through dense thickets of willows and cottonwood groves. We came about eight miles and crossed a very bad slough. One of Brother Young's horses mired down. He had to unhitch him to get him out.

We then ascended a steep hill and found a billet, left by Brother Pratt, which read as follows: "July 20th, Canyon Creek, Tuesday morning: To Willard Richards, G. A. Smith or any of the Saints: From this point it is five miles west to the

Aspen Forest in Wasatch Range.

summit of the dividing ridge. The road will be of a moderate descent, and considerable better than the one you have passed over for a few miles back. The ravine up which you will go is without water, except two or three small springs, which soon loose themselves beneath the soil. You will pass through groves of quaking asp, balsam, and cottonwood, more than you have seen for many days. From the dividing ridge, you will make a more rapid descent. The hill for a short distance will be quite steep, though straight and smooth. We have descended worse since we left Fort Bridger. You will go down about six miles when you will find a camping place, the grass being middling good. You will find a small spring about 100 rods after leaving the dividing ridge, which soon loses itself in the soil. The bed of the stream remains mostly dry for two or three miles, where you will strike a stream nearly one-third as large as the one where I leave this note. Your road in descending will lead through quite a timbered forest, of principally aspens, but some underwood of oak and small maple. The soil is extremely rich. About one and one-half miles beyond the camping ground, above mentioned, you will find quite a lengthy hill, to avoid passing through a rough rocky canyon. You will then descend in a ravine for three or four miles onto a broad and comparatively level valley, and which is probably an arm of prairie, putting up among the mountains from the western outlet. Most respectfully—Orson Pratt.''

''Elders Amasa Lyman, Charles C. Rich, and the saints: I leave you an extract of a letter from Orson Pratt found at this camping ground, for your benefit and guidance. Yours very truly, Thomas Bullock, Clerk of Pioneer Camp.''

We then descended a steep hill and encamped on the banks of Ogden's fork about a quarter of a mile beyond where we found the letter, having traveled seven and one-half miles. The sick are getting better this evening.

Friday, July 23rd.—The morning was warm and pleasant, and we proceeded on our journey about 6:45, the road leaving the stream here and turning short to the west, and passing up a ravine, about a west course over a gradual ascent. The road is rough, rocky, and sideling in many places, and leads through dense thickets of underbrush, and quite a forest of hemlock and poplar trees. At length, after traveling about four miles, we attained the summit of the hill. Here we had a fine view of the snowy mountains and the open country in the distance. We have passed two or three springs during our travel this forenoon. We have begun to descend a long steep hill (*Big mountain), part of the way we had to chain both wheels. The descent is winding over a rough road, there being many stumps to annoy us.

About half way down Brother L. Young's ox wagon turned over. His two little boys were in the wagon at the time, but providentially escaped uninjured, though part of the load, having been disarranged, rolled upon them, stopping up the entrance, but they were liberated by cutting a hole in the wagon cover.

As we descended, the road bearing to the south, we crossed a small stream six times, which ran along the base of the hill through a ravine (*Parley's canyon), and after having come six and one-half miles down a gradual descent we encamped on an open area of ground, spoken of by Orson Pratt, as being an arm of prairie, putting up among the mountains from the western outlet, about 12 o'clock, having come this forenoon about eight and one-half miles.

While we were stopped here, J. Pack and Joseph Mathews rode up on horseback. They reported both companies of the brethren to be about fourteen miles ahead, encamped in a valley about twenty-five miles from Salt Lake, which could be seen in the distance to the northwest. When they left this morning the brethren were preparing to move four miles farther, and then stop and commence planting. They say the soil is very rich and fertile. They also brought a letter from O. Pratt, G. A. Smith and W. Richards to President Young, giving an account of the road and the general features of the country, etc.

After a halt of about two hours we again proceeded on our journey, going south of west a short distance, the valley becoming more confined in its limits as we advanced, until we began to ascend a long steep hill, which is about one and one-half miles to the top. Here Brothers Pack and Mathews left us and went ahead. We began to descend a long steep hill (*Little mountain), bearing a southwest course. The most of the way we had to chain both wheels. As we descended the above hill we saw an abundance of service berries. At 5 p. m. we encamped at the base of the hill, on the banks of a small clear stream of cool water (*Emigration Canyon creek). Its banks are thickly skirted with quaking asp and cottonwood trees. We have come this afternoon three miles, and during the day eleven and one-half miles.

A short time after our arrival at this place, the sky became overcast with clouds, and a strong wind, setting in from the southwest, gives the appearance of a very heavy storm. The grass here is rather tall and rank, though in places is pretty good. The sick are gaining strength as fast as could be expected, considering the fatigue of the journey. The day has been the hottest we have experienced since we left Winter Quarters. There was not a breath of air in the ravine, and the dust was almost suffocating.

SEC. III.—WHAT WAS DONE AT SALT LAKE AND RETURN TRIP.

Saturday, July 24th.—The morning was pleasant. In getting up our horses we discovered that some were missing, two of Brother Whitney's and two of Brother Smoot's. The camp started, leaving Brothers Whitney's and Smoot's wagons behind. I rode ahead about a mile and could not find them, nor see any tracks. I then returned and went back about three miles and found them. After I got to the wagons, Brother Whitney and I got on our horses and rode ahead. The road was rough and uneven, winding along a narrow ravine, crossing the small stream, which we last encamped on, about fifteen or twenty times. We then left the ravine and turned to the right and ascended a very steep pitch, where we beheld the great valley of the Salt Lake spreading out before us.

My heart felt truly glad, and I rejoiced at having the privilege of beholding this extensive and beautiful valley, that may yet become a home for the Saints. From this point we could see the blue waters of the Salt Lake. By ascending one of the ridges at the mouth of this canyon, the view over the valley is at once pleasing and interesting. These high mountains on the east side, extending to the head of the valley, about fifty miles to the south, many of them white on the tops and crevises with snow. At the south end is another mountain, which bounds the valley in that direction, and at its western extremity it is joined by another range, forming its western boundary to the valley and extending in a northerly direction until it ceases abruptly nearly west of this place. The valley between these mountains is judged to be twenty-five to thirty miles wide at the north end of the last mentioned mountain. The level valley extends to the Salt Lake, which is plainly visible for many miles in a western direction from this place.

In the lake, and many miles beyond this valley, are two mountains projecting high in the air, forming a solemn but pleasing contrast with the dark blue waters of the lake. Beyond these two mountains and in the distance, in a direction between them, is another high dark mountain, supposed to be on the western boundary of the lake, and judged to be eighty to one hundred miles from here. At this distance we can see, apparently, but a small surface of the water, extending between this valley and the mountains referred to, but that surface is probably thirty miles wide. Looking to the northwest, another mountain appears, extending to the north till hidden by the eastern range. At the base of this mountain is a long ridge of white substance, which from its bright shining appearance is doubtless salt, and was probably caused by the dashing of the waves, and then hardened by the sun.

The whole surface of the valley appears, from here, to be level and beautiful. The distance from here to the lake is judged to be forty to fifty miles. Throughout the whole extent of the valley can be seen very many green patches of rich looking grass, which no doubt lays on the banks of creeks and streams. There is some little timber also on the streams, and in the direction of the great lake many small lakes appear upon the surface, the waters of which are doubtless salty. From a careful view of the appearance of the valley from this place, it cannot be concluded to be otherwise than rich and very fertile.

After leaving the canyon about two miles we came in sight of the other camps, a few miles to the west. Proceeding on we found the road descending gradually but very rapidly. At 11:45 we arrived at the camp of the brethren, having traveled nine and one-fourth miles today, making the total distance from the guide board at Pratt's Pass to this place 41¼ miles, and from Fort Bridger 115½ miles, and from Fort John (*Laramie), 512½ miles.

On our arrival among the brethren we found them busily engaged in plowing and planting potatoes. They have already plowed a number of acres, and got considerable planted. Others of the brethren are engaged in building a dam on the creek to turn the water on the land, so as to supply the lack of rain by irrigation, for which this place is admirably adapted, on account of the many streams descending from the mountains. The descent being rapid, the water courses can easily be turned to any portion of the land at pleasure and little labor.

About 5 o'clock this evening the sky became overcast with clouds and the rumbling of thunder could be heard in the distance, and to all appearance there was a heavy storm approaching. The wind blew up strong from the southwest, when it began to rain, the wind changing to the north, but the heaviest of the storm passed to the southwest of us. Nothwithstanding, we had a sufficient rain to moisten the soil, which is quite encouraging to us.

This valley is bounded by high mountains, some of them covered with snow, and from what knowledge we have of it at present, this is the most safe and secure place the Saints could possibly locate themselves in. Nature has fortified this place on all sides, with only a few narrow passes, which could be made impregnable without much difficulty. The scarcity of timber has probably been the reason that this beautiful valley has not been settled long since by the Gentiles. But I think we can find sufficient timber up the creeks for present purposes, and also coal in the mountains. The saints have reason to rejoice, and thank the Lord for this goodly land unpopulated by the Gentiles.

Result of This First Start of Irrigation.

Sunday, July 25th.—The morning was warm and pleasant, and at 10 o'clock the bugle sounded for the brethren to come together for meeting. Elders Kimball, G. A. Smith and E. T. Benson spoke on different subjects and gave some general instructions. After meeting Brother Kimball gave me a list of names of persons which he wished me to notify, and have them retire to a grove a short distance from the camp. The following is a list of the names: William King, Hosea Cushing, Orson

Whipple, George Billings, Thomas Cloward, Robert Biard, Carlos Murray, Orson K. Whitney, Hans C. Hansen, Jackson Reding, H. K. Whitney, Philo Johnson, Charles Harper and myself.

Heber C. Kimball.

We met about 1 p. m., when Elder Kimball addressed them in substance as follows: Most of you here present have become adopted into my family, except a very few (calling them by name), and Harris, who has become connected by marriage with my family. But I do not care for that, you are all the same to me, and your interest is my interest, for what is mine is yours and what is yours is your own. If I have the privilege of building a house, I want you to help me and I will help you. Harris will want to build a house for his father's family, if they should come up, and there is plenty of timber in the hills. When my family comes up, we may conclude to settle somewhere else; if so, there will be plenty to buy us out, if we shall have made any improvements. I want you all to be prudent and take care of your horses and cattle, and everything entrusted to your care. It would be a good plan and probably will be done, for those who stay here, to go back on the Sweet Water and kill buffalos for winter consumption. We shall go tomorrow, if Brigham is well enough, in search of a better location if, indeed, such can be found. If not, we shall remain here. There should be an enclosure made for the purpose of keeping our horses and cattle in nights, for there are plenty of Indians in the vicinity. I should advise you to keep the Sabbath day holy, whether others do or not. I want you to put all the seed into the ground that you think will come to maturity. I am satisfied that buckwheat will do as well here as any other seed we can sow. I want also some peach stones and apple seeds to be planted forthwith. Brothers Biard and Hanson I would like to have immediately engaged in making garments of buckskins, and Brother Cloward in making shoes, and Brother Johnson in making hats as soon as possible.

If you wish to go hunting, fishing, or to see the country, select a week-day for that purpose. Do not let us get giddy and light-minded, as the Nephites did of old, but strive to work righteousness in the beginning, inasmuch as we have reached "the promised land." If it is advisable to work in a family capacity we will do so, and, if in a Church capacity, we should be equally willing to do that. I am going out on a scout with the brethren and I shall probably want one or two of you to go with me, and also one or two wagons. I am not going to take anything back with me to Wniter Quarters, only what is really necessary. Even some of my clothes I shall leave behind. I shall leave Bishop Whipple with you. He is quite a steady and economical man, and as such I recommend him to you. I want every man to be as industrious as possible while I am gone, and get into the ground all the turnips, cabbage and other seeds you can.

In case a storm of snow should come on, it would be advisable to drive all the cattle among the willows, where they can remain till the snow goes off. I want you all to work together until such time shall come that every man shall have his inheritance set off to him. I feel toward you as a father toward his children, and I want you to banish all peevishness from among your midst and accommodate yourselves as much as possible to each other's wishes. I have it to say; my boys have been faithful to their various duties on this journey, and other people have noticed it and expressed their opinions, that they never saw such an attentive set of men in their lives, and I consider their conduct is worthy of imitation. I want you to be sober and prayerful, and remember me and my family in your prayers.''

A number of other good ideas were advanced by Brother Kimball of an edifying nature, and then he closed the meeting by prayer. At 2 p. m. we all retired separately to the camp, having enjoyed one of the happiest and best meetings we have had for a long time. A meeting was again held this afternoon in the circle. The brethren were successively addressed by Elders Woodruff, Pratt and W. Richards on subjects of a general nature, and in particular, the good fortune that had attended our safe arrival at this place without the loss of any individual by death or otherwise on the road. Brother Young advised the brethren to tie up their horses every night. About 6 p. m. the meeting was dismissed.

Brother Young called the attention of the brethren a few moments. He said he hoped all those who had found articles of any description on the road would make it known, that the owners might get them. He said a dishonest man was a curse to the saints, and he might live with them 969 years and go to hell and be damned at last. He said that if a man retained anything which did not belong to him, it would leak out in the course of time, and it would prove a curse to him, and would be a stain on him and his posterity that never would be wiped out in time and throughout all eternity, and the stain never would be wiped out until it was burned out in hell.

Monday, July 26th.—The morning was somewhat cloudy, and at 6 a. m. the bugle sounded for the brethren to collect their horses and cattle to recommence plowing and planting, the teams to be relieved at intervals of every four hours during the day. Fifteen men were selected to go and make a road through a defile in the mountains, where we expected to find timber for building. We put up our tent this morning, in the grove where we had our meeting yesterday, for the brethren to work in. Brother Biard has commenced making a pair of pants for me out of buckskins, and Brother Cloward is mending the Elders shoes.

President Young, Kimball and others rode this afternoon to view the country. They went up a hgh mountain about three miles from the camp, which is about northwest from here. They appeared to be delighted with the view of the surrounding country on their return. Elder Kimball missed his spy glass and returned back in search of it, accompanied by Brothers

Benson and Richards. He went to the top of the mountain in search of his glass, but could not find it.

At the foot of the mountain is a hot spring, where Brothers Benson and Richards bathed. They report it to be as hot as they could bear. Brothers Clayton and G. A. Smith went about two miles further than the brethren and came to a stream (*Jordan river), about 5 or 6 rods wide and about 3½ feet deep, which comes from the south end of the valley and runs into the Salt Lake. Brothers J. Brown and J. Mathews started out early this morning to explore the country. They returned this evening and reported that they had been on the mountain that is southwest of us. They found a horse near the mountain, about six years old, and brought him to the camp. Elder Kimball found his spy glass as he returned home.

Tuesday, July 27th.—The morning was warm, but somewhat cloudy. The bugle sounded as usual for the brethren to go to work, plowing and planting. There was a small company sent back on the road five or six miles with two wagons to get logs to saw up to make a boat. Soon after breakfast two Indians of the Eutaw (Utah) tribe came to camp. They were somewhat slightly clad in skins, and are quite small in stature. J. Redding exchanged a gun with one of them for a horse. Brother G. R. Grant also exchanged a gun for a pony. They gave us to understand by signs, that there was a large party of them about forty miles from here.

The Twelve and some others started on an exploring expedition this morning. Before they got out of sight three horsemen were seen coming toward the camp. Brother Kimball waited a few minutes until they arrived. It proved to be Brothers Amasa Lyman, Brannon, J. Stevens and Rodney Badger. They report the Battalion to be about two days' journey from here. Brothers Lyman and Brannon joined the expedition. This afternoon five or six more Indians came into camp, and staid all night.

Before Brother Kimball left he informed me, that Brother Brigham was going to move his wagons about three-quarters of a mile northwest, and he wanted me to move three of our wagons also. Soon after they started I commenced hauling the wagons up, crossing a small stream and encamped on the banks of another stream (City creek). We also moved our tent up this evening, and I hauled Brother Benson's wagon up. Dr. Richards is also going to move up, which will make quite a number.

The brethren are all busily engaged, plowing and planting. Elder Kimball keeps an ox team and a four mule team plowing, and is going to start another four mule team. Brother Cushing and Brother Johnson are plowing today. Brothers Whipple and Billings are planting. Brother King accompanied the expedition. Brothers Cloward and Baird and Hanson are at their usual occupation. Brother Clayton is engaged in writing up H. C. Kimball's journal. Brother C. Murray is waiting on Ellen (Saunders). There are five prairie teams kept constantly plowing and three teams harrowing. The longitude of the Warm Springs is 42 degrees 15 minutes 6 seconds.

Wednesday, July 28th.—The morning was warm and pleasant, and the brethren were engaged in plowing as usual. This

Exact Size, Facsimile of July 28th, 1847, as Written by Howard Egan in His Diary, the Original of Which We Have.

morning Brother Redding and myself harnessed up a mule that never had been worked, in order to brake him in so he could be used to plow. He worked very well, and we hauled some poles to make a bowery over our wagons. Last night I was out late hunting our horses, and I took supper with Brother Redding and lodged with him. Brother Brannon returned this afternoon and reported that the Twelve were on their way back to camp. Brother Joseph Hancock brought in a deer, which he killed today, to camp.

The brethren of the Twelve arrived at the camp this evening very much fatigued by their journey. They report seeing a number of large caves in the rocks along the mountains, one of which they could ride their horses in forty or fifty feet. They also saw a number of wild goats. Brother Woodruff lost his whip, and went back about three miles, and saw a party of Indians a short distance off. One of them rode up to him and shook hands with him, and made signs that they were going to the north part of the lake. The brethren bathed in the lake, the waters of which are so extremely salt that a man could not sink in it, if he should try. On the margin is vast quantities of salt of a superior quality, a sample of which Brother Young brought home with him. They reported it as one of the most beautiful places they had ever seen. I will give a general description of the lake and the surrounding country hereafter, as I expect to visit it before I return to Winter Quarters.

The brethren of the Twelve wished me to notify Brother Markham to have the brethren meet close by our camp at 8 o'clock this evening. They were addressed by President Young pertaining to our locating here. He said he wanted the brethren to express their feelings on the subject. Many of the brethren did so, and were in favor of settling here. It was moved and seconded that we should locate in this valley for the present, and lay out a city at this place; which was carried without a dissenting voice. It was also voted that the Twelve act as a committee to superintend the laying out of the city, etc., the plan of which I will give in another place. President Young expressed his feelings warmly to the brethren on different subjects. He was filled with the Spirit of God and spoke with power, which caused the brethren to rejoice.

Thursday, July 29th.—The morning was warm with a strong wind blowing from the southeast. Last night C. Murray and myself slept in the tent, and the wind became so violent we were under the necessity of striking our tent (lowering it). This forenoon we moved our other three wagons up to where we are encamped. The Twelve and some others, rode out this morning to meet the detachment commanded by Captain Brown. Brothers Whipple, King and myself engaged in sowing seeds in a garden spot about three miles southeast of the camp. This afternoon we had a heavy shower, which wet the soil to the depth of about three inches. Soon after the shower was over Captain Brown's company came in sight.

I understand that ther is fourteen government wagons, and twenty wagons that belong to the Mississippi company, who wintered at Pueblo. Brother Kimball informed me that the slight rain we had raised the water in the canyon so high that some of the wagons could not cross for some time. The Battalion detachment has encamped on the other side of the creek between the two camps. Brothers Cushing and Billings are engaged in plowing, Brother Philo Johnson is also engaged in farming. The other boys are engaged at their usual occupations. After supper Brother Kimball asked me to come into his wagon, and read the minutes of last Sunday's meeting, after which Brothers Kimball, Whipple and myself took a walk. We had a very pleasant evening's conversation, then joined in prayer and returned to camp about 11 p. m. The evening was pleasant.

Friday, July 30th.—The brethren were engaged as usual plowing and planting. Brothers Whipple, King, Redding and myself went up to the garden and sowed some more seeds. We have put in a few of almost all kinds of seeds. This afternoon the Twelve and officers of the Battalion, with some others rode out as far as the Hot Springs. They had been in council about three hours. There is an appointment given out for a meeting this evening at 7 o'clock at the upper camp. Brother H. K. Whitney moved his wagons up to our camp this evening. I have tried on a pair of buckskin pants made by Brother Baird, which are the neatest and the best fit I ever had. All the brethren, including those who belong to the Battalion, met according to previous appointment, near our camp. The brethren were addressed by President Young in his usual interesting and instructive manner. The meetng was opened by a Honsannah to God, three times.

He addressed the brethren of the Battalion very warm and affectionately. He said the council had proffered their assistance to the government to go to California, but they were always silent on the subject, until they heard we were driven from our homes and scattered on the prairie. Then they made a demand for five hundred men, that they might have women and children to suffer, and, if we had not complied with the requisition, they would have treated us as enemies, and the next move would have been to have let Missouri and the adjoining states loose on us, and wipe us from the face of the earth. This is what they had in comtemplation, and your going into the army has saved the lives of thousands of people, etc. President Young requested the brethren of the Battalion to turn out tomorrow and build a bowery to hold our meetings in.

Saturday, July 31st.—The weather was pleasant, and the brethren were engaged at their usual occupations. Brothers King, Whipple and myself were sowing turnips, buckwheat, oats, etc. The brethren of the Battalion are engaged in building the bowery, at the spot where the brethren first commenced plowing. Brother Markham thinks there is about fifty acres plowed, and the most of it is planted. At the garden spot there is about ten acres plowed and nearly all sowed. We have sowed for Brother Kimball's family three acres of buckwheat, one acre of corn, one acre of oats, half an acre of turnips, one-fourth acre of different kinds of seeds, and one bushel of potatoes.

Brothers G. Billings and Pack rode about six miles back on the road that we came on, and cut forty-one logs for building. There is some thirty or forty Indians at our camp today. There was a misunderstanding between two of them about a horse that was traded to one of the brethren for a gun, when one of them struck the other on the head with his gun. One of the old Indians, who is supposed to be a chief, horsewhipped both of them. A short time after, the one that got struck with the gun, took one of their horses and started off. They saw him and six of them rode after him. After they had been gone a few hours they returned and made signs that they had killed him. They said they had shot both him and his horse.

Brother King and myself spent the evening with the brethren of the Battalion. I learned that President Young gave some general instruction to the Battalion pertaining to trading with the Indians, and their future course, etc.

10.—WORK AT SALT LAKE, START BACK AUGUST, 1847.

Sunday, August 1st.—The morning was pleasant, with a strong breeze blowing from the northwest. A meeting was held in the Bowery, commencing at 10 a. m., and another this afternoon, commencing at 2 p. m. I was absent, but learned after that the revelation given early last spring in Winter Quarters, was read by Dr. Richards, and a vote taken that they would abide by the principles contained therein. The idea was suggested and finally adopted that we employ the Spanish mode of building houses with adobies, clay or durt moulded and dried in the sun.

Monday, August 2nd.—It was fine weather with a cool breeze from the northeast. This morning William King, George Billings and myself went into the mountains with teams for timber, with which we returned about sunset. Agreeable to previous arrangements, the two camps below commenced to move to this place. Prof. O. Pratt, Father Sherwood and others commenced surveying the ground for the city. Eight or nine men were today detailed or chosen to guard our cattle during our stay here, who are exempt from all other labors. The brethren are principally engaged in plowing, planting, sawing lumber for a boat, making coal pits, preparing to make adobies, etc.

Brother E. T. Benson, O. P. Rockwell and three others started on horseback, about noon to go back and meet the next company, expected soon from Winter Quarters. Brother Clayton wrote a letter for Brother Kimball to James Smithies, the substance of which was, that he wished him to forward by the bearer (Brother Benson) the general news in Winter Quarters, particularly as regards his (Heber's) family, and also all letters that have been written by our friends from that place. The wagons of the three camps, including the soldiers, were all formed into a compact circle, a short distance from this spot.

Tuesday, August 3rd.—It was warm and pleasant as usual, but the last night was the coolest one we have experienced for a long time. The brethren are engaged in their usual occupations. Considrable of the corn and beans planted has already made its appearance above the ground, and is in a flourshing condition. J. Redding and myself went this morning with a team eight miles up the pass, within one mile of the last camping place, where we cut down and brought to camp, two cedars, for the purpose of making bedsteads, pails, etc. We arrived at home about 9 p. m. We had quite a hard time of it, the road being almost impassable on account of the bridges having floated off.

President Young stated today, his intention of having the ox teams start back on Monday next, and the horse teams two weeks from that time. L. B. Myers returned from the Eutaw (Utah) Lake yesterday. He reports it to be about thirty miles south of this place, and that on the east side of it is plenty of timber, which might be easily floated down the river to this place, the outlet of the lake being a river passing near here. A number of huntsmen have gone back, within a day or two, some forty miles in pursuit of game.

Wednesday, August 4th.—The weather is pleasant with a slight breeze from the south. J. Redding, G. Billings, H. Cushing and myself, with three teams, went six miles to get timber. We returned this evening soon after dark with three loads of good logs (balsam), got for the purpose of building a store house. Brother William Clayton, with the assistance of William King and Orson (Whitney) was engaged today in making a new Roadometer, as he intends to start back with the ox teams on Monday next.

Brother Brannon, J. C. Little, Lieutenant Willis and one or two others started this morning on an excursion to the south, intending to go to the Eutaw (Utah) Lake. I learned that a case was brought before the Twelve for trial today. It referred to one of the soldier brethren, William Tubbs, who was accused of improper conduct with two females, who accompanied the Battalion. I did not learn particulars. but understood that the accused acknowledged that he had done wrong and was sorry for it; when the case was dismissed, and he was told to "go and sin no more."

Thursday, August 5th.—It was warm as usual. This morning G. Billings, J. Redding, H. Cushing, Andrew Gibbons, Philo Johnson and myself again went into the woods after logs with three teams. We returned toward night. This evening Samuel Brannon, J. C. Little, and Lieutenant Willis returned from their excursion to the Eutaw Lake, of which and the adjacent country, they gave a similar account, to that of Lewis B. Myers. During their travel, about ten miles from here, they saw lying by the side of the trail. the dead bodies of two Indians, supposed to have been killed in the affray mentioned to have occurred on the 31st ult. They also discovered the dead body of a horse with its throat cut, some six miles from here. This probably belonged

to one of the Indians, and had been first shot, while they were
endeavoring to make their escape. A number of Indians came
into camp this evening and stopped for the night.

Friday, August 6th.—It was warm and sultry. The brethren
were engaged in their usual avocations. This morning considerable alarm was created in the camp by the report that the
Indians had left during the night and taken with them all our
loose horses. This, however, proved groundless, as upon thorough
search the horses, supposed to be missing, were found. They
were not easily seen from here on account of the high grass on
the bottoms. The preliminary arrangements, having been completed, the brethren this morning commenced making adobies on
the bottoms a mile below here, and during this forenoon,
moulded and laid out 750 of them. H. Cushing, G. Billings,
Andrew Gibbons and myself with four teams went after more
logs for building. We got mostly balsam fir tree logs, and we
returned toward evening.

Saturday, August 7th.—The hounds to G. Billings wagon
having been broken, were repaired this morning. J. Redding,
John Tibbits, G. Billings, Andrew Gibbons and myself, with
three teams, again went into the woods. We returned about
noon with a quantity of poles, of which we made a horse yard
this afternoon on Brother Kimball's lot, which is situated on
the other side of the creek, a few rods hence. Hosea Cushing
made a hay rake today. William King is still engaged in constructing a roadometer for Brother Clayton. Horace and Orson
(Whitney) took their teams and went up the pass, near here,
about half a mile and got a load of bushes, with which to cover
the blacksmith shop, the first house built with logs, which stands
a short distance from here.

Today a number of brethren made a dam, a few rods above
the wagons, on the small stream, which runs along the north
side of the camp. After this two dikes were made communicating
with the dam, the water of which will irrigate the whole camp
ground, and laying the dust renders everything more cool and
pleasant. This evening Brother Kimball invited all the members
of his family to the dam, above here, where he administered to
them the ordinance of baptism. A number of the other brethren,
making, I believe, fifty-four in all, were baptized this evening
by himself and others of the quorum of the Twelve.

Sunday, August 8th.—The morning was cloudy with considerable of rain. The ceremony of baptism was recommenced,
and all who felt disposed were invited to come forward and
receive the ordinance, which they did in great numbers, both
men and women. A number of Indians again made their ap-

pearance in the camp this morning. They came for the purpose of reclaiming a horse, one of them had sold to Brother J. Hancock for a gun, which the Indian had some way broken by accident and still wished to keep it. By the president's advise, Brother Hancock refused to give up the horse, for, if we yielded to their claim in this instance, we might make up our minds to submit in future to every other demand they might make, of a like nature.

First House Built In Salt Lake City.

A meeting was held in the Bowery, commencing at 10 a. m. Brother Kimball first addressed the congregation, exhorting them to abide by their covenants, and to the observance of various duties devolving upon them as saints of God. He was followed by Elder Woodruff, who gave them a good deal of good instruction and advice of a like nature, and the meeting was dismissed at noon, being adjourned until 2 p. m. A council of the Twelve was held in a tent near here, at which an "Epistle of the Twelve" to the Battalion and the saints in California was read. This is to be transmitted by Elder Samuel Brannon, who starts on his return tomorrow.

Meeting held pursuant to adjournment at 2 p. m. There were present of the quorum of the Twelve: President Young, H. C. Kimball, Willard Richards, W. Woodruff and O. Pratt. Sacrament was administererd, during which time Brother Lorenzo Young made some remarks, after which Brother Kimball arose and said: "There is some business to bring before the brethren. First—In regard to building the stockade of adobies; and now the idea is to call out a company of men to be under a leader, who shall attend to that business. Sixty to hoke, twelve to mould and twenty to put up walls. I think it best to beat up for volunteers." The names of seventy-six were taken as volunteers.

President Young said: "We now propose to put up some log houses, and plaster them up outside, perhaps build one side with logs." Brother Kimball moved that we put the log houses on the line—seconded and carried. Brother Robert Crow moved that we have four gates, one on each side—seconded and carried. President Young said: "We want five or six men to assist Father Sherwood in surveying the city. Every man shall be credited what he does on the adobie houses, and then when others come in, they shall pay the price for it. We expect every man will have his lot and farm and will attend to it himself. A few men came with Thomas Williams when he came to Fort Bridger, when they came they borrowed flour of the Pioneer company, most of them refuse to pay what was borrowed for them. They ought to return the compliment."

Thomas Williams said: "There are only two or three who have paid their portion. Those were the persons who returned to the Battalion." Captain Brown said: "Thomas Williams suggested the propriety of going ahead to overtake the Pioneers and get back a couple of stolen mules. If Williams had asked for volunteers he could have had half the Battalion."

President Young said: "You came and would not have eaten more if you had staid. Is there a man that would not have borrowed on the strength of his rations. Brother Rockwood let them have twenty pounds of flour, **that** we don't want, but the twelfth ten have not ten pounds of flour among them, and that **ought** to be paid." He then related the "Sim" Goodel affair, and said "I anticipate the time will come when I shall enjoy good health in this valley, and be able to speak to the brethren. I deprive myself of preaching to the brethren in order to keep on this side of the vail. If the wind had not blowed so hard, I should have spoken upon the sealing principle. I perceive that I fail, that my bodily strength is decreasing. If I had spoken it would have hurt me. There are many things I want to say before I go. I feel thankful that I am here, words and actions cannot exhibit what is in me. The hand of the Lord is stretched out. He will surely vex the nations that has driven us out. They have rejected the whole council of God. The nation will be sifted and the most come out chaff, and they will go to the firey furnace. They will go to hell. This is the spot I had anticipated. We will not have a hard winter here. The highest mountains are near one and one-quarter miles high. We shall find that sugar cane and sweet potatoes will grow here. The brethren from Pueblo advise us all to build adobie houses. There never was a better or richer soil than this. Last fall we found there were lots of persons who had not two weeks provisions with them. If we had come on then, we should have led a people to the mountains to suffer. We told the pioneers to bring at least one hundred pounds of bread-stuff. If men have not bread, let them go where it is. There are some that would lie down and die before they would complain, and again others who would take the blood of man for it. The first company were charged to bring a sufficient quantity to last them through the present season. I calculate we shall bring as much as will last us until we can raise food. We want all the brethren who are going back, to go to the Salt Lake and have a swim. The water is almost equal to vinegar to make your eyes and nose smart.'' After a benediction by the president, the meeting was dismissed at 5:20 p. m.

Monday, August 9th.—It is fine weather this morning and Andrew Gibbons, George Billings, Horace Cushing, William King, Horace Whitney and myself, with four teams, went up the pass about six miles from here, where we got four loads of poles and took them to the yard, about a mile below here, where the brethren are engaged in making adobies with which to build the stockade or fort, which is to enclose ten acres. Captain Brown, Samuel Brannon, William H. Squires and some others started this morning on pack horses for California. Brother J. C. Little and some others went with them, intending to accompany them as far as Fort Hall, and a few only as far as Bear River.

Tuesday, August 10th.—It was a pleasant morning. Horace and myself with two teams went to the place where we got poles yesterday, and cut three loads of logs, which he, myself and Ozro Eastman with a third team, took to the adobie yard, where we arrived at 5 p. m. and found Brother Kimball, J. Redding, A. Gibbons and G. Billings engaged in laying the basement of a row of log buildings on the east side, which side of the stockade is immediately on the line, and I understand is to be entirely built of logs. President Young's row of buildings joins Brother Kimball's.

I omitted to mention that last evening Brother Kimball invited Horace (Whitney), Brothers Whipple, William Clayton, William King, H. Cushing and myself to a walk over the creek, a short distance hence, to view the building lot he had selected. It is situated on a small elevated bench of ground, which commands a beautiful and extensive view of the valley to the north and south. Brother Kimball informed us that it was his intention to select two lots for Brother Whitney to the west and adjoining his own, and next to him Brother Clayton, if he chooses, could have a lot. He said that most of the Twelve had selected lots in the vicinity of the temple lot, which consists of forty acres (*changed after to twenty acres). After spending some time in conversation on different subjects, chiefly relating, however, to the prospect of our return to Winter Quarters, he proposed that we should pray. Accordingly he made a beautiful prayer, returning thanks to the Lord for the preservation of ourselves, horses and cattle, and for conducting us to a goodly land, possessed of a rich and fertile soil, even "a land of promise." He also prayed for our families in Winter Quarters, that they might have no sickness among them, and finally for the saints throughout the world.

After he had closed we returned to camp. This afternoon the weather has been quite cloudy, and toward evening we had quite a gale of wind that prostrated quite a few of the soldiers' tents, but the wind did not last long.

Wednesday, August 11th.—It was a fine day. and Orson (Whitney) and myself went into the woods after logs. We returned just after sun down with two loads. The rest of the boys were engaged in laying up logs at the adobie yard. That part of the wall to be constructed of adobies was commenced today. A large band of Indians made their appearance in camp this morning on horseback. Not being permitted to come within the circle, after staying some time, they went down on the bottoms and encamped, about three miles below here. Four wagons (ox teams) started for Winter Quarters this morning, under the command of Captain Jacobs. These, I suppose, will remain on the Sweet Water and hunt buffalos till we come up.

This afternoon we were much surprised and grieved by the unusual occurence among us of an afflicting and domestic calamity. The following is a brief relation of the affair: Brother Brown Crow while getting a pail of water out of the small stream, which flows by on the south side of the camp, discovered the dead body of his nephew, Milton Thirlkill, (a lad of about 3 years of age) lying in the deepest part of the water near the dam. The body was immediately taken out, and, notwithstanding every remedy usual in such cases, was resorted to for its resuscitation for an hour or more, but they were at length obliged to give up the case as hopeless. The child had been seen playing with a young brother a short time previous, by the side of the stream; hence, they inferred that he must have been in the water some ten minutes.

The grief of both of the parents was great, but that of the agonized mother baffles all description. She laughed, wept, walked to and fro, alternately, refusing all attempts at consolation from her friends, being, apparently unable to become resigned to her domestic and melancholy bereavement.

Thursday, August 12th.—This was a very warm day, and we did not go after logs. The most of the boys, as usual, were engaged in laying up logs at the adobie yard. The funeral, or burial of the child of George W. and Matilda Jane Thirlkill, took place about 2 p. m. Brother H. K. Whitney gave me the following account of the ceremony:

"Myself with some others, accompanied as assistance, went to the place of burial, which is on Brother Crow's lot, about two miles below here, nearly opposite the adobie yard. As soon as we reached the grave, we all knelt and a beautiful and affecting prayer was made by Elder O. Pratt in behalf of the bereaved parents and friends; after which, by request of Brother Crow, he made a few remarks by way of exhortation and instruction to us all, and concluded by a brief consoling address to the parents and friends of the deceased. About 3 p. m. we returned to the camp.''

Two loads of salt arrived from the Salt Lake about 3 o'clock. It is the best kind I have ever seen, being as white as snow, though somewhat coarse. The brethren who brought it in, remained on the shore of the lake for a day or two boiling down the salt together with water, in order to separate it from the particles of dirt with which it abounded. A number of brethren started today on horseback for Winter Quarters. Most of them were soldier brethren.

Friday, August 13th.—It was warm and sultry as usual. Brother John Tibbits and myself started for the woods about noon to procure timber for sawing. Just as we arrived at the mouth of the pass, we met Horace and Orson with their teams going to the adobie yard with a load of logs.

Brother Kimball's row of buildings, consisting of five rooms, is already built up five logs high. Adjoining to the end of those, Dr. Richards and others of the Twelve, are building houses. There were two additional loads of salt brought in by the brethren this afternoon from the lake.

Saturday, August 14th.—This is a pleasant day. As it is the intention to start the ox teams on Monday next, all who are then going back, started this morning on an excursion to the Salt Lake. Some others were also permitted to go, among whom were Orson Whitney and Brother Clayton with his wagon. When they returned this evening Brother Clayton reported the distance to be twenty-two miles. The shaft or screw of the roadometer was broken on his return. Brother J. C. Little, Joseph Mathews, John Brown, Lieutenant Willis and John Buchanon, who accompanied Captain Brown and others as far as Bear River on their way to California on Monday last, returned today. They had been as far as Cache valley on an exploring expedition, of which place they give a favorable account, although, they say, there is no more timber there than here, and that like this, being up the ravines in the mountains.

Lewis B. Myers also returned today from the same country. Both parties report the game to be very scarce, neither having killed any. Some of them visited the settlement made by a man by the name of Miles, before referred to, and report the American corn to be as high as ones shoulders, and the Spanish corn tasseling out.

G. Billings, H. Cushing and myself again went into the woods for logs today. While on the road we met with quite an accident. H. Cushing's team, being ahead stopped suddenly, when one of the oxen of G. Billing's attached to the wagon immediately behind, ran with full force against the reach of the former wagon, which projected out considerably behind. The reach penetrated the breast of the ox nearly six inches, inflicting a wound large enough to admit a man's clenched hand, but, notwithstanding, having bound it up, we think he will get well. The fortification, or stockade has progressed bravely during the past week from the united diligence and industry of the brethren, and we indulge hopes to be ready to start back soon after Brother Benson returns.

Sunday, August 15th.—It was beautiful weather as usual, and a meeting was held at the Bowery, commencing at 10 a. m. President Young addressed the congregation on the sealing principles, or more particularly, on the law of adoption. He told them: It did not detract from a man's glory to be sealed to another, but added to it, for he still held that of his own and adopted parents at the same time. Meeting was adjourned at 12 noon, to meet again at 2 p. m.

Meeting met pursuant to adjournment and the congregation was addressed by Elder H. C. Kimball and O. Pratt on various subjects. The meeting was dismissed at 6 p. m., with the request by President Young that all those who intend to start back tomorrow should meet at his tent this evening at the sound of the bugle, which was accordingly done, and all the soldiers going brought their guns, ammunition, etc., and surrendered them into the president's hands, for the reception and safe keeping of which there will be a house built hereafter. I do not know the number going, but of those about Brother Kimball are the following: William Clayton, J. Redding, Robert Biard and Thomas Cloward. It rained considerably soon after we returned for the night, accompanied with a little wind.

Monday, August 16th.—It was somewhat cloudy and rained at intervals throughout the day. I was engaged in hunting up cattle this forenoon. Brother Biard and Cloward got started today, each having a wagon with two yokes of oxen attached, one yoke of which Brother Kimball got of Brother Huntington. William King repaired the roadometer this afternoon, and Wliliam Clayton, J. Redding and myself rode in the former's wagon as far as the Warm Springs, one and one-half miles distant. This we done to see how the machinery would work. Quite a number of wagons started today besides the two above mentioned. Brothers Whipple and Allen went up the hollow where we have been accustomed to get logs (Emmigration canyon), and procured a large piece of sandstone, out of which this afternoon Brother Allen is fashioning a grindstone. There was quite a wind and storm soon after we retired for the night.

Tuesday, August 17th.—The sky was somewhat cloudy this morning. Brother Clayton started with his wagon from here today. He is accompanied by J. Redding and E. Lamb.

Brother Kimball, Dr. Richards, Colonel Rockwood, Thomas Bullock, Stephen H. Goddard and myself went up the Pass, about ten miles from here, where the brethren were encamped. They were soon called together, when Brother Kimball gave them some instructions for their observance and guidance on their journey. This company is intrusted to the commands of Captain Roundy and Tunis Rappleyee. The list of men and teams composing same is as follows: Fifty-nine men, thirty-two wagons, fourteen mules, sixteen horses, and ninety-two yokes of oxen. Brother Kimball and the rest of us returned toward night.

This evening he called most of his boys together at Brother Wilkie's tent, where each chose his respective lot and Horace wrote their names on the blanks, representing the lots on the city plat or map. Brother William Clayton having left, Horace is hereafter to keep Brother Kimball's journal. The brethren are as usual engaged today at work on the adobie wall, which, when completed will be nine feet high and twenty-seven inches thick. Professor Pratt has taken observations and found the latitude of this place to be 40 degrees 45 minutes 50 seconds. The altitude above the level of the sea is 4309 feet, and above the Eutaw outlet (*head of Jordan) sixty-five feet. This evening after we returned, we again had quite a heavy wind from the southwest, accompanied by some rain, and, mingled with the latter last night, it is said, there was considerable snow. This heralds the approach of cold weather, and in the opinion of all, we ought not to remain here much longer.

Wednesday, August 18th.—There was fair weather this forenoon, though somewhat showery this afternoon. Nothing of importance occured today, except the usual work going on at the adobie yard, at which place I, for the first time, worked on the buildings, together with the rest of the boys. President Young has announced his intention that we shall start back on Tuesday next, and had his horses shod yesterday in preparation for that event. This afternoon Hosea and myself went to work at odd jobs about the wagons, unloading them, etc.

Thursday, August 19th.—It was a warm and pleasant day. Hosea and myself were engaged part of the day in drawing gravel with which to cover the houses. The remainder of the boys were also at work finishing them off. We had our horses and mules shod today, preparatory to our starting on Tuesday next. A party of Mountaineers (consisting of four white men and two squaws) arrived in the valley this afternoon from Fort Bridger. Their ostensible reason for coming here was "to see how we get along," as they expressed themselves; but undoubtedly the real object of their visit was to trade with the Indians. They were encamped this evening about a mile below here on the bottoms.

This afternoon Horace copied the names of those who had selected lots, as also the number of lots and block, opposite each one's name. Hans is engaged in making me a coat of buckskins.

Friday, August 20th.—It was pleasant weather, and Hosea Cushing and myself were engaged in hauling some loose logs that lay near here down to the adobie yard. Horace took a bar of iron to the blacksmith shop, had it cut in two, and carried it to the stockade to be used in constructing a chimney in one of Brother Kimball's rooms, which is being built by Brother S. Goddard. Brother Dockman is engaged in making a door. They have the covering laid over the top of one of the rooms, and the remainder are nearly ready for covering. Brother J. Mathews is engaged in sawing lumber at the saw-pit near by, with which to make the floors.

The laying out of the city is now completed. It is composed of 135 blocks, each containing ten acres, which is subdivided into eight lots, each containing one and one-fourth acres. The streets are eight rods wide. There are three public squares (including the adobie yard) in different parts of the city. The Temple block, like the rest contains ten acres. Father Sherwood returned from an exploring expedition to Cache valley this evening, whither he went day before yesterday, for the purpose of trading with the Indians. With him came a man by the name of Wells, who has lived some years in New Mexico among the Spaniards. I understand the brethren have given him the privilege of choosing a city lot, if he wishes to dwell here.

Brother A. Carrington, John Brown and one or two others started this evening on an exploring expedition to visit the high mountains called the Twin Peaks, lying some distance to the southeast of this place. It is their intention to proceed to the base of the mountain and there encamp for the night, and on the morrow ascend the same in search of coal, etc.

Saturday, August 21st.—It was fair weather as usual. President Young and Kimball moved their wagons and effects down to the stockade today. Hosea Cushing, E. Whipple and myself assisted in the same . Nearly all of Brother Kimball's rooms are now covered, and the floor of the one appropriated for Ellen Saunder's use is nearly laid. The most of the afternoon was employed by Brother Kimball, H. Cushing and myself in packing, unpacking, repacking and storing away the things in the house. The remainder of the boys as usual were engaged in working on the houses. Horace took his wagon to the blacksmith shop, where, by my intervention Brother Burr Frost repaired the skein to the axle tree, and also some of the hounds that had been broken, for which Horace gave him two-thirds of a pail of corn.

Sunday, August 22nd.—It was a pleasant day, though thunder could be heard in the distance this afternoon, and it probably rained considerably in the mountains. A meeting was held at the Bowery, commencing at 10 a. m. The congregation was addressed by Elder A. Lyman upon the subject of our present situation as a people, the blessing we had received at the hands of the Lord, our further prospects, etc.

A few remarks were made by President Young, stating the necessity of our holding a conference in order to transact some church business, which it was important should be brought before the people before we leave this place on our return to Winter Quarters. The meeting was then adjourned till 2 p. m. In the interim a council of the Twelve was held under the tree on Brother Kimball's lot.

Pursuant to adjournment, conference met at 2 p. m. The following is the minutes of said conference, as reported by the clerk, Thomas Bullock: Sunday, August 22, 1847, 2 o'clock p. m. A special conference of the Church of Jesus Christ of Latter-day Saints, held in the Bowery on the Temple block in the Great Salt Lake City. Present: President Young, H. C. Kimball, W. Woodruff, A. Lyman, W. Richards and O. Pratt, also Thomas Bullock and J. C. Little, clerks of said conference.

President Young called the meeting to order and the choir sang "The Spirit of God Like a Fire Is Burning." Prayer by W. Woodruff. The choir sang "From All That Dwell Below the Skies." Elder Kimball called for the business to be transacted before the conference and requested the brethren to be free and open, that it may be well for those that remain and those who are to come here. It is necessary to transact a few items of business; to have a presidency to preside over this place, and to appoint such officers as are necessary to watch over and council them for their well being. Also the stockade; shall we continue our labors, and concentrate all our efforts in the building of that, or scatter, and every man work for himself? Shall we cultivate the earth in the vicinity of the city, or go three or four miles and make farms and fence them so that our crops can be secure? Shall we scatter our labors? One man build his house, another fence his lot, another go hunting, etc., etc. These are matters for your consideration.

If the brethren have any interest we want an expression of it; if they have not, be silent, and we will transact the business. H. G. Sherwood said: "It meets my feelings to cultivate the city and fence it in with an adobie wall, and a high one will make a guard against the Indians and keep our cattle out. I am in favor of fencing in the city and cultivating it."

N. Higgins said: "The Indians supposed the land to be all theirs, and are in the habit of taking a share of the grain for the use of the land."

President Young moved that the brethren fence in the city and such portions as they had a mind to in sections and cultivate it. It was seconded by Dimick B. Huntington. H. C. Kimball said: "We have talked considerable about it, and the most prudent and economical way of doing it. It is best to farm in that portion which is tillable and that which is the most convenient for us. Suppose we divide it into three sections.

Put the fence upon the line of the city just where we want it; and that which is not wet enough can be irrigated, and can raise 100 to 1000 bushels for ourselves and those who come after us, and they shall pay you a **good round price for it**. I would rather fence a block of ten acres and have the crop, than plant 100 acres for the cattle to destroy. Will you put your "mites" together for that which is the best for every man, woman and child? Will you **do it?** (Cries of "Yes") I say put our fence together and fence the city, and sow our wheat safely." The motion was carried unanimously.

President Young said: "I move that there be a president to preside over this place." Seconded and carried. "That there be a High Council." Seconded and carried. "That all other officers that are necessary be appointed for this place." Seconded and carried. "That we call this place the Great Salt Lake City of the Great Basin, North America. That we call the postoffice the Great Basin Postoffice." Seconded and carried. H. C. Kimball said: "I move that we call the river the 'Western Jordan.' " Seconded and carried.

President Young said: "It is the right of the Twelve to nominate the officers, and the people to receive them. We wish to know who is coming in the next company. If Uncle John Smith comes it is our minds that he preside. Colonel Rockwood is my principal man, attends to all my duties." H. C. Kimball said: "I move that Colonel Rockwood be honorably released from his duties as overseer of the Stockade." Seconded and carried. "I also move that Tarleton Lewis be appointed to that office." Seconded and carried. President Young said: "There will be thousands of instances of men being discharged and who are never shown on record as being appointed. It is the business of all clerks to write the business that is transacted, and not to ask questions. Colonel Rockwood is my aide-de-camp. I was acknowledged as their General and their dictator. If I appoint him to do a thing and don't tell the clerk, the clerk is not to blame, and when he is discharged it can be recorded.

"The brethren are not requested to labor for nought. You don't know what dangers you are in. I am full of caution. I wish this people may grow and increase and become a great nation. It ought to suffice the elders of Israel to go and do as they are told. Is it not necessary that the yard should be secured, that the Indians cannot get in? About forty persons are going to live in those houses; that would only be one-fourth of the whole, and have three sides exposed, but common sense teaches us to build it all around. Men laboring here will be glad to buy a cow, some sheep, clothing, and other things. Some wealthy men are coming and will want rooms. The men who build them are entitled to their pay.

"Don't be so devilish hoggish as to be afraid to do a day's work without getting pay for it. And I can prophecy in the name of Jesus Christ, a man having such a spirit will be damned; and I say further, that such a man shall not live here. Get up your walls four and one-half feet high and that will keep the cattle out. Who is there sick in this camp through living in your wagons? Now, if you go and leave those walls and build up your own house, and I venture to prophecy that you or some of your family will be sick and you will have to watch over them. I had rather they sleep in the Bowery than in a close house. We propose to fence in thirty rods square that, in case of necessity, the cattle can be placed in, and in the inside stack your hay. In the spring remove your fence. Plow a trench about twenty feet from the houses and the women can raise a multitude of garden sauce.

I want to engage 50,000 bushels of wheat and other grain in proportion, and I will pay you 50 cents per bushel for corn, $1.25 for wheat and 25 cents for oats. Why not? I bring glass for you and you raise grain for me. Raise all you can. You can buy sheep, teams, or a cow or two. We want you to live in that Stockade until we come back again, and raise grain next year. If you only fence in forty acres, make it so an Indian cannot see in, and then they won't be tempted."

Elder O. Pratt said: "It would be impossible to fence in this city with a fence so an Indian cannot see in it. It will take 2300 rods to fence in the whole city, and it would take a good many months." H. C. Kimball said: "There are some creeks that have no names." President Young said: "I move that this creek be called the City Creek." Carried. "That the large creek about eight miles south be called Mill Creek." Seconded and carried. "That the little creek, a little south, be called Red Bute Creek. "Seconded and carried. "That the next be called Canyon Creek." Carried. "That the next be called Big Canyon Creek." Seconded and carried.

"Now I want to know if the people are satisfied with the labors of the Twelve?"

T. Lewis said: "I move that we give them our approbation, that we are satisfied with their labors, and give them our blessing." Seconded and carried.

Lorenzo Young reminded those brethren who did not pray, that it was a good time for them to begin and fulfill their covenants that they have now made. When we covenant to do a thing, be careful and always do it.

President Young said: ''I want to know who are going back to winter quarters? Those who are going to stay, will you finish that adobe wall? If so, stand up. (A number arose.) I should have no hesitation in taking five men and build a mile of adobe wall eight feet high this fall. Keep it in mind: 50 cents for corn, $1.25 for wheat, and other grain in proportion.''

H. C. Kimball said: ''My feelings are for the welfare and wellbeing of all this people. I am your brother and you are my brethren, all being born from the same parents; and I am now approximating back again to those feelings, in them again being restored to their parents. You should throw away selfishness for it is of hell, and I say in the name of Jesus away with it to hell. (Cries of Amen.) A man possessed of such feelings stinks worse than a skunk. I want to cultivate a feeling of union, of peace, toward my brethren, and, if they knock me over, I'll try to forget it.

The Holy Ghost will rest upon you and I shall see the day when the heavens will be opened and we will render up our stewardships to our Heavenly Father. Brother Brigham is going to be greater than he was. He will be greater in strength, in beauty and in glory. A man don't know how to appreciate a thing until it is taken away. A man don't appreciate a wife until she is away, nor a wife appreciate a husband until he is gone. Call upon God and we shall increase here. Away with the spirit of alienation and let us be united. I believe I shall receive power to thrust everything beneath my feet and rise in glory. I wish to God we did not have to return. If I had my family here, I would give anything I have. This is a paradise to me. It is one of the most comely places I ever beheld. I hope none of us will be left to polute this land. I had rather depart than do as a great many do.''

President Young said: ''I move that Brother MacIntyre be clerk and keep an account of public labors.'' Carried. ''In regard to our starting—get ready as fast as possible, and on Tuesday night we will start out and see if we are ready to go. I move that we adjourn this conference to October 6, 1848, at 10 o'clock a. m., at this place.'' Carried. ''I also move that Edson Whipple attend to the distribution of water over the plowed land.'' Seconded and carried. Elder O. Pratt dismissed the conference by benediction.

After the meeting the rest of the boys and myself assisted

Horace in taking his wagon by hand from the blacksmith shop down to the Stockade.

The Twelve held another council this evening in front of the buildings. Brothers Carrington, Brown and others returned during the session of conference from the exploring expedition to the mountains, on ascending which they had found no coal, but plenty of black slate.

Monday, August 23rd.—It was somewhat cloudy with a little rain. George Billings and A. Gibbons went after poles with which to cover the buildings. The rest of the boys and myself were at work on the houses, getting the wagons ready for the journey, etc. Ellen Saunders has moved into her room, and the other rooms will soon be finished. Thomas Williams and others returned from Fort Hall today. The former was the bearer of a letter from Captain Brown to Brother Kimball, merely stating his health, prospects, etc. Brother Kimball has recently got a good wagon of Brother Shelton. This he loaned him for the purpose of assisting in bringing up the families.

Tuesday, August 24th.—It was fair weather until about noon when it suddenly became cloudy and we had quite a heavy shower. The boys this forenoon were usually busy at work on the houses. About 2 p. m., it having cleared off, Horace and myself, with his wagon, and Hosea Cushing, G. Billings and Carlos Murray, with one of Brother Kimball's wagons, started on an excursion to the Salt Lake. It is unnecessary to relate particulars connected with our visit, or give any farther description of the lake, as there has been sufficient mention made of it already; but suffice it to say, that we had a fine bath in its waters, and staid all night on its shore, together with a number of others who had come in wagons and on horseback.

Wednesday, August 25th.—It was a bright and clear morning and we arose early, got our breakfast and, after waiting a short time to fill a bag with salt, we started back and arrived at the Stockade about noon, where we found the brethren making preparations to go back to winter quarters, as it is the intention to start about 6 o'clock in the evening. After our return from the lake we busied ourselves this afternoon in getting up the horses, cutting grass for them, that we may hitch them up for all night in order to be ready with the rest to make an early start. Brothers Kimball, Whipple and myself met in Ellen's room a little after dark to talk over business matters, after which we had prayers and retired about 10 p. m.

Thursday, August 26th.—The weather was beautiful and as fast as they got ready this morning they started out, one by one, the first about 9 o'clock. The last of our wagons started about 10 o'clock. I remained behind to settle some business with Brother Whipple, who concluded to accompany me on horseback to the camp. We overtook the wagons about nine miles from the valley, and traveled six miles further and encamped near the cold springs on Canyon Creek, on the arm of prairie spoken of by O. Pratt in his letter as we came out.

Friday, August 27th.—The weather was somewhat warm and sultry. We arose early and got our breakfast and resumed our journey. Brother Whipple returned to the valley. We ascended the long, steep hill, spoken of heretofore, and at length we attained its summit, having traveled four miles. We halted a short time for the last teams to get up, many of which had to double in order to do so. We then traveled down about four miles and came to Ogden's Fork. After crossing the stream, we traveled a short distance and stopped to bait about 4 p. m. Here we continued about one hour and proceeded on and encamped about sundown, having traveled about fifteen miles today. We found the feed tolerable good.

The following are the names of those going in Brother Kimball's wagons: Hosea Cushing, William King, George Billings, Andrew Gibbons, Carlos Murray, Ralph Douglass, Able M. Sargant, William Ferril, Albert Sharp, Thurston Lawson, Edwin Holden. Brother Markham is hauling Porter's wagon for us until we meet the companies.

Saturday, August 28th.—It was pleasant weather, we started about 7:30 a. m., traveled about twelve miles, forded Weber Fork, and halted to bait. This stream has fallen considerably since we were here last. We proceeded on our jurney about 3 o'clock, traveled about four miles along the banks of the river, and then turned abruptly to the left and traveled through a narrow pass about four miles and encamped, stopping in single file on the road a little after dark. Some of the brethren, who had been out hunting, found a steer, which had strayed from the Battalion. They killed it and divided it among the camp. Brothers King, Cushing and myself made up our bed on the grass and slept in the open air.

Sunday, August 29th.—It was pleasant weather and we proceeded on our journey at 7:35 and traveled about twelve miles to Redding's Cave, where we halted to feed about 1 p. m. Soon after we halted, Brother Benson rode up, the brethren were very glad to see him and gathered around him to hear the news. He met the company about forty miles this side of Fort John, (Laramie), which consisted of 566 wagons. He brought a list of names from 1200 to 1500 in number. These were divided into nine companies. He and Porter left the forward company on the Sweet Water, where they had lost a number of their cattle by sickness, and many had strayed away. He brought a number of papers and letters. I received one from my wife dated 14th June, leaving them all well, which rejoiced my heart. I thank my Heavenly Father that He has blessed them with health and strength, and I pray God that He may preserve them from evil and from sickness and death, that we may enjoy each others society again.

About 4 p. m. we proceeded on our journey, came about four miles and met Porter (Rockwell), four miles further we encamped in a small valley about dark, having come about twenty miles today. We had wild sage for fuel. Porter took supper with Brother Kimball, whom I cook for and mess with. The evening was cold and some frost.

Monday, August 30th.—It was cloudy, gloomy and cold weather. We started on our journey at 7:40, and after traveling six miles we came to Bear River. After fording, we stopped to feed at 11 a. m. During the bait, Brother Bullock read the names of six of the camp that were coming on, after which we proceeded and traveled on eight miles and encamped in the valley at 4 p. m., making fourteen miles during the day. The feed here is pretty good and two good springs of water, and plenty of cedar on the mountains for fuel. The evening was cloudy and drizzling rain.

The following is a list of the names in this company: Brigham Young, Alvarus Hanks, John Y. Green, Geo. Clark*, Truman O. Angell, J. G. Luse*, Joseph S. Schofield, John G. Holman, A. P. Rockwood, G. R. Grant, Stephen H. Goddard, D. Laughlin*, Millen Atwood, Wm. Dykes, Thomas Tanner, David Grant, A. Everett, Thomas Woolsey, Geo. Wilson*, Haywood Thomas*, Jessie Johnson*, Samuel B. Fox, Willard Richards, John Brimhall*, Thomas Bullock, A. S. Huntly*, B. B. Richmond*, Rodney Badger, Eli Harvey Peirce, W. W. Rust*, Ezra T. Benson, Joseph Mathews, Daniel Powel*, James Camp*, Wm. Pack*, Erastus Snow, Green Flake, Wm. MacIntire*, Benjamin Stewart*, Geo. W. Brown, John Crow*, Porter Rockwell, P. T. Mashek*, Chas. Shumway, Wm. Rowe*, C. Rowe*, Andrew P. Shumway, Burr Frost, B. L. Adams, Wm. Carter, A. P. Chessley, Wm. Wadsworth, Thomas C——*, Datus Ensign, John Gould*, Samuel Gould*, John Dixon, Simeon F. Howd, Amasa Lyman, Seth Taft, Albert Carrington, John Brown, Stephen Kelsey, G. A. Smith, J. J. Ferill*, Wilford Woodruff, S. Chamberlin, Dexter Stillman*, Wm. Senill*, Wm. C. A. Smoot, Nath. Fairbanks, J. E. Stewart, C. A. Harper, Robert T. Thomas, Perry Fitzgerald, Isaac N. Weston*, James Case, Ozro Eastman, J. C. Earl, Monroe Frink, Judson Persons, Levi N. Kendall*, Orson Pratt, S. Markham, Joseph Egbert, Geo. Mills, M. B. Thorpe, C. Kleinman, H. K. Whitney, S. Larsen*, Geo. Billings, H. C. Kimball, Ralph Douglass*, Howard Egan, Edwin Holden*, H. Cushing, Wm. Gifford,*, Wm. A. King, Albert Sharp*, Carlos Murray, A. M. Sargent*, O. K. Whitney, Andrew Gibbons, comprising 103 men, 36 wagons, 42 horses and 35 mules.

*Those not marked were returning members of the original band of Pioneers. The others were probably "Mormon Battalion" men, with some exceptions.

President Young called the brethren together this evening for organization, when the following persons were elected to office: S. Markham, captain of one hundred; Barnabus Adams and Joseph Mathews, captains of fifties; Brigham Young, John Brown, Howard Egan, Geo. Clark, Geo. Wilson, E. Snow, Thomas Tanner and E. A. Harper, captains of tens. President Young selected his ten, which included six of the Twelve, A. P. Rockwood, S. H. Goddard and J. Schofield. It was moved that we travel in order, after we had thus organized. Brother Young advised the brethren to gather up their horses and tie them, as it was his intention to start as early as 6 o'clock in the morning, which we accordingly did. Thomas Bullock then read a portion of the names of those coming on in the companies expected.

Tuesday, August 31st.—The weather was pleasant and we proceeded on our journey at 7 a. m. and traveled ten miles and crossed Muddy Fork, the bed of which we found to be quite dry; came seven miles and halted to bait at 1 p. m. Here we remained for two hours and then started on. The wagons arrived at Fort Bridger about 5 p. m. Brother King and myself and a few others rode ahead on horseback and arrived early in the afternoon. After the wagons had halted we discovered that one of our horses was missing and also one of Brother Snow's. The company moved on about a mile further and encamped, having come twenty-three miles today. Brother King and myself started back to look for the horses. Brother Snow overtook us about five miles from the fort. The evening was very cold. We traveled back within three miles of where we encamped last night and found our horses about 11:30 o'clock. We made a fire to warm ourselves and let our horses feed for about half an hour, and then started back, arriving at the camp a little before sunrise. We got our breakfast and laid down to sleep, in order to give our horses a chance to feed, the camp starting ahead. Brother C. Murray remained with us.

11.—MEETING THE TRAINS, SEPTEMBER, 1847.

Wednesday, September 1st, 1847.—It was pleasant weather. I understand the brethren found an ox belonging to the government at Fort Bridger. They killed it and divided it among the soldiers and others. At 10 o'clock Brother Porter, who had been back at the fort, came along and woke us up. We saddled our horses and started after the camp, bringing E. Snow's horse with us; traveled about three miles, when Brother Snow's horse started back. Brothers King and Murray went back to drive him up. They met a Frenchman, who helped them to catch the horse. He is one of three who are going back in company with us.

We crossed Black's Fork twice, and came seventeen and three-quarters miles, and found the camp stopped to feed. Soon after we arrived the camp proceeded on again. I went ahead with the camp, leaving Brothers King and Murray to bait the horses. We crossed Black's Fork three times this afternoon, came fourteen and three-quarters miles and encamped on the banks of Ham's Fork, having traveled thirty-two miles today. The evening was very cold.

Thursday, September 2nd.—The weather was warm this morning. The other two French men arrived at the camp. They had staid back to hunt up some of their horses that had strayed away. At 8 o'clock we proceeded on our journey, crossed Ham's Fork and traveled twenty-two miles and camped on the banks of Green River about 4 p. m., having traveled over a barren desert country during the day. We found an Indian here who had left his tribe (Snakes) two days before on the Sweet Water. He was going to Bridger's (Fort). Soon after we arrived it suddenly blew up very cold. I wrote a letter this evening to send back to the valley.

Friday, September 3rd.—It continues cold and cloudy weather. We started at 6:30 o'clock, came two miles and forded the river, which we found to be very low; proceeded ten miles and stopped at 10 a. m. to feed on the banks of Big Sandy. Here we remained about two hours and then proceeded on seventeen miles, forded the Big Sandy and encamped on its banks, having come twenty-seven miles today.

At this place we found Daniel Spencer's company, consisting of about fifty wagons. They reported P. P. Pratt's company to be encamped six and three-quarters miles back on the

Little Sandy. Brother Spencer's camp was called together and Brothers Young, Kimball, G. A. Smith and others made some remarks and gave a general description of the Valley, etc. The evening was very cold.

Saturday, September 4th.—The weather was cool, but pleasant, and at 8 a. m. D. Spencer's camp was in motion. Some of our company here met with their families and returned back to the Valley. The following are some of their names: Wm. McIntire, Burr Frost, Datus Ensign, Seth Taft. About the same time we proceeded on our journey. After going seven miles we encamped at noon on the banks of Little Sandy. Here we found P. P. Pratt's company, consisting of between seventy and eighty wagons, a messenger having been sent to delay them this morning until we arrived. I saw many old friends.

The Twelve were in council this afternoon. The people were again called together and similar instructions and information to that of last evening were given by the Twelve and others. Geo. Mills and E. Holden returned with this company to the Valley. I took supper with Brother Samuel Moore this evening. Sister Moore washed some clothes for me. The evening was pleasant.

Sunday, September 5th.—The weather was fine and we pursued our journey at 9 a. m. One of our horses was missing and I went down the creek about a mile and a half and found him and also one of Brother Brigham's and E. Snow's. We crossed the Big Sandy and came about twenty-six miles and encamped near the Pacific Springs. Here we found two companies, Brothers Smoot's and Wallace's. Soon after we arrived Brother Rich's company came up. Here we found Brother Kimball's wagons. James Smithers, Peter Hanson, Mary Helen Harris and Mary Fosgrene were along. The brethren were called together this evening and received similar instruction to that which was given to the other companies. Brother Young said it was his intention to remain here tomorrow and have a meeting at 11 o'clock. The evening was very cold.

Monday, September 6th.—It was a pleasant day and the brethren came together about 11 a. m. and were addressed by E. Snow and others, who gave instructions similar to what were given to the other companies. The Twelve and some others met in council this afternoon. I took a list of the provisions in Brother Kimball's wagons, which amounted to 2519 lbs. of breadstuff, besides groceries. James Smithers has 1031 lbs. of breadstuff, besides groceries. Brother Kimball thought it best to send back Thurston Larsen, one of the soldiers, to help Brother Whipple. Carlos Murray was also sent back with F. Granger, who has the charge of Hiram Kimball's teams.

Brother Whipple will have over 3000 lbs. of provisions for five persons—Hans C. Hanson, Peter Hanson, Thurston Larson, Mary Fosgrene and himself. Ellen Saunders and M. E. Harris have two barrels of flour, groceries, etc. They will not want much assistance from him. The evening was very cold. I wrote some in a letter for H. C. Kimball to send to Brother Whipple. A number of the brethren met their families and turned back.

Tuesday, September 7th.—The morning was very cold. The wagon we had belonging to Neff was sent back in Brother Wallace's care, and Brother Nebeker let us have a lighter one. About 9 a. m. we started on our journey. A messenger was sent ahead to stop Brother Taylor's company. Soon after we started it blew up very cold and began to snow, which continued until after we encamped, having come about fourteen miles. Here we found Brother Taylor's 100 encamped on the banks of the Sweet Water. When the brethren had learned that the Pioneer Company would encamp with them this evening, they immediately made preparations to give them a supper, which was done up in style. Toward evening the weather cleared off.

(Here the Diary ends abruptly.)

*The Diary ends very abruptly and we have no more written on the trip, which probably was because, as we learn from other sources, the Indians had commenced to be troublesome, stealing horses and committing other depredations.

"An exciting affray took place between the Indians and the pioneers on the morning of September 21st. The brethren were just getting ready to start, when the alarm was given by the men who had been sent out to gather up the horses, that the Indians were 'rushing' them—driving them off. The camp flew to arms just in time to receive the onslaught of the savages, who, emerging from the timber and firing their guns, charged upon them at full speed.

"There were at least two hundred mounted warriors. A return volley from the Pioneers broke the Indian charge, and the brethren then gave chase. The sight of their daring courage spread consternation among the Indians, who broke and fled incontinently. The old chief who had directed the attack now shouted to his band and proclaimed peace to the Pioneers, telling them that he and his warriors were good Sioux, and had mistaken them for Crows or Snakes, with whom they were at war. The brethren thought it good policy to accept the excuse, transparent though it was, and to appear satisfied with the explanation."—Life of Heber C. Kimball, page 394.

Continuing on their way, the Pioneers of the returning company arrived in safety at Winter Quarters on the 31st of October. The joy of their meeting was no doubt very great, and they found that during their absence that peace and prosperity had generally prevailed. Horace A. Egan was born August 17th, 1847, and Helen Egan August 28th, 1847, at Winter Quarters, just before their return. The winter was spent there with their families. We now turn to H. R. Egan's recital.

Dave Kimball and Wife.

SEC. IV.—SECOND TRIP WITH FAMILY.

12.—WINTER QUARTERS.

How and when we left this place I do not know, or how we got to Winter Quarters, and I do not remember of seeing father from the time last seen in the rope factory to the time we were living in our log house in Winter Quarters. How well I remember the excitement of us boys when we saw the smoke of a steamboat rising over the trees that were on a point of land just where the river made a great bend below the town. The boat was coming up stream and made a great cloud of smoke. It came on and passed between our shore and the island that lay opposite the town, then stopped at the next point above for wood. It was about a mile away. Some of the boys went up there to get a closer view, but I was afraid I would get my jacket dusted if I went, so refused to go with them. While at Winter Quarters I saw the largest fish I have ever seen in my life. It was a catfish caught by a man named Sheets. They had to load it in the wagon by hauling it up with ropes. It was about two-thirds the length of the wagon bed, and oh, what a mouth! I do believe if it had not been for the very long and sharp teeth I could have crawled into that fish very easy. It was still alive when I saw it, and the men warned us boys against putting our hands near enough to be struck by his bayonet, that was laying on his back about one-third of his length from his head to his tail, and on a hinge or joint, so he could strike with it at will, or raise it and dive under an enemy and rip him open. That sight caused me ever after to be afraid of swimming in waters that I was not acquainted with.

It was here that I did my first agricultural work. There was a path back of our house that ran straight through the field to the next street. Mother gave me a package of sunflower seeds and told me to go down one side and back the other and stick my finger in the ground at every step and drop one seed in the hole and cover it up, and keep about one foot from the path. This I did and afterwards saw two rows of large sunflowers with pan-like heads. The rows were not exactly straight, for this was my first gardening and I had no line.

One day I heard that the hazel nuts were ripe, so next day David Kimball and I went to the Bluffs after some. We found a nice patch that had not been culled over. We each had a small sack that would hold about two quarts. We had these about half full when Dave went to about the middle of the patch and said, ''I claim from that tree to that bush and to that tree,'' and so on, turning and pointing out a circle that took in the whole patch except a small margin around the described circle. He kept watching that I did not trespass on his claim. The nuts were just as good and just as thick outside of his claim as inside. If they had not been I might have got a drubbing for stealing. At that time I was a little afraid of him, although we had never quarreled.

Well, we had filled the sacks and were piling the nuts inside our shirts, having tightened our belts to keep them from falling out. We had gathered about all we could handle, and Dave had not covered one-hundredth part of his claim, when there came up a heavy rainstorm and we had to leg it for home, where we arrived with clothes soaked through, and had lost all the nuts but those in the sacks. We never went after hazel nuts again.

One day, with a boy named Levi Green, we were peeling the bark off a slippery elm log that was laying in the back yard. We boys used to get the bark to eat or to dry for future use. Levi, on one side of the log, had a hatchet with which to cut off the outside rough bark and cut across the ends. Then the bark could be peeled off in long strips.

He had made a strip ready for peeling, when I asked him to let me take his hatchet to get some ready on my side of the log. He let me have it, and as I was working with it he said, ''Give me the hatchet.'' I said, ''Just a minute.'' ''I want it right now,'' he said, so I handed it to him and laid both of my hands on top of the log. ''Why didn't you give it to me sooner?'' he said. ''I will cut your fingers off,'' and made a motion as if to strike at my left hand, which I drew quickly off, but he changed the stroke and the hatchet cut off my two middle fingers of my right hand at the first joint. One finger was hanging by a little piece of skin.

I ran to the house crying, and as Mother wanted to cut the skin that still held the finger, I put up a big cry and begged her to put the finger on again. She decided to do so, but hardly believed it would knit and grow there. She did the best she could with splints and bandages; then went out and found the other piece, but it was so dirty she decided not to try growing it to its place, but put it in a bottle with some liquid to preserve it.

My fingers were not examined for three days; then Mother

saw that I, in my playing, had twisted the piece partly around, but it was too late to attempt to straighten it, as it was joined again good and fast. Many a time since then I have wished she had taken it off, for it would have saved me much trouble by being out of the way.

So you see a small part of me lays buried at Winter Quarters, where at the resurrection I must go to make my body whole. But if that is the plan, what a job some people will have to collect the pieces and get them into place. There are some few other things I can remember about Winter Quarters, but will pass them by. .

13.—ON TO SALT LAKE.

*On the 24th of May, 1848, the First Presidency organized the main body of the Saints on the Elk Horn, preparatory to the second journey to the Rocky mountains. The camp consisted of over six hundred wagons, the largest company that had yet set out to cross the plains, and were under the care and supervision of Brigham Young and Heber C. Kimball. We have no family Diary of this trip, but Howard R. writes from memory as follows:

I recollect getting in the covered wagon that took us away from Winter Quarters, but don't remember of seeing Father till later. We had arrived at the Horn River and crossed the ferry and camped for the night about two hundred yards from it. That evening there was much excitement in camp, as a report had come in from the herders that a band of Indians were running off all the stock. The next morning we heard that the men had saved the stock, but a couple of our men had been wounded. Before noon, as I was sitting in the front of the wagon, I saw two men holding Father up and leading him towards our wagon from the ferry. His arms were hanging down and his chin was on his breast. I heard the men say that the Indians had shot him through the wrist. He had swum the Horn River that way, and had lost so much blood he could not do it again, so they had to bring him around by the ferry. I now could see him every day and watch Dr. Bernhisel dress the wound and trim the ends of the cords with a pair of scissors where they stuck out of the flesh. Father had been shot in the wrist of his right hand, and the bullet cut every cord of the thumb and fingers in the course, but broke no bones. It was here that Thomas Ricks was shot in the back with buckshot, but not killed.

14.—SCENES BY THE WAY.

We left the Horn River, and the next I remember was seeing Fort Laramie. We were on the opposite side of the Platte River from the fort. We saw it for the most of two days, first in the west and then in the east.

Buffalo Stampede.—The next thing I remember was one day we had camped for noon. I was playing near the end of the wagon tongue. Our wagon was the first on that wing of the corral. Mother caught her boys, and before I knew anything more we landed in the wagon, and she followed, and just in time, for a stampeded herd of buffalos was coming straight for the camp. They divided just a little way from the camp, some passing the back, some the front of the corral. Some of them passed over the end of our wagon tongue, doing no damage, but the part that passed the back end struck and broke a hind wheel of the last wagon in our wing. We staid there to repair damages till next day.

Prairie Dogs.—I remember the first colony of prairie dogs we passed through. The whole earth seemed to be covered with little mounds, on which we could see the dogs sitting sometimes. There was a warning given out that if anyone shot one of these dogs and the body fell into a hole, not to reach for it with the naked hand, as the rattlesnakes lived in the same holes as the dogs did.

When a dog was shot, while standing on one end on top of a mound, it always fell into the hole, and it was dangerous to try to get it, other than with a stick. These dog colonies would cover acres, but the colonies would be miles apart. It seems to me now that we could see dozens of the dogs at a time all sitting upright and watching our train, and if a person started towards them there would be a general barking chorus and instantly every dog would disappear and not appear again till the intruder had left to a safe distance.

Antelope.—One day as our train was passing the open part of a bend in the river, I was sitting in the front end of the wagon, when Father, who was driving, ran to the side of the wagon and said, "Mother, quick, my gun," Mother was as quick as she could be, but before she could pass the gun out Father said, "too late." There had been an antelope in the bend and as the train reached from one point to another he could not pass out only by running between the river and the train, in doing this it brought him within five or six rods of us, and all the train back of us. I saw the animal and Father told us it was an antelope, and, if he could have got his gun quick enough we could have had some nice meat. Mother said it was a shame to kill such a pretty animal as that. We heard a number of shots but I did not know till suppertime that someone had killed it, when Mother said. "This is some of that pretty antelope you saw when Father wanted his gun."

One afternoon we camped close to the river bank. There was a large island at this place separated from our bank of the river by a slough or small stream of very clear and deep water and about three rods wide. The men wanted to see if the grass was better on the island. It was very poor everywhere else, having been grazed off by the large herds of buffalo and other grass eating animals.

The bank of the river here from the water to the top was higher than a man's head. I was standing on this bank when one of the men volunteered to swim over and see how it was on the island. I saw him go down to the water edge. There was just enough room for him to stand between the bank and the water. He took all his clothes off and slipped into the water. That was the first time I ever saw every motion a person makes while swimming. I saw him get out on the other side and disappear in the timber, but remember no more about this affair.

One day our wagon was the last in the train and Mother, who was driving the team, let me get out and walk behind the wagon. I took my time and gradually fell back till I could hardly see the wagon, when I noticed this it scared me so I ran at my fastest speed, but soon was out of wind and went very slow again to gain my breath, and took another run, but I was getting farther behind all the time. As the train was nearing a rolling country, where I couldn't be seen, Mother got George Redding to come back and get me.

He took hold of my hand and tried to make me run the whole distance to the train, but finding I was about all in he swung me on his back and tried to rattle my teeth out by running at a dog trot, stamping his feet as hard as he could to give me a good jolting, and something to remember him by, which this proves I do, for I never got very far from the wagon again.

I remember of helping Mother gather "buffalo chips" for fire material, as there was nothing else and they made a good fire. When we camped where there was plenty of them we would collect a couple of sacks full and carry them to the next camp, for sometimes they would be very scarce.

Now this is what I heard at the time, but did not see: Some one in the camp had lost part of a sack of beans. Some one had stolen them. Part of them were found in the feed box of a certain man, where he had placed them for his team to eat, thinking it was corn. He had stolen them after dark and by his mistaking beans for corn was detected. I could mention the man's name, but think it best not to.

Chimney Rock From the Pioneer Road.

I recollect seeing **Chimney Rock.** It was on the opposite side of the river, but quite plainly seen from our side. Some of the men went across to get a close view of it.

One day we camped a little ways from a dry **Salaratus Lake.** Mother took me along with her to get some. It was very hard and smooth and we had only table knives to dig it out, but I remember we got as much as Mother could carry to the wagon. It lasted for a number of years after we arrived in the valley. This place is not far east of **Independence Rock,** which I remember very well. The road passes around the southern end of the rock and only a couple of rods from it. To me it appeared to be the shape of the Salt Lake Tabernacle, only very much larger. There was hundreds of names of people written on it. Some in large letters and far out of the reach of anyone standing on the ground. The men had been warned about climbing on top, as there were a number of large cracks running crossways that were very deep and to fall in one of them was sure death and probably the body could never be found.

Next we came to the Sweet Water, that runs through the Devil's Gate. Traveling up this stream, which was very crooked, Mother was driving when the next wagon ahead of ours turned over into a creek or bog hole. The driver (a man named Holt, I believe), did not swing out far enough to strike the bridge fair, so two wheels missed the bridge. There were two children in the wagon sitting on top of boxes and bales, but in a twinkling this was reversed, children under and only the wagon cover to keep them from drowning. The man called for help and soon the men came running from both ways. The children had not been severely hurt and all was on the move again soon after.

Devil's Gate, we could see as we climbed the bluffs to the west. The very deep and narrow cut through which the water ran, it seemed to me, was over a hundred feet deep, with almost perpendicular walls and about twenty-five to forty feet apart at the top.

Fort Bridger is the next place remembered, with its low dirt covered houses near the bank of the river. Indians and white men all dressed in buckin clothes, and more dogs, half-

Camping at Echo Canyon.

bred wolf, than you could shake a stick at. It was here that Father traded for the same pistol he had held in his hand and dropped, when shot, in the fight at the Horn River. It had passed from Indian to Indian and arrived at Bridger long before we did.

I remember **Echo Canyon,** the high perpendicular rocks on the off side of the road most of the way through. We could hear the men calling and dogs barking from one cliff to another, although the ones starting the sound was far ahead of us, it went bounding from cliff to cliff, repeating the sound perfectly.

*Mother has related the following many times about Echo Canyon: At the head or summit, before entering Echo Canyon, Father was called to assist in some repairs that were necessary on Heber C. Kimball's wagon, which made it necessary for Mother to drive the team until he should catch up, which he expected would not be long.

She had two yoke of cattle and a yoke of cows, which she drove down that canyon, and she missed more stumps and rocks than any other driver, so it was said, crossing the stream twenty-seven times. Some times she would be ahead of the team, some times between the cattle and wagon, to pass brush, trees and, rocks.

Her son Erastus was in the wagon, having been run over. It seems he was being lifted into the wagon, but slipped in some way and fell under the tongue and would have escaped all right, only on account of a pig that was tied under the back of the wagon. In trying to get out of the way of the pig his foot got under the wheel.

Those of the family who could walk were on ahead and Mother's was the lead team. Those ahead would holler out, "Here is another creek," and Mother would say, "D——n the creeks!" This she used to tell many times. Howard R. further states:

Then we came to Weber River and when we left the camp here Father said we had to climb a mountain for seven miles, and I thought before we did get to the top we had come seven hundred miles, for he had us walk up every step of it, and not only that, but down the other side, where it was awful steep, and everything loose in the wagon was liable to attempt to pass the team. The next day we were on the little mountain, where Father took us to one side of the road and pointed out the place where we would live in the great Salt Lake Valley. It was two more days when Father drove the team and landed the wagon near to the door of a house, near the middle of the south side of the north fort, where we lived for a couple of years.

*Before their arrival, the Fort at Salt Lake Valley contained 423 apartments and 1670 people and 875 acres had been sown to winter wheat. It was in June of this year that myriads of big crickets came down from the mountains and would have devoured the crops, but for the arrival of immense flocks of seagulls, which devoured the crickets.

Native Utahn in Pioneer days.

1871 UTAH CENTRAL R.R.

1847

ENSIGN PEAK

PART II.

SALT LAKE: INCIDENTS OF EARLY SETTLEMENT.

SEC. I.—OUR HOME LIFE.

15.—THE OLD FORT.

*It was in September, 1848, that the family arrived in Salt Lake Valley and moved into a room of the Old Fort that had been provided for them. This Old Fort had been commenced when Father was at Salt Lake on the first trip and was built on the square now called Pioneer Park. Howard R. goes on to say:

I remember the rainy season, when the sun was not seen for nearly a month. The roof of our house was a shed roof, covered with inch lumber, plastered with clay on the outside. The roof had sagged so that there was quite a depression in the center. This had filled with water and was leaking through to the room below.

Heber C. Kimball called in to see how we were all getting along. He had not sat there long when the roof settled more with a loud crack. Kimball jumped out of the door and called Mother to come out quick or the roof would fall on her. No she would not go out, but invited him to come back in out of the rain, but no, he went off in a hurry.

When he had gone Mother placed a tub under where the drip was, then stood up in a chair and run a table knife up between the boards, so letting the water come down in a stream faster than she could carry it in the bucket to the door. Soon the weight on the roof was lessened enough to allow the roof to spring back some, and the danger of it falling in was removed.

A few minutes after this had been done a man came running to the door with a post to place under the sagging roof to hold it up. He said Brother Kimball had sent him. Mother told him she would not have a post set up in the middle of her parlor and for him to tell Brother Kimball that the danger

was passed and he could now return and finish his visit if he
so desired.

Of late years I often think of what a hard life Mother
had in pioneer days, but I suppose that was the lot of all
the pioneers; digging roots and gathering greens, catching
fish in the Jordan River, collecting anything eatable to make
what little flour and cornmeal we had last till another supply could be procured, was the common lot. Wood was also
scarce, even the bark of the fence poles was stripped off for
fuel, for the men could not spare the time to haul wood from
the canyons.

Father was away most all the time working for the church
and Mother would never ask for help if she could avoid it.
Possibly she could have got along easier and with less trouble
if she had not been so independent. I have heard her say that
she would work her finger ends off before she would ask for
assistance.

16.—OUR NEW HOME.

After we moved out of the Fort to our new home, on the
second lot south of the corner of First North and Main
Street, in April, 1849, Mother had a little better time of it
than before. We had a house built of adobes with a shingle
roof. There was but one large room that was plastered sides
and ceiling, and a lumber floor that Mother used to mop every
day. She took quite a pride in her white floor. It was in
this house, June 13, 1851, that W. M. Egan was born. Here
we could keep a pig and some poultry, which helped along
very nicely, besides we were now able to keep a cow.

Oh, we were just beginning to live fat, and we had our
garden in. It was here that I saw the largest spider that I
ever did in my life. Mother heard the chickens making a
great fuss back of the house. She looked out of the back window and saw the chickens standing in a ring around a large
spider. It was standing as high as possible with one leg
raised, and striking at the hens when they ventured too close.
Mother got a tin box about three by six inches, and one and
a half inches deep, laying this on the ground she drove the
thing over the box. Where it stood its legs reached the ground
each side of the box without touching it. Mother gave it a tap
with a stick and it pulled its legs in and settled down in the
box, which it nearly filled. Mother slid the cover on the box
and set it in the window and when she went to let a visitor
see it, found that the sun, shining on the box, had killed the
spider. Its body was about the size of a silver quarter.

Mother pinned it to a board with a needle and kept it for a long time for people to see.

Laying Cornerstone of Temple.—It was while we lived here that I witnessed the first breaking of ground for the foundation of the Temple (February 14, 1853), and a few months after, the laying of the cornerstone (April 6, 1853), when there seemed to be thousands of people there to witness it. There was an immense mound of earth near the southwest corner of where the Temple was to be built. This earth was what had been dug out of the place for the foundation. The day was set for the laying of the cornerstone. This mound as well as the whole surrounding space was covered by a very large number of very happy people. Some had come many miles to witness the ceremony. With some of my boy friends I stood on the northeast side near the top of the mound, and had a good view of the southeast corner, where the stone was laid. And since that time I have seen the gradual growth of those heavy walls up to the capstone, being about forty years from the breaking of the ground to the capstone.

Late View of Salt Lake Temple.

There are a great many events that come to my mind, while we lived just across the street from Heber C. Kimball. I shoveled dirt with the rest of the boys to dig out the place for the foundation of the large adobe two-story house of Brother Kimball's. I remember when the first grading of Main street was being done north of Temple block, how sorry I felt to see a man cut down a very large oak tree that was standing in the middle of where they wanted the road. There was only one more tree as large and that stood some distance to the southeast, I think, in Bishop Whitney's lot.   Each year they were loaded down with acorns.   I have climbed both of these trees to gather them.   I can't see now why such landmarks should not have been preserved.

17.—GRASSHOPPERS AND CRICKETS.

It was while we lived here that we had the grasshopper invasion. I remember that during the heat of the day they were so thick in the sky that at times you could not see the sun, and where they would light for the night, or when the wind was too strong from the direction they wanted to travel, they destroyed everything green. All of this mighty army of hoppers were traveling in a southeasterly direction and in two or three days had finished their work here and passed on. Over at the great lake they did not fare so well. There along the shore could be seen great windrows of their bodies that had been washed ashore by the north winds. Near Black Rock there were three such rows, so wide and high that a man could have filled a wagon bed with them as quick as he could have shoveled that much sand, and the whole shore line facing the north was just the same. Millions of bushels of preserved or pickeled grasshoppers, that would do no more harm.

Crickets.—Oh! yes, I must not forget them! Well they hatched out all along on top of the bench land, and as they grew kept working down hill, leaving nothing green behind except sage brush. The road north of our place ran along the lower level of the bench, the grain and hay fields being still farther down and a fence between the road and fields. When the crickets got near the road, war was declared and the fight was on; men, women and children walking back and forth swinging brooms made of willows or bunches of grass, trying to drive the enemy back, but with very little success.

This kind of warfare only made the enemy more hungry, and every morning would find them nearer the grain, till at last, was put in operation, our biggest gun, which consisted of all the sheep, cows and horses that could be collected. These were crowded together and driven back and forth the length of the field slaying the enemy by the legions. Thus it only required about a week to save part of the crop, but a little was better than none those days. The next year this was repeated, only on a smaller scale, for the enemy's ranks had been sadly depleted by the large flocks of sea gulls that used them for food.

*This was in following years after the sea gulls had saved the first crop.

18.—ANOTHER HOME.

When Father returned from one of his trips he got acquainted with a couple of men named Mr. Moore and W. E. Horner. Together they bought a city lot in the Nineteenth ward. On this lot had been built a very large barn intended for a livery stable. The man Horner was some of a horse doctor, and Father and Moore gave him the reins to do as he thought best. The lot was a corner lot and directly cata-cornered from the northeast corner of union square.

The barn was built cross ways of the lot and about a third of its length down from the south end. There had been an adobie house built about sixteen feet south of the southeast corner of the barn, leaving a space for a shed, which was supported at the corner of the barn by a large squared log for a post on which were placed the plates to hold the roof. Afterward it had been decided to make another room of this by laying up three adobie walls, joining onto the first room and of the same width, and one roof to cover all. There was a door in the first room facing the south street and a window in the west side. The new room had a door and window on the west side, a door on the east side, and a window in the north end. From the barn south was all open ground, sometimes used by emigrants for camping. From the barn north the lot was fenced with a strong fence, making a secure corral to turn animals in, to feed.

Mr. Moore did not stay long in the partnership and Horner went east to bring his wife across the plains, and all this time there was not much done with the stable. When Horner came back he built a house on the next lot north of the barn, and for a while business was flourishing, at least in the summer time, but taken all together, Father, when they tried to settle up, was not satisfied and bought Horner out, calculating to make a dairy barn of it as soon as he could make the proper arrangements.

The barn had been built on large flat rocks placed at intervals along the outer side principally under the joints of the heavy bed timbers. The rocks had been sunk in the ground so there was but a small space between the sills and the ground. Earth had been placed all around to stop the draft. Us boys, and many of the neighboring boys, used to spend many an hour under there crawling from one place to another. Sometimes digging trenches in the hard ground so we could crawl under a beam to get to another corner that we couldn't reach without.

19.—THE BURNING OF THE BARN.

One day us boys took our little cart and went up on the hillside to get some oak brush for firewood. We were about to start for home when we chanced to see a small blaze at the east end of the barn, watching this for a very few moments we saw the flame spread all over that end. We were about a half mile away. We dropped everything and ran as fast as we could for home.

When we arrived there the job had been completed, nothing left of the barn but a huge pile of live coals. Mother was sitting out in the yard surrounded by her household goods that had been quickly removed to a safe distance. They had not been handled very carefully and I remember Mother saying they might as well have been left to burn as to have been smashed to pieces as some of the things were. The house was saved, but somewhat damaged. The large corner post I have mentioned was nearly burned out. The north window was burned, and the glass melted and run to the ground. The shingles near the north end were badly scorched. The whole place would have been swept clean if it had not been that there was a large stream of water at hand which was turned in the lot and the whole house was kept under a sheet of water.

Now the cause of the fire was learned from Mother. But first let me say that there was no stoves in the house. All the cooking was done by an open fireplace, one such being in each room. The wind was blowing quite a gale from the south. This helped to save the house, but caused the blaze.

The woman that lived in the south room had let her fire die out, and came to Mother to get some live coals to start a fire with. She got some on a shovel and went out of the back door, but soon returned for more, saying the others had all blowed away. She had just passed out the second time when the alarm of fire was given and people from all directions came running with buckets and ladders and the fight was on. For days the stream of water was running into that pile of coals. There was three horses in the stalls. They could get out, but two which were turned loose in the corral ran back through the flames, one reaching his stall, the other getting only part way, as shown by what was left of them after the fire had been killed.

We lost all of our chickens, and our pig had lost all of his bristles, while his pen was burning so he could escape. There was about thirty tons of hay in the barn, and the grain room was full of oats and barley. There were four sets of harness and some saddles in the harness room. All went up in smoke, besides a good many carpenter tools. The flames had spread so rapidly that it was imposible to save much that was in the barn. The two horses might have been saved if they had been tied to a post when taken out.

Well, we slept in our house that night, a blanket being put up at the north window hole, but I don't think Mother slept much. There was plenty of help offered to replace the furniture back in the house, but Mother wanted time to consider if it would not be just as well to finish the smashing and breaking business where it was.

Upper Main Street, Salt Lake City, 1860. Bishop Hunter's Residence, Telegraph Office, Etc., Just North of Deseret National Bank Building.

SEC. II.—RELICS.

20.—INDIAN MOUNDS.

There was a couple of small mounds on the south side of the lot just where the fence was to be placed. These had to be cut down to the level of the surrounding land, and by doing this there was dug up a large number of human bones, and also quantities of some kind of berries that were petrified. There was quite a number of arrow spikes made of black and white flint, and some few pieces of pottery of a dark brown color. This part of the lot was covered all over with large cobble stones, while all around it for some distance there were none.

21.—THE INDIAN PORTRAIT.

In the largest red ravine that leads down from Ensign Peak bench, and about half way to the bottom, was a cliff of rocks from side to side, and about twenty-five or thirty feet high. It was more than perpendicular, for the top leaned over to such an extent that water coming down the gulch would fall clear off the face of the cliff, which was composed of a conglomeration of different kinds of stones all cemented together with hardpan.

On the right hand side as you go up, and some ten feet above the steep sloping earth at the bottom, was embedded in the walls a boulder about three feet in diameter, flush with the face of the wall. On this boulder was painted, with red, blue, and black material, the figure of an Indian sitting on his horse. He was a big, broad-shouldered man, dressed in the Indian fashion, large plumes of feathers on his head, a long spear in one hand, the other held the bridle reins. Just close back of him on the same rock was a small band of Indians all on horses, apparently some distance away, but all could be seen very plainly.

The horses were almost as perfectly drawn as could be by a camera. The Indian was in the correct position for sitting a horseback, and must have been taken from life, but by whom? and what kind of paint used, to stand the weather so long? It could not be washed off and when I last saw it, it was just as bright as ever, only where the boys had tried to chip off a piece that would have some of the paint on, by throwing small boulders at it, thus marring the painting badly.

That is another thing that should have been preserved. It could have been easily chiseled out and carried away.

The Tannery.—Father owned an interest in the Margetts tannery, but when and how he got out of it I do not know, but I do know that the venture never made him a millionaire. This tannery was just across the street west of our home.

*The tannery was started by Richard Margetts, Father and Robert Golding, the latter of whom had a tannery a block and a half north of our home. I think Father put in a piece of Main street property and finally took it out in boots and shoes for his Deep Creek store.

Deep Snow.—**Cattle Starving.**—One morning in 1857 I awoke to find a heavy snowstorm had set in, and it continued all day, all night, and all next day, and until some time in the night. The next morning when I was able to go out I found that the snow was up to my waist or about two and a half feet deep on a level. Some places eight feet deep in the valley. It was some days before the roads were broke open so travel could be resumed.

Some of us boys heard that there were a good many cattle caught out on the range, west of Jordan, and were dead or dying and that boys could make something by going over there and getting the hides off the dead ones. Three of us got our sleds and ropes ready and when the snow had settled and crusted so it would bear our weight we started on our exploring trip.

When about four miles northwest of the Jordan bridge we found a bunch of ten or twelve cattle, every one dead, and laying close together. By helping each other we were able to start for home about 3 or 4 o'clock p. m., each with a hide on his sled. We repeated this the next day, but the next a thaw wind called a halt as far as boy sleds were concerned. We sold the hides for $3 apiece, which we considered millionaire wages.

***Freezing and Starving.**—In the winter of 1857, probably just before the snowstorm mentioned in the preceding paragraphs, Father went east after some cattle that he had heard were for sale. His business was buying cattle in winter to drive to California for Beef, in summer. He had a man with him and when in the mountains this heavy storm caught them and they got lost.

While endeavoring to save his companion from freezing by rubbing his feet, his own froze. He lost one of his little toes entirely, and I have cut the calloused parts from his heels and toes many a time afterward. They were three days with but a pinch of cracker crumbs and after that ten days without anything to eat. His companion often said he would lie down and die, but Father would coax him and say I will try and save my life, and would go ahead and set down in a hollow and his companion would finally come along.

When they got in sight of Fort Bridger the snow was crusted and their clothing and shoes were cut to pieces breaking the crust and they would leave blood in their tracks, but they tore up their blankets and wrapped their feet and legs as best they could. They finally arrived at Fort Bridger and were used up for many days. The skin of the calf of their legs could be wrapped around the bone.

*Federal Army.—Father had scarcely recovered from the exposures of freezing and starving when the Federal Army was sent to wipe out the ''Mormons'' and as he was an active militia man with title of major he was much concerned in the activities that brought about a settlement in this affair.

In May, 1858, Father was sent with a company to escort Colonel Kane to Florence, having the following recommendation, which was signed by Governor Cummings:

Executive Office
Great Salt Lake City U.T. May 12. 1858

I beg to reccommend to your favorable attention Messrs Egan, Murdock, Nebt, Knowlton, Van Ettan, Worthing & Mather the company escorting my friend Col. Kane to Florence—on their way to the States and upon their return. Any assistance which you may furnish in providing forage, for animals if they stand in need of them I will oblige
Yours truly
P. Cummings
Governor of Utah Territory

To

Commanding at Ft. Laramie

Facsimile of Recommend from Governor Cumming.

From California Father obtained ammunition for the Nauvoo Legion, as is shown by the following receipt:

Ordnance Depot
Nauvoo Legion. G.S.L. City
Feb 3 1858

Received at this department on the 19th January ult. from Mr. Howard Egan

27 Kegs (TEEC) Rifle Powder 25 lbs each
30 M Percussion Caps
100 lbs Lead—

J. W. Ollerbeck,
Chief of Ordnance
N. L.

Facsimile of Receipt for Ammunition for Nauvoo Legion.

We do not have any. farther details of his personal activities in the matter and do not wish to take up space in rehearsing what has many times been said respecting it.

*The Move.—While Father was east escorting Colonel Kane, the family moved south with the rest of the Saints, all of whom abandoned their homes, while the army the United States had sent here to clean them out, was passing through Salt Lake City, the preparation being made to destroy every home, if the army attempted to take possession. The family went to Provo, but soon returned as far as Mullener's Mill, where the Lehi Sugar Factory now stands, and lived in a dugout. Mullener's Mill dam broke away three times while we were there. After the Federal Army had passed on to Fort Crittenden in Cedar Valley we returned to our home in Salt Lake City.

Immigration Fund.—Father at one time gave W. H. Sherman $100 gold coin to help poor English converts to emigrate to Utah, and to assist as many as possible. Sherman went on his mission to England and on his arrival there commenced sending back notes for the various amounts loaned to the different people that did not have quite enough money to pay their fare, each giving their note for the amount received, with the promise to pay Father out of the first money earned after their arrival in Utah.

About four years after the date of the last note, Father gave them to me to figure up the amount of the thirty notes, to see how close to the $100 the total would come, as he said it would cost something to change the money to English. We found that the notes amounted to exactly $100. We could not figure out how it had been done without the cost of exchange had been divided to each note as interest in advance.

Father had intended the money to act on the perpetual plan, by sending it back to help more, as soon as paid. Father said he might be able to collect the most of it by calling on each person owing him, but said probably they

Deseret News and Tithing Office Corner in 1860, Where Hotel Utah Now Stan

needed the money, and so told me to take these notes and burn them, which I did, but it destroyed his perpetual assistance plan.

*Before Mother died a note for $50, which had been given for the same purpose, was found and it was given to John Morgan for a life scholarship in his college, which he used to pay a painter that had been immigrated by it.

A short time ago a man, who said he had been secretary of a theatrical organization, said he remembered counting the door receipts and found a $10 gold piece among the silver coins and asked the doorkeeper how he got that, who said it was given by Howard Egan for his entrance fee and to help them.

In 1862 he was made a deputy clerk of the United States Third Judicial District Court in and for Utah Territory, as attested by the following certificate:

Facsimile of Appointment as Deputy Clerk of the U. S. Third Judicial Court.

Many things of interest could be placed here, but our space is too limited and we are more concerned with the Pioneering features. If we had all of Father's papers that were kept during Mother's lifetime we would need several volumes to contain them, to say nothing of the many thrilling incidents of his life that now cannot be told.

SEC. III—STORIES OF EARLY SALT LAKE.

22—THE COLD SWIM.

When I was a boy I thought if any one started for a certain place and backed out it showed that they were cowards, and this opinion has caused me at different times some hardships and discomfort. So if any one makes up his mind to do something or go somewhere and it is not really necessary, don't act bull-headed and face all kinds of trouble just to say you didn't back out, for in after years, when some ailment gets a good hold of you, think what a fool you were, though you didn't at the time, know that it would get it back on you with ten-fold the suffering you first experienced.

I could mention a good many times that I should have backed out, but will tell you of but one at this time. A number of the boys that used to go hunting down Jordan river said they never killed anything but they got it. This, because sometimes a duck would fall on the opposite side of the river. Now, I had shot a big mallard duck. He fell just on the edge of the opposite bank. There was another hunter with me, who said, ''Now I guess you won't get that one, for there is mush ice floating down the river and its three miles to the bridge, and before you could go around some coyote would get it.'' ''I'll see about that.'' So, taking off all my clothes I rolled them in a snug little bundle with my gun in the middle and fastened them on my head with my belt over the top and under my chin. The other hunter said, ''I wouldn't go after that duck for half a dozen like him. He is not worth it.'' ''I know that,'' I said, ''but I always make it my business to get what I kill.'' I waded in as far as I could and had only about one rod to swim, but that was through the mush ice and was quite a plenty for me. The air was warmer than the water. I was soon dressed again and, picking up the duck, said good-bye to the hunter that had watched the whole proceeding.

I started up the river for the bridge, not feeling any the worse for my bath, but in fact somewhat refreshed, but let me say right here, I would not advise any one to take that kind of health treatment. I was a little lucky that day, for before I reached the bridge a flock of geese flew over me and I brought down a nice big fellow and he didn't fall the other side of the

river, and when I reached the bridge I got a chance to ride
most of the way home, besides selling the duck to the man
that drove the team for 50 cents, that being the amount we
usually got for a large duck.

23.—SETTING A GUN FOR BEAR.

There was a man by the name of Cragan that had lived
a couple of blocks south of my home, who had been killed in
north Mill Creek canyon while going after firewood. He was
riding on the front hounds of his wagon when the king bolt
broke and the front axeltree rolled over and pinned him down
under the heels of his horses. They were frightened and ran
away, kicking the man to death and making a complete wreck
of the front part of the wagon and the harness, besides nearly
killing themselves.

The man had another team of oxen and a strong heavy
wagon that the widow used to let out to haul wood on shares,
so getting her fuel for winter. I got the team to haul a few
loads one summer, from what was called Coons Canyon,
eighteen miles west of Salt Lake City. It took two days to
make the round trip and hard work and late hours. At that
time of the year the team had to be turned out to feed on
the grass, as no feed of any kind was carried for them. One
day there was twelve or fifteen boys in the canyon cabin,
mostly for the purpose of getting wood. A few had come to
hunt bear for, as some of them said, the canyon seemed to
be full of them.

That morning a boy had seen one not far up the left hand
fork, going up. He had been down to the spring to drink and
his tracks were very plain in the dusty road, and it was said
by some of the boys that, every day they would drag their
load of maple down that road, the next morning there was the
bear tracks where he had come down to the spring and back.
So that evening the whole lot agreed to go after Mr. Bear and
the boy that shot him was to be given ten rounds of ammunition by each of the other boys.

I and my chum, and bedfellow, talked up a scheme that
we thought might earn us the ammunition promised, if we
could carry it through. This is what we did. Slipping out
unobserved we took a chunk of bacon of about two pounds, a
long twine fish line, a hatchet and our guns, and went up to
the spring. The moon was shining brightly and we could see
no bear tracks in the road, and knew that bruin had not yet
come for his drink, so we looked around for a place to suit
us for what we wanted to do.

We soon decided that a good sized tree close to the road and about two rods above the spring would answer our purpose, so we placed my gun up in this tree, muzzle pointed down, tied it firmly, then one end of the twine to the trigger, then passed the other end up and over a limb and then down to the ground, where we drove a hooked stake in the ground and passed the string under the hook, tied the string around the bacon so it would lay just outside of the wheel track and about one foot outside of where the bullet would strike, if we had made correct calculations.

When this was done we went back to camp and bed. We had not been missed nor had we been long at the job. The next morning, we were the first to get up, and went up to the spring and found that Mr. Bear had been there and pulled at the bacon and fired the gun. This we could see at the first glance, as the bear had wallowed in the road and left a good deal of his blood there and all along the road as he went back up the canyon.

We took the gun down, pulled up the stake and moved all signs of a trap, which was not many. Then loaded the gun and fired it off, loaded again and followed the bloody trail to where the bear had left the road and taken to the thick brush. We now supposed he had been stunned by the bullet, but by now might be able to put up a good fight, as we thought he must be a grizzly, as that was the kind that had been seen there, but he must be getting weak losing so much blood.

We concluded to return to camp for breakfast, and to report that we had shot and wounded a large bear, and he had gone into a thick brush, where it was hard to trail him and thought we would give him time to bleed to death. The other boys done considerable grumbling, and said if we had not been in such a hurry, and waited till they were all together they could have filled him so full of lead that he could not pack it away, and now, it was chance if we ever found him, even if he was dead.

Well, we all went on the hunt, but the thorn brush was so thick that it was very slow work to find the trail and follow it. In some places we found where the bear had rolled around quite a space, then it would take a long time to find what direction he had gone. This went on till after noon, when we went to camp for dinner and found there was only enough provisions left to last two meals. There we were, up against it, only about half a load of wood ready and eighteen or twenty miles from home.

Well, after holding council as to what we should do, we decided to get our loads and go home. We did, but not all of the boys. Next week I heard that some one found the bear dead and a hole down through his neck. They said he must have been shot while standing up with his back to us. We let them guess.

24.—THE HORNETS.

In 1847, after the Pioneers reached the valley and began their fort building operations, Father was one of those that hauled house logs from Red Butte canyon. On one of his trips, going up the canyon, he saw a little up the road, what appeared to be a good tree, large enough to cut for saw logs for timber, and as the other teams were way back, he thought he would climb the steep sidehill and take a near view of it. When he reached it he sounded it with the back of his axe. Immediately there arose a buzzing sound. He had stirred up a nest of hornets.

Making a rapid retreat down the hill, followed the biggest part of the way by a string of hornets, that were trying to get a line on him, he made his escape without getting hit. He determined to say nothing to anyone about it. Some few days after, while going up the canyon, the man driving the lead team turned out of the road just below this tree. Father asked him what he was going to do. He said, ''Get that tree, its dead easy. It will roll right down to the road.'' Father said, ''You had better not, but wait a few days till I get out what I have chopped, and then I will help you. That tree will make two good loads.'' ''No,'' he said, ''I can get it alone,'' and started up the hill with his axe.

Father and the other teamsters, driving a little further up, stopped where they could see the fun. The man reached the tree, took off his coat and swung his axe into the tree. He had not chopped out many chips when he was seen to jump to one side and grab his coat, and fairly fly down to the road. He was more like a large rock sliding and turning end over end till he reached his team, which he put on the run up the canyon till he thought he was safe from a further attack.

When he came up to where Father was he said, ''Darn you, Egan, why didn't you tell me there was hornets near that tree?'' ''You never asked me, and I told you I would help you get it and so I will.'' ''No, you won't the road is as close as I want to get to that tree. I have three pretty severe bayonet stabs that will take a week to heal Besides, I am not perfectly satisfied as to your innocence in this affair.''

A few days later Father started very early in the morning for the canyon and on his way up gathered a large armful of dry grass. When opposite the hornet tree he carried the grass up the hill and placed it on the hive, after plugging up with grass the door hole. No hornets had yet came out, as it was quite cold that early in the morning. After placing the straw to suit him, placing a few dry limps on top to make a greater heat, he set fire to the pile and enjoyed his revenge, while listening to the buzzing death song of the enemy, which could be heard above the snapping of the fire.

It didn't take long for the whole colony to become good hornets, and then Father attacked the tree, which made him two good loads of saw logs. One of which he got home early in the afternoon. The man that was stung by the hornets said, ''Nice logs, how far up did you go after them?'' ''These are a part of the tree you would not have.'' ''What! the hornet tree?'' ''Yes.'' ''How did you manage it?'' ''Oh, easy! This morning when it was cool I was afraid the poor things might suffer, so I gave them a little fire to warm up in. I think they were satisfied, for not one came out to complain.'' ''Well, by jinks, you had a joke on the hornets as well as on me.''

25.—THE STAMPEDE IS STOPPED.

(As told by Father, as near as I can remember.)

We were camped at a large horseshoe bend of the Platt River. The points of the shoe being about one-half of a mile apart. The wagons were placed about half way between the points of the shoe and the cattle and teams were put inside of the shoe. This arrangement would not call for but few guards, as the river was not fordable at any place in the bend, and if the stock attempted to pass out they could be heard at camp. This was thought to be a very good and safe plan.

It was a very dark night and everything was all right till a couple of hours before day, when Father was awakened by the rumbling sound of many animals running. He jumped out of bed and into his boots, buckled on his belt which carried his Colts pistol and knife, grabbed his hat and left camp on the run to head off the frightened animals before they could pass out of the bend. The night had grown still darker, as it most always does just before day. It was so dark that you could not have seen your hand a foot from your face.

Well, when running at top speed he ran up against a naked Indian breast to breast. He knew it was an Indian, for he felt his naked skin, but no damage was done and the rebound had instantly separated them. How far, he did not know. He dropped down as low as possible, but still on his feet and gun in right hand and knife in left, listened for the slightest rustle of the grass, not wanting to fire at random for fear of getting an arrow in return.

Representative Pioneers. Brigham Young and Brothers.

Lorenzo, 1804; Brigham, 1801; Phineas, 1799; Joseph, 1797; John, 1795.

After waiting some time and hearing no sound from his friend, he side-stepped very carefully for about a rod, and as he could hear the animals still running, he placed his left hand on his breast holding his hunting knife point forward, made a dash ahead, determined that if he ran up against his friend again there would be something doing. He ran this way until he saw the glistening waters of the river, which he came near running into. He now knew that he had turned the animals back in the bend, where they could run in a circle till tired enough to stop.

He did not return to camp till after daylight and did not see any Indians, but plenty of their tracks in the dusty road where the train had turned off to make camp. A count proved that no animals had got away and camp moved on. But just try and imagine the thoughts and feelings after the contact with the Indian, not knowing of his actions, or when he would hear the twang of his bowstring and feel the point of his arrow. No doubt but the Indian was expecting the white man to shoot, when he could see by the flash of the gun where he was and return the fire with greater success than taking chances. But all's well that ends well.

The place where this happened could be located by reading Father's journal giving a description of the camps and country along the Platt River. This was a few years after the Pioneers.

How Salt Lake Has Grown.

26.—TABY WE-PUP.

In the early days of Grantsville, in Tooele valley, there was an Indian chief of a band of Go-Shutes, whose country was from Salt Lake valley on the east, to Granite Rock on the desert on the west, and from Simpson's Springs on the south, to the Great Salt Lake on the north.

This Indian was a great diplomat, and always claimed to be a good friend of the whites, who were trying to establish their homes in his country. There were frequent raids on the settlers' stock, when small bands of twenty or more would be stolen and driven off, supposedly by hostile Indians. When this happened a delegation of the whites would visit Taby's camp, which could always be found within a few miles of Grantsville.

At the request of the whites he would agree to send a party of his own men after the thieves and kill them, and bring back the stolen animals, but he must be paid for the job by giving him a beef, two or three sacks of flour, five or six blankets, a stated amount of sugar, coffee, matches, a few shirts, and always a stated amount of powder, lead and caps.

After the agreement was made, the white men would go back home feeling sure that Taby would get their stock back and that the thieves would be punished. They generally did not have to wait over two weeks before a rumor would come from Taby's camp, saying the stolen animals would be brought in the next day, and sure they would, but most always a few short of the number stolen.

Taby would come from his camp for the promised reward and at the same time would tell of the hard fight his men had had with the thieves, and how many they had killed and wounded, and how a few of his own men were slightly wounded, for which he ought to have more blankets, which of course the white men couldn't see that way, for a bargain is a bargain. This kind of business would happen about every six or eight months and wind up about the same way.

The white men were getting more numerous and their herds needed more grazing land. So a party of young men built a few cabins in Skull Valley over the first range of mountains west of Grantsville and made it their business to herd the stock for the settlers. These young men were most always in the saddle, watching their stock and exploring the country west of them, where they found numerous signs of where bands of stock at some time had been driven out on the desert, and some places back again, where Taby had brought them home.

Well, the time came that the herd boys missed about forty head of horned stock, and four or five of the boys went in search of them. In circling around they soon found the trail leading west, and they could find but three pony tracks, so they supposed there were only three thieves that was doing the stealing.

Preparing themselves with a couple of canteens of water each, four of the boys determined to see if it was possible to save the animals. They started on the trail from Cedar Mountains, which is on the east edge of the desert. A due west line from there, of seventy-five or eighty miles, is a patch of ground of about a quarter section, and a little higher than the level of the desert. Near one end is a small spring of brakish water. The next nearest water is twenty miles further west.

The next morning about daylight the boys were getting quite close to this first water place. They could see cattle scattered all over it, and when they got on the higher ground they could also see three Indians just starting from the spring going west. They gave them some scare, besides wounding one of their ponies. The boys, after resting till the next day, afternoon, made their way back home with all of their animals but one. That the Indians had killed for grub when they stopped at the spring.

This put an end to old Taby's double-faced transactions. It was afterwards learned that he was the father of the whole stealing operations, but the friendly Deep Creek Indians were afraid of him, and did not dare to tell of his doings till the old man got his last call.

Then it was found out that when he wanted a new blanket or two and some provisions, he would send some of his men to steal and drive off a band of stock, and after a bargain was made send a rumor out and have them brought back, that is, what they did not kill for food, or the hides for footwear, or to make ropes and lassos. There probably are some people now living that may remember old Taby We-Pup, but that never knew of his doings.

Jebow and Squaw.
Early Salt Lake Character.

PART III.

PIONEERING: SALT LAKE to CALIFORNIA.

SEC. I.—ROUTE SOUTH AND NORTH.

27.—A DIARY.

By Howard Egan, of His Trip in 1849-50, From Fort Utah
(Provo City) to California, With the Distance, Water,
Feed and Suitable Camp Grounds, Numbered
From 1 to 89, Etc. Kept for a
Future Traveling Guide.

Sunday, November 18th, 1849.—We started from Fort
Utah in company with Brothers Granger and Hills, having
three wagons and fifteen head of animals and forty souls, for
California. It stormed for three days previous to our starting,
which has made the roads very bad. After traveling seven
and a half miles we came to a small spring branch, and we
traveled up a little further and camped at Hobble Creek
(*now Springville), which is a good camp ground with feed
and wood in plenty.

Monday, 19th.—The morning was warm and pleasant.
Brother Orlando Hovey started in company with us this
morning, having a wagon, four yoke of cattle and four men.
Our company numbered fourteen men and boys. We traveled
eight miles and came to a creek about ten feet wide (*Spanish Fork), which is a good camp ground, with wood in plenty.
We came nine miles and camped at a small spring branch
(*near Salem), where the feed was good and plenty of willows
for fuel.

Tuesday, 20th.—This morning we had a severe storm of
rain and sleet, which made the roads very bad. This afternoon
the road is much better. We passed several good camp
grounds. No. 6 (*Payson) is a beautiful stream, there being
two branches with wood in plenty. All the streams and

springs up to No. 10 were good camps. We came twenty-three miles and camped on No. 10, where there are plenty of willows. There is a branch of this creek a quarter of a mile ahead.

Wednesday, 21st.—This morning Brother Badger and Brother Burnett came to our camp with a letter from Salt Lake. We traveled twelve miles over a bad road and came to No. 11, a spring at the right of the road, which is a good camp ground, with plenty of grass and sagebrush and plenty of wood one mile away. We came five miles to No. 12, a spring branch, and camped. The feed was good and wood in plenty. This is the last camp in the Utah Valley.

Thursday, 22nd.—Last night it commenced snowing and continued until this morning. Today we crossed the dividing ridge between the Utah and the Sevier Valleys. We traveled twelve miles and camped at the Sevier River, No. 13. The river is about four rods wide and three and one-half feet deep, with the south bank steep. The feed was good, and plenty of wood and willows for camp use.

Friday, 23rd.—The morning was pleasant and we traveled twelve miles over a beautiful road to camp 14, where feed and water was plenty. In the dry season you will have to go two miles east, where there is a good spring. We traveled fourteen miles and camped at No. 15, a spring, with feed good and plenty of cedar. The road is good between the Sevier and this camp, with the exception of about four miles.

Saturday, 24th.—The morning was pleasant, and we traveled three miles and came to No. 16, a good camp, with plenty of willows. We went on two miles further and came to No. 17, a creek, with plenty of wood. We traveled ten miles and came to No. 18, a spring, and good camp, with plenty of willows. We then came six miles and camped at No. 19, a brackish spring and poor camp ground, with no wood and less sage, and feed very short.

Sunday, 25th.—This day's travel has been over a crooked, rough and stony road. We traveled two miles and camped at No. 20, a spring branch, with wood and feed in plenty.

Monday, 26th.—The weather was very cold. We traveled six miles and came to No. 21, a small creek, a good camp ground, plenty of wood and feed. We traveled fourteen miles and camped at No. 22; plenty of wood and feed short. We are now traveling in company, with six horse teams and twenty-eight men.

Tuesday, 27th.—We traveled five miles and came to a small creek, No. 23, a good camp ground, plenty of feed and willows. We came a quarter mile and crossed No. 24, a good camp ground; a half mile further we came to Beaver Creek, No. 25. It commenced snowing and we camped. This stream is about one rod wide; wood and feed plenty, a beautiful camping place. Our company is now organized. H. Egan is captain, and Brother Orlando Hovey has joined our company. Brothers Granger and Egan take his provisions.

Wednesday, 28th.—Last night we had a severe snowstorm. We traveled about seven miles down the Beaver and found the road was not passable. We then traveled seven miles east, close to the foot of the mountain, where we struck a road that bore south through the mountains. We traveled about four miles and found good feed and plenty of wood, no water. We traveled eighteen miles, but were only eight miles from where we camped last night.

Thursday, 29th.—The morning was pleasant, and we traveled about thirteen miles and camped at a spring, the feed being good and plenty of sage. Ten miles of the road today was through a rough mountain country and very rocky. Brother John Hills broke his wagon tire in two places. Spring No. 26, where we are camped, is about one mile from the road and about three miles from where you first enter the Little Salt Lake Valley.

Friday, 30th.—We traveled ten miles and came to No. 27, a creek with plenty of willows and feed. It is a good camp ground. We came six miles and camped at No. 28, a creek about one rod wide, with plenty of wood and feed. The road has been very good today. We are in sight of the Little Salt Lake. The weather is warm and pleasant.

DECEMBER, 1849.

Saturday, 1st.—We traveled six and a quarter miles and came to creek No. 29. It is a good camp ground, with plenty of wood and feed. We caught up with Mr. ———'s company at this creek. He laid up to do some blacksmithing, and kindly offered to have our wagon tire welded, and any other work we wanted.

Sunday, 2nd.—We traveled four miles and came to No. 30, a spring and good camp ground. Then we came seven miles to Muddy creek No. 31, a bad creek to cross; wood plenty, feed short. We traveled six miles and came to a spring branch, feed and wood plenty. We met four men belonging to Captain Smith's company, who had lost their road and had been living on mule flesh for sixteen days.

Monday, 3rd.—We traveled sixteen miles and camped at No. 33, a spring branch; wood plenty and feed short.

Tuesday, 4th.—Last night it commenced snowing, and the morning was cold and stormy. We traveled thirteen miles and came to No. 34, a spring branch, with feed and willows plenty. We traveled nine miles and camped at No. 35, a spring branch; feed and wood plenty.

Wednesday, 5th.—This morning was cold and stormy. We came eleven miles to No. 36, a spring branch. The feed was short, but wood plenty. We came about three miles and camped in a valley. The feed and wood was plenty, but no water. The storm was very severe, and the last end of the road very bad.

Thursday, 6th.—Last night we experienced the hardest storm we have had since we started. We traveled about eight miles over rough roads to Santa Clara. We came about two miles further and camped near the Santa Clara, where feed was poor, but wood was plenty. It has stormed all day.

Friday, 7th.—The morning was very cold. We traveled three miles down the Santa Clara, where one of my wagon tires broke. Brother Granger unloaded his wagon and went back with me to Mr. ———'s camp, about thirty miles. We were gone three days, the weather being very cold.

Saturday, 8th.—The weather was extremely cold, being 12 degrees below zero.

Sunday, 9th.—This morning we arrived at our camp. The wagons had gone ahead. The weather was still cold and feed very poor.

Monday, 10th.—We traveled ten miles down the Santa Clara, the road being very hard. We came a mile and a half and camped at a spring, plenty of wood but feed very poor.

Tuesday, 11th.—The morning was cold, but we traveled about fifteen miles over a very rough road, snow being about one foot deep. We stopped two hours and fed. The feed is very good up to the right of the road in a ravine from where we stopped. We traveled fifteen miles further and camped on the Rio Virgin, plenty of wood, but feed very poor. There is some little bunch grass one mile up the hill.

Wednesday, 12th.—We traveled down the Virgin over a heavy sandy road through the most barren, desolate country I have ever seen. We came about eight miles and camped. Plenty of willows and some salt grass. The Virgin is about two rods wide here.

Thursday, 13th.—The weather was warm and pleasant. We traveled about eighteen miles down the Virgin. The road was sandy and we crossed the river ten times. The fords were good and there was plenty of willows and some little feed, the first we have seen since we started this morning.

Friday, 14th.—The morning was cloudy with some rain. We traveled about twelve miles down the Virgin River. The road was sandy and we crossed the river four or five times, then turned short to the right and went over a very heavy sandy, crooked road. We came about six miles and found some feed to the left of the road on the side of the mountain.

Saturday, 15th.—It was pleasant weather. Brother J. Bill's team gave out and he left his wagon and put his load in different wagons. We traveled a half mile and camped at the foot of a very steep mountain that we had to cross. We took out part of the loads and doubled teams, and with a rope 250 feet long to the top of the mountain and twenty men to assist the teams we got up. We came five miles and bated, and then came to the Muddy. The feed was good, but wood scarce. Part of the road was very sandy.

Sunday, 16th.—The weather was pleasant, and we remained in camp. We saw a number of Indians in the evening.

Monday, 17th.—About noon today we moved camp up the creek about three miles and came to a river. It is called fifty-five miles to the next water after we leave here. The weather is rainy and the roads are bad.

Tuesday, 18th.—It has rained all night without any ceasing, which makes the roads very bad. We remained in camp today, and it has continued raining nearly all day. Last night the guards fired at what we supposed to be an Indian on the opposite side of the creek. It is with difficulty that we can get our animals to feed, it is so rainy.

Wednesday, 19th.—It was clear, pleasant weather, and we traveled ten miles, finding some feed, we bated. For half this morning we had to help the teams with ropes made fast to the wagons. The road then was gravel and sandy. We came about eight miles, the road being very bad. The animals sank to their knees every step. We found some water in holes and some bunch grass.

Thursday, 20th.—We traveled ten miles and found some feed on the sand bluffs. The road was much better, and we came twenty-five miles. The last three or four miles of the road was very bad. We arrived at the springs at 2 in the morning. Loot and Parks left their wagons, and Brother Granger left his and took Foot's wagon, it being lighter. The feed is scarce, it being buried over with sand. The wood also is scarce and the water is milk warm. There has been five animals and three wagons left since we started.

Friday, 21st.—This day we remained in camp. Mr. Noyle left his wagon and packed. We left our wagons and took his, it being lighter. The weather is warm and pleasant.

Saturday, 22nd.—Today we moved camp up the branch about three miles, the road being very bad and steep. There is plenty of feed.

Sunday, 23rd.—We traveled about eighteen miles, part of the road being rough and stony, and camped near a beautiful spring branch. There was plenty of bunch grass on the mountain and plenty of wood. Two of our company were run by some Indians, who were behind.

Monday, 24th.—About 2 o'clock this morning our animals were fired at by a party of Indians, which caused them to scatter. They ran off, but two of our men pursued them so close they got all but three belonging to Mr. Carr, which the Indians killed and quartered. One of the three was shot four times. Here I left the wagons and took Mr. Carr's. We traveled four miles and came to a spring branch, a poor camp, but we went on eight miles to a spring, where there was plenty of feed. We then came about twenty-five miles over a rough road and camped at a spring, the water being bad and a poor camp ground.

Tuesday, 25th.—We started at daylight this morning with the intention of stopping at a spring five miles ahead. After traveling about eight miles we stopped at last and found that the road ran about five miles east of the spring. Some of the company had started without eating their breakfast or taking in water. We came about twenty-five miles and camped at a spring, where the feed was nearly eat off, but the water was good and plenty of wood. We arrived here about half past 4 o'clock in the evening.

Wednesday, 26th.—We remained in camp today. Mr. Carr's horse that was shot by the Indians was left at this place, he being unable to travel.

Thursday, 27th.—The weather was pleasant. We found a man here with an arrow stuck in his side, and saw fresh Indian tracks. One of the guard saw an Indian in the brush just before daylight and fired at him. We started at 3 o'clock this afternoon and came ten miles, part of the road being sandy, and part of it run over a low, wet bottom. We crossed a small stream several times, but the water was not good. At 7.30 we camped at a spring, where the feed and water was good and wood plentiful.

Friday, 28th.—We started at 3 o'clock and came thirteen miles over a bad road and camped at spring No. 48, at the left of the road, where the water was brackish, poor feed and brush for fire. We arrived in camp about 9 o'clock. It rained about three hours this evening.

Saturday, 29th.—We started at 8 o'clock, and came twelve miles over a sandy road. We stopped to rest, but there was no feed. We came twelve miles more and stopped and got supper. We came twenty-five miles and camped at spring No. 49. There was no feed and the water was brackish, the latter part of the road being good. We arrived here at 4 o'clock in the morning, but some of the company did not arrive until after daylight. We passed a number of cattle today and some wagons that were left.

Sunday, 30th.—We remained in camp today. There was a little coarse bunch grass one-half mile west near the road. We found three wagons with nearly all their loading in, left by some of the company ahead.

Monday, 31st.—We started this afternoon at 4 o'clock, came ten miles and stopped to rest, the road being sandy and uphill. We traveled all night and arrived at the Mohave at 8 o'clock in the morning. We had come forty miles.

TUESDAY, JANUARY 1, 1850.

Tuesday, 1st.—We arrived in camp today, part of the company coming up about noon. There is some pretty good feed about a mile across the river. There is good water and plenty of wood. We have seen several wagons that were left and a number of dead cattle. One of the company found a mule here in pretty good order. Most of our company are short of provisions. We divided with them all we had to spare.

Wednesday, 2nd.—We started at 10 o'clock and came about fourteen miles, crossed the river and came three miles and camped. The first ten or twelve miles the road was sandy and ran a half to a mile from the river. The feed is good and plenty of wood. There was a company camped here last night. Their fires were burning when we arrived. Some of our packers remained in camp, among whom were Parke, Neagle ' and Fair.

Thursday, 3rd.—We started at daylight this morning and came about seven miles, where we found Captain Davis' company, as they had laid up for the day. I started for the settlement in company with Mr. Loot. We traveled about twelve miles over a sandy road and came to the river, traveled four miles further and stopped for the night. The feed was good and plenty of wood.

Friday, 4th.—We started at daylight and came about fifteen miles and stopped to feed, then we came twenty-five miles to Cahoon Pass. The latter part of the road was very rough. We camped at a spring where the feed was all eaten out, but there was plenty of wood. This afternoon it commenced raining and continued without any cessation all night.

Saturday, 5th.—We started this morning at 4 o'clock. The water was rushing through the pass about three feet deep. It was with great difficulty that we could get along. Some places the water would roll our horses over. We came fifteen miles and found a wagon and camp there. We stopped to feed, after which we came fourteen miles and stopped at a ranch. It rained nearly all day.

Sunday, 6th.—We camped at William's Ranch. Here I found Brothers Rich and Hunt and some eighteen or twenty of the brethren all well. This is a beautiful valley. The hills look as green as they would in Salt Lake Valley in May.

Monday, 7th.—The weather was pleasant and the brethren were all preparing to start.

Tuesday, 8th.—It is still pleasant weather. Brother Rich is procuring wheat and getting it ground for our company. Brother Stoddard came in the evening and reported the company ten miles from here.

Wednesday, 9th.—The weather is fair. Our company arrived about noon, all well.

Thursday, 10th.—The two ox teams belonging to Brother Rich's company started this afternoon. We spent this day in getting our grinding done. The distance to this settlement is about 769 miles from the Utah Lake.

Friday, 11th.—We commenced our journey again today, and came ten miles and camped with the two ox teams belonging to Brother Rich's company. The feed is much better here than it is at William's Ranch. It commenced raining this evening. We are camped near the stream, where there is plenty of wood.

Saturday, 12th.—We remained in camp today. Brothers Rich and Hunt came up this evening, and we organized. J. Hunt was chosen captain.

Sunday, 13th.—We came ten miles and camped near a stream, where there was feed and wood plenty. The forenoon was rainy, which made the roads bad, but the afternoon was fair.

Monday, 14th.—The weather was pleasant and we came about seven miles and stopped to feed at the intersection of St. Gubrith, which is a most beautiful location. We found plenty of oranges on the trees. The Mission has been partly deserted since the move. Some of the fields are fenced with prickley pears that are planted in straight rows and grow from five to twenty-five feet high. We traveled three miles and camped near a small stream, but there was no wood.

Prickley Pear or Cactus used for fencing.

Tuesday, 15th.—We came about four miles and camped near the stream about a mile and a half from the City or Pueblo de Los Angeles.

Wednesday, 16th.—We remained in camp today, and laid in our groceries. Brother Davis and some two or three others arrived from the Tormage Train, and reported them in distress, and they sent in for assistance.

Thursday, 17th.—We came twelve miles and camped near a small stream and a deserted ranch, where there was good feed.

Friday, 18th.—The weather was pleasant this morning, and we killed a heifer. Brothers Rich, Hunt and some others are preparing to pack and go ahead of the wagons. The brethren were called together, who were to remain with the wagons and Howard Egan was elected captain by a unanimous vote of the company. We traveled twelve miles and camped near a spring, where there was plenty of feed and wood.

Saturday, 19th.—We traveled about twelve miles today and camped near a spring, there being plenty of wood and feed. The roads today have been rough and crooked. Brothers Rich and Hunt let me have $53.00 this morning for the use of the company. The weather is beautiful for this season of the year.

Sunday, 20th.—We traveled about fourteen miles and camped near a small stream in an oak grove, where the feed was good. The pack company left us today and went ahead. We passed several small streams that would answer for camp grounds. The road was pretty good and the weather was pleasant.

Monday, 21st.—We traveled about twenty-one miles and camped under the St. Altave. There were four or five ranches in sight, but poor feed, though plenty wood. The head of the river is about one hundred yards wide. We came down one of the steepest mountains today that I ever saw a wagon run over.

Tuesday, 22nd.—Last night we had a heavy rain, but the morning was pleasant. We traveled about six miles and stopped to feed. We then came about three miles and camped. There we inspected the Mission Buenentrance, near a stream within a quarter mile of the sea shore. There was plenty of feed and wood. The road has been good today. Our camp numbered 35 men, 1 woman, 20 horses and mules, 20 head of oxen and 5 wagons.

Wednesday, 23rd.—It was pleasant weather and we traveled about sixteen miles, most of the way down the beach. The roads were rough. We camped near a small stream in a grove where the feed was good. This is a beautiful camping place. About two miles back there is a creek and a good camp ground.

Thursday, 24th.—Last night it commenced raining and continued without any cessation all day today, so we remained in camp.

Friday, 25th.—It rained all night last night, and cleared about 9 o'clock this morning. At 12 o'clock we proceeded on our journey. The roads were bad and we came about six miles and camped near a stream, where wood and feed was plenty. We passed several good camping places.

Saturday, 26th.—It was pleasant weather and we came about five miles and stopped to feed. One mile further we passed St. Abantres and traded one yoke of our cattle that were broke down, paying $10.00 to boot. We came six miles and camped in a grove near a creek, where there was first rate feed. The road has been very hard today.

Sunday, 27th.—It was fine weather and we came between nine and ten miles, the road being very bad. We crossed seven creeks, all of which are good camp grounds, there being plenty of wood and feed. Our camp ground this evening is a beautiful place on the seashore, and the best place we have had since we started, and a beautiful grove to camp in.

Monday, 28th.—It was fine weather, and we traveled about eleven miles. The road has not been so wet today, but very hilly. We camped near a spring branch, where there was plenty of feed and wood. We are within a half mile of the sea.

Tuesday, 29th.—We traveled about five miles and turned up a ravine, the road being very rough and rocky. It is about three miles to a ranch. We traveled about eight miles further and camped near a creek.

Wednesday, 30th.—Last evening we killed a beef. The fore part of the night was rainy. This morning five head of our cattle were missing. Most of our camp have been out hunting but could not find them. We got back to the camp about 10 o'clock and learned the cattle were about four miles from the mission.

FEBRUARY, 1850.

Friday, 1st.—We moved down across the River St. Yuness, which is about fifty yards wide. The mission of the same name is about half a mile from the river. The road we passed in the forenoon was very good. We crossed a very steep mountain, and from there to the ranch I rode with the company. About a mile past the ranch there is plenty of good wood and water; feed not so good. We traveled about eighteen miles today.

Saturday, 2nd.—It was pleasant weather. We traveled about sixteen miles and came to a river about six rods wide, came about two miles further and camped near a small stream, where there was plenty of feed, but wood scarce. The last two or three miles of the road was very bad.

Sunday, 3rd.—The weather was pleasant, and we came about three miles to a ranch. The road was bad in many places. We traveled twelve miles and camped in a valley near a spring branch, where there was plenty of wood and feed.

Monday, 4th.—It was a dandy morning and we traveled about one and a half miles over a very hard road and came to St. Luke ——, a mission and a store. We traveled up the stream about six and a half miles and camped. Most of the road ran through a canyon. This is a beautiful camping place. The feed is very good and plenty of wood. We have traveled about eighteen miles today. All of the company are well except Brother John Bills, who is very sick.

Tuesday, 5th.—The weather is pleasant. We went about two miles up the canyon and crossed over the mountain. The

road was pretty good and we came about four miles to the old
mission. We have had very good weather today and have
traveled about twenty miles. Two miles back we crossed the
St. Miguel River, which is about fifty rods wide. At a ranch
and store we purchased two beeves and paid $25.00 for them.

Wednesday, 6th.—Last night we camped under a white
oak tree that measured twenty-two feet in circumference and
the boughs measured 495 feet in circumference. The weather
was fine and we traveled four and a half miles and came to
the St. Miguel Mission, which is deserted. We came eight
miles further to a large river about one hundred yards wide,
which we crossed and camped, there being plenty of feed and
wood.

Thursday, 7th.—The morning was cloudy and we came
four miles to a river about fifty yards wide, traveled up the
river about eight miles and camped at a deserted ranch. We
crossed the river and traveled four miles further up the river,
seven miles to a ranch, Las Hoetis, and camped. making twenty-three miles today. The feed is very short here, but plenty
of wood. We have been traveling through a very poor country today. Two deer have been killed.

Friday, 8th.—It was fine weather and we came about
eight miles and crossed the mountain and traveled down a
beautiful valley. There was plenty of grass, but no water.
We came ten miles to a deserted ranch, one mile further we
came to the river Monterey and camped. We traveled about
nineteen miles today, and the roads were first rate, with feed
and water in plenty.

Saturday, 9th.—We came three miles to an Indian ranch,
and nine miles further to a large river; eight miles to the Mission Soladen. Six miles from there we crossed the River Monterey. By raising our wagon boxes we got over without any
difficulty. We traveled about twenty-one miles today, the
roads being good, and there was plenty of wood and feed
tonight.

Sunday, 10th.—The weather was fine, and we traveled a
half mile and came to a ranch. The road leaves the river and
runs parallel with it from three to five miles to a ranch to
the left. Saw several ducks along the river. We came about
twenty miles and camped in a grove, where there wa : plenty
of feed, but water scarce.

Monday, 11th.—We traveled three miles and came to a
ranch, then came fourteen miles over a very rough road, and
from there on to San Juan Mission. We then came one mile
further and camped.

Tuesday, 12th.—Last evening I received a letter that Brother Rich left at the mission, dated the 10th, one day ahead of us. Brothers Staden, Edward and myself started about 10 o'clock at night and found Brother Rich and company one mile from San Jose, about 8 o'clock this morning. The distance being forty-five miles. We made arrangements to get provisions.

Wednesday, 13th.—We sent Franklin Edwards back to meet the company and stop the ox teams and send the other teams up after the provisions. Brothers Rich, Pratt, Hunt and Rollane started for San Francisco.

Thursday, 14th.—About noon the horse teams arrived, loaded up and started out a mile and camped.

Friday, 15th.—It was fine weather, and we traveled seventeen miles and came to the company. The brethren killed a heifer and several deer.

Saturday, 16th.—We started back about fourteen miles on the road, where we came to Gillar's ranch. We then turned to the right and came four miles on the road to the Marapars diggins, part of the road being very wet.

Sunday, 17th.—We came six miles to Patgher's ranch. I rode ahead. We traveled ten miles up the Patgher's Pass and camped in a beautiful valley.

Monday, 18th.—The morning was cloudy, and we traveled about two miles and came to the foot of the mountain. Here we had to double teams for about two miles. We came about ten miles and camped in the Jousain Valley. The roads have been very hilly and hard to travel. There is plenty of feed and wood.

Tuesday, 19th.—Last night we had a light rain. This morning Brother John Bills was much worse. The company remained in camp and about 10 o'clock this evening Brother Bills died. We moved camp about five miles.

Wednesday, 20th.—We traveled twenty miles and came to the San Jouaquin River, took our wagons apart and crossed them in a whale boat, for which we had to pay $87.50.

Thursday, 21st.—We traveled about eighteen miles up the Mercelda River and camped in a bend of the river, where the feed was good. The roads were sandy.

Friday, 22nd.—This morning six of our company went ahead to explore. We traveled about wenty miles and crossed the Mercelda River and camped.

Saturday, 23rd.—We traveled about ten miles and stopped to feed. Then sent four of our company out to explore. We traveled about four miles and camped near a spring branch.

Here this journal or diary breaks off abruptly, except places and distances are given, which is of no interest now.

*At this point it may be well to review some of the facts
in relation to the early settlement of California wherein Mormons had some hand. The ship Brooklyn sailed from New
York with 235 Saints aboard in February, 1846. They stopped
at Honolulu on the 26th of June and arrived at Yerba Buena
(now San Francisco), California, July 29, and soon commenced
agricultural work.

The Mormon Battalion, that Father had returned from as
they left Santa Fe, reached Pueblo de los Angles March 23,
1847, where they were ordered to erect a fort on a hill nearby.
They were honorably discharged July 16. A number of them
were employed by Capt. John A. Sutter to dig a mill race
in September where gold was discovered in January, 1848,
which excited the whole country and brought thousands across
the plains.

Upper California, which included Utah, was ceded to the
United States by Mexico in February, 1848. In the middle of
June, 1849, parties from the east began to arrive in Salt Lake
on their way to California gold mines, and the people were
much enriched trading with them. Father and others returned
in the fall of 1850. Missionaries were sent there at different
times and quite a number were sent to make a settlement, which
was finally abandoned.

28.—"TECUMSEE."

I will now try to tell you how Father got the Indian,
named by him, Tecumsee. But first I will say that Father was
employed by some Salt Lake merchants to travel through the
settlements both north and south in the winter time, buying up
all the extra animals, cows and steers, that the people would
sell. They were to keep these animals till spring brought the
grass up, so he could collect them as he came along on his
start for California.

He had been very successful in buying, and when he had
gone as far north as Malad river, where he camped for a few
days, he had a bunch of about fifteen hundred head and a train
of fifteen wagons, a hundred horses and mules, and thirty-five
men, all to be looked after and taken care of till they arrived
in California.

It used to be Father's plan, after he had got the camp
under way in the morning, and when the stock were well strung
out, he would select a good position and count the whole bunch,
and if there were any missing he would send men out to hunt
them up and bring them in, and sometimes they were not successful in finding them. If the lost animals were very few, it

would not pay to lay over to hunt them, but if there was a bunch lost, the train would camp at the first water until the stock was found or accounted for.

They had traveled past Promontory Point and camped near Sage, or Indian creek, about sundown. There is a narrow, sharp, rocky ridge makes down from the mountains on the north of the road, and the camp was made just after rounding this rocky point. Father had been, with some others, back to look for missing animals, and as they were nearing the camp he gave his horse to one of the men to lead to camp and take care of, as he wished to take a little foot exercise.

He climbed the steep ridge a few hundred yards from the point near the road, and he knew that the camp was close to the opposite side of where he was climbing up, and when he reached the top would have a fine view of the surrounding country. When he reached the top he saw the camp as he expected and the stock spreading out to feed.

On looking down the ridge the way he expected to go to camp, he saw what he first thought to be the tail feathers of a bird, but in looking a little closer with his field glass he saw that there was an Indian under those feathers, who seemed to be trying to keep out of sight of anyone in the camp, and at the same time get close enough to some of the animals that were grazing near to stick an arrow in them (an Indian trick to get the carcass after the train had moved on).

Father was directly above the Indian, and the Indian between him and the camp. Father lost no time in getting within a few yards of the fellow, and just as the Indian was preparing to shoot the nearest steer, Father gave a "Hugh!" The Indian turned round and faced a sixshooter, dropped his arrows and said "Hugh! Hugh!" Father placed his sixshooter in his scabbard and motioned the Indian to pick up his arrows; then motioned him to go down to camp, where Father had him sit down by a campfire and placed a guard over him, gave him a good supper, and then blankets to sleep on; and made to understand that he must stay there till sunrise next morning or the guard would shoot him. The next morning the Indian was given all he could eat, and some flour and bacon for his squaw (if he had one) and told to go.

Just before 12 o'clock noon, as Father was counting the animals as they passed along by a certain point of the road, he chanced to look around and saw the Indian of the night before, with two others, standing near watching Father. Father went on with his count till all the cattle had passed. After summing up his count he found that there were five or six animals missing. He turned to the Indians and held up six fingers, then pointed to the cattle, then motioned his hands over the country; the Indians uttered a sigh and soon disappeared.

Father, contrary to his usual practice, did not send any men to find the lost animals. He made camp about 3 or 4 o'clock.

Washikee, Peace Chief; near relation to Tecumsee.

About sundown there could be seen a cloud of dust coming down the road. It might be a pack train, for it was coming pretty fast. It was only Father's Indians bringing in the lost animals, but instead of only five or six, they had brought in fifteen head. Some of them did not have the company brand, but were animals that had been lost by other trains or immigrants.

The three Indians did not leave again until they had passed over the line of their country, which was along the Humboldt river, and Father placed no white men to herd and guard the stock, the Indians doing this from sundown to sunrise. Father had killed three head for beef, giving one to the Indians, and there had been two or three poisoned, and two or three drowned in the spring holes in Thousand Spring Valley, and at his last count in California he had one animal more than he left Malad Valley with. (So much for being kind to Indians.)

The next year as Father was making another trip with stock for the California market, about the same place, the Indians came again and did the same as the year before, leaving as usual, except Tecumsee (as Father called him). (That was the Indian Father held up on the rocky ridge.) He did not leave when the rest did, but kept as close to Father as he could day and night.

In California he had to do a good deal of traveling, and when stopping at a hotel it was always understood that Tecumsee slept on the floor by his bedroom door. One night when they were thus fixed, Father heard a slight sound of someone walking in the room. The moon made it light enough to see farely well. He saw the Indian come to the chair on which Father had placed his clothes, and proceeded to go through his pockets. Father said nothing about it, and next morning found that the Indian had only taken a few dimes, leaving all money larger than that. After that Father would only leave a dime or two, which were sure to be gone in the morning.

As he had never seen or heard of the Indian buying anything, he wondered why he would steal money and not spend it. So one day Father went to a store with the Indian and gave him to understand that he was going to buy a hat and a shirt for him. After the things were fitted on, Father in paying for them pretended he did not have money enough. The Indian went down in his own pockets and brought out a rag in which were tied up two or three dollars in dimes. He untied the bunch and slid it along the counter to Father to take out what was needed to fill the bill.

One day, in Sacramento, Father wanted the Indian to wear shoes while in the city, so took him to a shop and got a pair fitted to him; then when they came to pay for them it took money from both of them. An hour after that they were walking down the street, the Indian trailing behind. Father chanced to look back; the Indian was there all right, hat in hand, shoes slung across his arms, eating candy and taking in all the sights that were to be seen from the sidewalk.

As a general thing he tried to imitate Father's walk and actions, which caused many a smile among spectators and many a hearty laugh from Father's acquaintances. He could not bear to wear shoes long at a time, when they were new, and off they would come, no matter where he was; the same with his hat.

Well, the old fellow was at one time the "war chief" of the "To-So-Witch Band" of the "Sho-Sho-nees Indians." He came with Father to Salt Lake and never went back to his tribe.

NOTE.—To Wm. M. Egan: Probably you know what became of him. I don't remember. He was sometimes at Mother's, and at other times I have seen him at different mail stations.—H. R. Egan.

*I remember him well. He used to sleep in our back kitchen, and do chores, and was quite an old man then, but I do not remember about his death.—W. M. Egan.

Kanosh Pavant Chief.

SEC. II.—STORIES OF TRAVEL AND HAPPENINGS.
29.—"INDIAN SNAKE EATING."

When Father was returning from one of his trips to California by the southern route, my brother Erastus was in the company, and from some of them I got this: We were in the desert and had made camp near a small spring. We had nothing to make a fire with but scrub greasewood. We had our fire made and were getting our supper about ready, when there appeared a couple of the Desert Indians, clad in their Sunday attire, which consisted of a grass string around their loins. A kind of fringe about eight or ten inches long hung from the string clear around them. This was all of their covering except a mass of coal black hair on their heads about the size of a bushel basket.

They came up close to the fire and stood like posts, but watching every move of the whites. One of them had a live rattlesnake which he held by the tail, letting the snake hang down very close to his leg, but paying no attention to the squirming reptile whatever. This put the spectators on their nerves. They said nothing, but expected to see the snake at any moment bury his fangs in the Indian's leg. After the whites had removed their cooked supper from the fire, the Indian that held the snake kicked, with his bare feet, the embers together, and then laid the snake on the coals. It crawled off. He picked it up and put it on again. This was repeated several times before the snake died; and when it was roasted enough to satisfy the Indian, he took it off the fire and pinched its head off with his fingers and threw it away; then broke off a section of the body and commenced eating it like a boy would a carrot. The two made short work of the snake and licked their fingers as if they liked it, and I suppose they did.

At another camp, while they were cooking a meal, three or four of the same kind of Indians came up and stood watching the cooking arrangements. Father told Erastus not to notice them or they might take too much liberty. When the meal was all ready and spread on the blanket, all but the frying pan of gravy, Erastus was told to get it off the fire and bring it to the table. He lifted it off the fire. The handle was hot and burned his fingers, so he laid it down to get a better hold. As he did so he looked at one of the Indians and grinned. That was enough. They all jumped at once around the pan, and bending their forefingers like a fishhook, dived into that gravy, and as hot as it was they soon cleaned it all up, and the white people had no sop that meal just on account of the grin on the boy's face.

30.—THE SLEEPING MULE (FATHER'S).

On Father's quick trip to California, straight across the great American desert, his rule was to stop but four hours out of every twenty-four, which soon made men and mules suffer for the want of sleep as well as rest.

One day, after crossing about a thirty-mile desert, they came to the bench or foothills of the next range of mountains, that appeared to be very dry. Father told his partner to ride a little ways off in that direction and he would go the opposite, and if either found any water to shoot his pistol off, that the other might come to him, and if neither of them found any water they must return and climb the mountain and search the other side.

After going as far as he thought advisable, Father took the back track, and when he got to the place where they had parted, not meeting his man, he followed his tracks as fast as he could. After going about one-half of a mile, and just over a small ridge, he saw the man and mule both standing up. The man had his hands on the horn of the saddle as if about to mount. The mule's head was down close to the bunch grass, but both man and beast were fast asleep.

The mule was the first to awake, but merely raised his head a little. The man slept till Father had dismounted and gave him a shaking up, and asked him why he had not fired the shot to let him know that he had found water. He said he was going to ride back to the top of the little ridge and do so, as the shot could be heard farther, but had lost himself just as he was about to mount. There was plenty of water there, so they rested for four full hours.

At another time on this trip they were suffering very severely for water, but fortunately came to a small stream of clear mountain water. Father's partner jumped off his mule and threw himself flat down with his lips to the water, sucking in huge mouthfuls. Father grabbed him by the legs and pushed him heels over head into the creek. Of course, when he scrambled out, he was ready to fight, but when Father said, "Now you can drink without killing yourself, and I hope you have learned a good lesson about drinking when thirsty.

Father said, at one time on his fast trip across the country, as he was traveling through a narrow, steep side canyon, it appeared to him that he was going through the street of a very large city. The buildings on each side appeared to be of many shapes, and some of many stories high, and occasionally a bridge would span the street, and so low down that he would duck his head to ride under them. Some of the houses seemed to be lighted up. He could see the lights in many windows, but there was no sound.

Then he knew that he was suffering for the want of sleep. That made the transformation. He had often when on the desert seen the mirage take the form of buildings, bridges, forests and lakes (the writer has seen the same things), but he knew this was not a mirage, but lack of sleep.

Father was of the opinion that man can go longer without sleep than the animals he rode, but he felt sure that the animals often slept while traveling slow. I don't know as to that, but I do know that I have ridden horseback for five or six miles while I was fast asleep, and only awakened by the pony changing his gait.

This was at the place where the two riders passed each other and reported that they had not met. Both had been fast asleep and the ponies had not changed their pace in passing, so the boys slept on till they did, which would be at some incline or decline, as if to receive further orders, which they generally got by a gentle touch of the spurs or a lifting of the bridle reins.

Suffering for Sleep.—When Father arrived in Sacramento, at the end of his ten-day mule trip, his first duty was to take a bath and then a good sleep, both of which he stood very much in need of. So, after engaging his room at the hotel, he turned the water on and did not wait for the tub to fill, but got in and sat down and leaned back and— Well, the first he knew the bellboy was in the room trying to wake him up, and the water still running at full force. The first thing the bellboy knew was a battery of boots directed at him, which caused his hasty retreat. But he had broken the first real comfortable sleep Father had enjoyed for over ten days. As there were only two of them on the last trip, and as they only rested four out of every twenty-four hours, and as both could not sleep at the same time, on account of the danger of being attacked by man or beast, there were only two hours out of each twenty-four for each to sleep. Too little to be much enjoyed, for the awakening was the hardest part of the job, for sleep came quickly but awakening came with a grudge and a surprise at the shortness of the length of two hours.

31.—A FEARFUL FALL.

In early days, when Father was at home for a brief time, they used to have a sociable evening at home with friends, at one home or another. As Father put in most all his time in going or coming, or in California, the good folks, especially the women folks, were always urging him to tell them some of his thrilling experiences, as they knew he must have had many of them. So, on one evening after much persuasion, he told this to the very attentive listeners:

"I was selling beef to the placer miners and had to do a great deal of horseback riding to visit the different camps to get their orders for beef. On going to one camp I found the trail so steep that I thought I would walk the balance of the way, about one-fourth of a mile. So I tied my horse close to the trail and footed it on up to the camp. On the way up I noticed a good many prospect holes that had been abandoned. Some of them with large dumps and some with their windlasses still over them. I remember of thinking how dangerous it was to leave such places uncovered, as men or animals that might fall in one of them, if not killed, could not be heard by anyone, and so die of starvation or thirst.

But to go on, I arrived in the camp early in the afternoon and was much pleased, as I had made contracts for a good amount of beef for each week for a couple of months, which meant ten or twelve head of beef sold. Well, they were a jolly crew of miners, and more so on account of their success. All of which meant money for me.

By the time I had made the round of the camp and finished up my business it was dark. Some of the miners wanted me to stay with them all night, but I would not, for I had left my horse tied so he could not feed, and I also thought I could find my way back down the gulch, although it had grown extremely dark.

"I followed a well-beaten trail and was making very good time, when all at once I felt that I was falling. Throwing out my hands I struck what I supposed was a windlass frame, and clung to it for dear life. But the thing was so rotten that it broke almost in two, and the least move I made it would crack, and was already pinching my hands. Now, if you can just imagine the horrible thoughts that ran riot through my head. How I should lie mangled at the bottom, or if dead, how long before I would be found. What would my wife and friends say as to the cause of my disappearance. Great beads of sweat came out all over me. All my life's doing, good, bad and indifferent, rushed through my mind at lightning speed, and the terror and agony of it all! My strength was going away, and I knew that the last moment had come, so commended my soul to the powers above, I closed my eyes and let go my hold and dropped (Oh, my! Dreadful! Horrible! And so on, from the ladies) **about six inches.** Needless to say, after resting a few moments I soon found my horse and rode home.''

DIARY.

*To show some of Father's activities selling beef in California we here insert some of his Diary of 1855, as follows: January 1—At the ranch on the San Joaquin; cloudy. 12th— Left the ranch with O. R. Stibbins and the Indian. 13th—At Stockton; stopped at the Slough House. 14th—Stopped at Sacramento. 15th—Stopped at Putah. 16th—Started with forty-four head of cattle. 17th—Stopped at the Slough House; commenced boarding at $9 per week. 20th—Found an ox on the east side of Cosmines river branded L K. 21st—Mexican Joseph came from San Joaquin. 25th—Sold ten head of cattle. 26th—Went to Sacramento and returned. 28th—J. H. Kinkead arrived this evening. 29th—Mr. Kinkead left this morning. February 2—Sold five head of cattle to Mr. Tudsbury. 4th—

First Salt Lake City Store, Livingston & Kinkead;
after Livingston Bell & Co.

Mr. Livingston paid us a visit. 7th—Sold fifteen head of cattle to Bill Williams of Diamond Springs. 11th—Received letter from home. 12th—C. Stibbins started north. 14th—Sold seven head of cattle to Mr. Spensir. Received a package of letters from Captain Hunt. (*This was another message from the Mormon Battalion.) 22nd—Sold twelve head of cattle. Started for Sacramento. 23rd—At Sacramento. 24th—Went out to Putah and got fifty-one head of cattle. 25th—Arrived at the Cosmines. March 1—Sold ten head of cattle to Mr. Crocker. 6th—Started to Sacramento. 8th—Went to Putah after cattle. Got fifty-one head. 9th—Arrived at the Slough House. 14th—Sold twelve head of cattle. 15th—Subscribed $5 for the Mormon Herald to P. P. Pratt. 19th—Sold fifteen head of cattle to Windall. 20th—Mr. Charles Warner got killed. 21st—Went to Sacramento; sent $2000 to Livingston & Kinkead. 22nd—Returned to the Slough House. 29th—Sold three head of cattle. April 1—Sold twenty-five head of cattle to Mr. Tudsbury. 2nd—At Sacramento: went to Five Mile house with a friend. 3rd—Went to Putah and got fifty-two head of cattle and stopped at Washington. 4th—Crossed the cattle and arrived at the Slough House. 6th—Started to Sacramento. 9th—E. C. Blodgett brought fifty cows from the San Joaquin. 10th—Sold a cow. 20th—Sold seven steers to Zimmerman. 22nd—Sold four steers and one cow to Donnely & Moffett. 26th—Sold four cows and four steers to Oliver Joyet. May 2—Went to Sacramento and sold thirty-eight head of cattle to Frank Tudsbury. 4th—Went to Putah and got fifty head of cattle. 8th—A man by the name of Bohler was murdered one mile from Dayton's ranch. Sold two cows to B. Hamenell. 14th—A man was executed at Dayton's ranch. (*Perhaps the murderer lynched.) 19th—Sold twenty-five head of cattle to Mines & Co. 21st—Sold twenty-five steers and seven cows. 27th—Sold fifty-seven head of cows and steers to Soseen. 28th—Started to Auburn and crossed the American river. Lost a cow and calf. 30th—Took stage for Sacramento. 31st—Went to Putah creek and drove thirty-one head of cows and steers to Sacramento. June 5th—Started W. Nash with fourteen head of cattle to Auburn. 6th—Sold nineteen head of cattle to King & Co. of Grass Valley. 11th—Started for Georgetown. Sold Frank Hereford fifteen cows. 18th—Stopper five miles from Rough and Ready. 20th—At Jordan Spring House. Sold to Mr. Morgan fifty-four head of steers. 28th—Received of H. Mudy & Warner $2500 for Mr. Brown. 30th—E. C. Blodgett arrived with the mules. July 1—Started the boys for Salt Lake.

¶ For certification of Diary see page 196, which was so placed to show search of Mail Line.

SEC. II.—THE CENTRAL ROUTE TO CALIFORNIA.

32.—A TEN DAYS' TRIP TO CALIFORNIA MADE BY HOWARD EGAN IN 1855.

From Salt Lake City, Utah, to Sacramento, Cal., in Ten Days on Mule Back, Through a Trackless and Desert Country. A Time Never Equaled Before or Since by Such a Mode of Traveling.

Wednesday, September 19, 1855.—We started from Salt Lake City to go to Sacramento, Cal., early this morning, and stopped at Tooele to breakfast. Then went on and stopped in Lone Rock Valley about 1 o'clock p. m. We started on again at 3 o'clock and stopped at a brackish spring to get supper, about two hours, and then went on again.

Thursday, 20th.—We stopped at the eastern edge of the desert about 2 o'clock in the morning and started at 5 o'clock, stopping to breakfast at the Granite mountain, where there are fine springs and good feed for a small company. We started from there at 11 a. m. and crossed the desert, stopping on the west side of the desert at Willow Springs at 7 p. m. We started again and at 9 o'clock the same evening we passed Peter Haws and company, who were camped about ten miles from the spring.

Friday, 21st.—We camped about 4 a. m. and started on at 5 o'clock, stopping to breakfast at 9 o'clock. We started again at 10 a. m. and stopped to bate about 3 p. m. for an hour, and started on again at 5 o'clock. Mr. J. Redding, who accompanied us as far as Redding's Springs, returned home.

Saturday, 22nd.—We stopped at 3 o'clock in the morning for two hours, and started on again at 5 o'clock, traveled two miles and stopped for breakfast. The morning was cold and cloudy. We started at 8 a. m. and stopped to feed at 2 p. m., starting on at 3 o'clock. We saw a large Indian camp in the valley. It commenced raining about dark. We went up a canyon and camped for the night.

Sunday, 23rd.—We started at 6 o'clock in the morning and met the Indians coming up the canyon on our trail. We stopped in the Humboldt valley at 2 p. m. to feed for an hour, and then started at 3 o'clock and traveled until 4 o'clock the next morning without water.

Monday, 24th.—We started at 6 a. m. and found a spring of water about 10 o'clock on the top of a mountain, and stopped to feed. We started again at 12 o'clock and stopped at 1 p. m. for an hour and left at 2 p. m., traveling all the evening.

Tuesday, 25th.—We stopped about 1 hour and 30 minutes to feed, and started at 3:30 p. m.

Wednesday, 26th.—We camped at 2 o'clock this morning and started at 6:30 a. m. and arrived at the Humboldt river, ninety miles from the sink.

Thursday, 27th.—We arrived at the Trading Post, at the Sink, about 11 p. m., and started at 2 o'clock to cross the Big Desert, arriving at Rag Town at 11:30 p. m.

Friday, 28th.—We started at 2:30 a. m. from Rag Town and stopped at Gold Canyon at 11:30 a. m. We started from there at 2 p. m. and arrived at Jack Valley at 7 o'clock; changed mules and started at 9 o'clock and went on.

Saturday, 29th.—We traveled all night and stopped at Slippery Ford to breakfast. We changed mules at Silver Creek and traveled all night, arriving at Placerville at 5 o'clock in the morning and at Sacramento at 6 p. m., making the trip in ten days.

33.—*FINDING THE EGAN TRAIL.

OVERLAND MAIL LINE. NOW LINCOLN HIGHWAY.

Original Trails.—Many original trails were blazed through the western country by early travelers. The trappers, as early as 1810, one year after the birth of America's immortal Lincoln, in whose memory this and subsequent trails were forged into this ocean-to-ocean highway, and if we include the present California—(it was all California at that time, as far north as the north line of that state now and east to the Rocky mountains)—much earlier than that. Peter Skeene was on the Weber river, near Great Salt Lake, in 1825, and W. M. Ashley on the shores of Utah Lake in 1826. In 1842 General John C. Fremont visited Great Salt Lake, and the trail to Oregon through the South Pass and down the Columbia river began to be traveled yearly. Mr. Sutter went down the coast, located in California, and then some travelers went by way of Fort Hall, Idaho, and up the Humboldt, through what is now Truckee pass, through the Sierra Nevada mountains.

In 1844 Hastings followed the Indian trail through the Rocky mountains and blazed a cutoff trail south of Great Salt Lake, which is the present link of the Lincoln Highway which during the last year has caused the most apprehension of any point on the route between New York and the Pacific coast, intersecting the north trail on the Humboldt. Walker, with ten men, followed this trail into Salt Lake Valley, and the Donner party in 1846 followed the Hastings cutoff, most of the company perishing in the Sierra Nevada mountains from cold and hunger on account of the impassable snow. In 1847 the ''Mormon'' pioneers followed this same trail to the Great Salt Lake Valley and began to make their home there. This trail and the Oregon trail they followed to South Pass, in Wyoming is part of the Lincoln Highway. There still were many trails to be blazed throughout the intermountain country.

Egan Trail.—Quoting from Bancroft's History of Utah, pages 751-2: ''Between Utah and California there were three principal lines of travel—the northern, the central and southern. The first skirted the northern edge of Great Salt Lake and thence after crossing an intervening stretch of desert, followed the valley of the Humboldt and Carson rivers, being, in fact, almost identical with Fremont's route of 1845. Notwithstanding its length, it was still preferred by travelers, as grass and water were fairly plentiful, with only two small tracts of desert land to contend with. (The southern route has been fully given in Father's Diary of 1849-50, in preceding article No. 27.)

''The central route, better known to the settlers of Utah by the name of Egan's Trail, and to California-bound emigrants as the Simpson route, though the two were by no means coincident, varied but a few miles from 40 degrees north latitude, until reaching Hastings pass in the Humboldt mountains where it branched off in a southwesterly direction toward Carson lake and river, and from Carson City south to Genoa. The South route was by way of the Sevier, Santa Clara, Virgin, Las Vegas, Indian rivers to San Bernardino.

''In 1859 J. H. Simpson, of the topographical engineers, received instructions from Gen. Johnson to explore the great basin, with a view to find a desert route from Camp Floyd to Genoa, in Carson valley. An account of the expedition will be found in his 'Exploring Great Basin.' For about 300 miles his route was identical with Egan's, except for a few unimportant deviations, but soon after reaching Ruby Valley it tended more toward the south. Egan's line was preferred, however, as on the one taken by Simpson grass and water were scarce.''

''**Howard Egan**, a Major in the Nauvoo Legion and a well-known guide and mountaineer, was for some years engaged in driving stock to California in the service of Livingston & Kinkead and afterward became a mail agent.''—Burton's City of the Saints, page 550.

In 1855 he was engaged in this business and in his diary, which I now have in my possession, he writes the following about his searching out the Egan Trail:

''July 4th— Started in the stage to Placerville on the way to Salt Lake; stopped at South Fork of American river. July 5th, stopped at Lake Valley, ate supper at Gold Canyon, traveled all night and stopped at Savin's to breakfast. July 6, crossed the twenty-six-mile desert, stopped near Rag Town and started over the forty-mile desert at 7:30. July 7th, traveled over the desert. July 8th, arrived at the sink of the Humboldt. Started at 11 a. m. and came thirty-five miles and stopped for supper. Started at 10 p. m. and traveled all night. July 9th, about 4 a. m., stopped to feed. Started at 8 a. m. and arrived at the trading post about 11 a. m. Left the Indian Tecumsee at this point. Camped at 9 p. m. July 10th, started about 4 a. m. and spent the day in hunting the Beckwith trail. This evening three of the mules ran off. Spent the night hunting them. July 11th—This morning I found the mules and started at 7:30 a. m., stopped to bait at 4:30 p. m. Started about 8 p. m. and camped about 12:30 a. m. and started at 3 a. m. July 12th, stopped to bait about 7 a. m. and started about 9:30 a. m. We had the pleasure of having some Indians to breakfast with us. Stopped about 5 p. m. July 13th, started at 3 this morning. Stopped to breakfast at 5:30 a. m. and camped at 4 p. m. Started to hunt a pass through the Humboldt range and got lost. Got to camp next morning, July 14th. Spent this day by all to find a pass through the mountains. July 15th, started at 5 a. m. and stopped at Peter Haw's and took dinner. Started at 2:30 p. m. and camped at 8 p. m. July 16th, started at 3 a. m., came fifteen miles and stopped at C. Munvey's to bait. Started a south course through a pass in the Humboldt mountains, traveled through a beautiful valley and stopped at 3 p. m. Traveled ten miles and camped. July 17th, started at 4 this morning and, traveling a south course, about 7 a. m. intersected Hastings trail, bearing east. Stopped to feed at 11 a. m. at Sulphur Springs. John R. Addams, traveling in company with horses, camped about 8 p. m.; no water. July 18th, started at 3:30 a. m., bearing north. Traveled about five miles and came to a large slough and stopped to feed. Started at 8 o'clock and stopped about 4 p. m., where there is a host of springs (no doubt Thousand Spring valley); feed good. Started at 7 p. m. and stopped on the desert about 12:30 a. m.; no grass nor water. July 19th, started at 3 o'clock this morning, traveled over a rough, barren country and stopped at a spring on the right of the road about 3 p. m. Started at 6 o'clock and stopped at 11:30 p. m. July 20th, started this morning about 4 o'clock and stopped to feed about 11 o'clock.''

From this on his diary contains little or nothing until after he arrived in Salt Lake City and had made a wager that he could ride to Sacramento in ten days a mule-back. He then gives an account of the trip commencing September 19th, 1855, and arrived at Sacramento at 6 p. m., September 29th, making the trip in ten days, as given in Article 32.

In the back of his diary for this year (1855) he makes the following memorandum: ''Commencement of trail,'' which, he says, ''was ninety miles to the right (or south) of the sink of Humboldt. Across a valley twelve miles—little water in canyon over a mountain five miles; little water to the right in the creek across a valley one mile from the road at foot of mountain, good grass and water. Thirty miles to summit of mountain. Ten miles to left, one mile over small mountain creek. Fifteen miles to Ruby Valley. Twenty miles down to valley; forty miles in same valley, creek fifteen miles (perhaps Shell Creek) on the side of a small mountain is a large spring. Twenty miles over mountain five or six springs (Spring Valley). Twelve miles to summit of a little mountain; twenty-five miles to Deep Creek; thirty miles to desert; twenty miles over summit of mountain; forty-five miles to Salt Spring. To creek sixteen miles.''

These were his notes in laying out the trail, and he also had a map, but as it is only a rude drawing, with no names of places, no one but him could make much out of it. He had also a list of figures, perhaps distances.

STATIONS AND DISTANCES

On the Egan Trail or Overland Mail Line as Finally Selected.

Names of Stations.	Names of Stations.
Miles	Miles
0 Salt Lake City.	12 Black Rock.
9 Traveler's Rest.	11 Fish Springs.
11 Rockwell's.	10 Boyd's.
9 Dug Out.	10 Willow Springs.
10 Fort Crittenden.	15 Canyon Station.
10 Pass.	12 Deep Creek.
10 Rush Valley.	8 Prairie Gate or Eight Mile.
11 Point Lookout.	18 Antelope Springs.
15 Simpson's Springs.	13 Spring Valley.
8 River Bed.	12 Schell Creek.
10 Dug Way.	12 Egan Canyon.

15 Butte.	15 Fair View.
11 Mountain Springs.	13 Mountain Well.
9 Ruby Valley.	15 Still Water.
12 Jacob's Wells.	14 Old River.
12 Diamond Springs.	14 Bisby's.
12 Sulphur Springs.	11 Nevada.
13 Robert's Creek.	12 Desert Wells.
13 Camp Station.	13 Dayton.
15 Dry Creek.	13 Carson.
10 Cape Horn.	14 Genoa.
11 Simpson's Park.	11 Friday's.
15 Reese River.	10 Yonk's.
12 Mount Airey.	12 Strawberry.
14 Castle Rock.	12 Webster's.
12 Edward's Creek.	12 Moss.
11 Cold Spring.	12 Sportsman's Hall.
10 Middle Gate.	12 Placerville.

Total 658 miles.

Overland Mail Line.—No doubt he was hunting this line out with the object of a mail line, for soon after he was in partnership, or more or less associated with W. G. Chorpening in carrying the mail. In "The Overland Stage to California," we read that W. G. Chorpening, in the 50's was proprietor of the mail line from Sacramento east to the Utah capital, there connecting with the route from St. Joseph, Mo. In the spring of 1858 Chorpening purchased ten stage coaches, with all the necessary supplies for the route, and the vehicles were received at Atchison, Kansas, in August, 1858, shipped by Missouri river steamboat."—Page 40.

· This was not a daily mail service, but was made daily in July, 1861, and was succeeded by Holladay Overland Mail and Express Co., and later Wells Fargo and Co.

34—*PONY EXPRESS.

The first "Pony Express" from the west arrived at Salt Lake City, April 7th, 1860, having left Sacramento, California, on the evening of April 3rd, 1860, and on the 9th it arrived from the east, having left St. Joseph, Mo., on the same evening April 3rd, 1860." Brother Howard writes:

"**Father's First Express Ride.**—When all was supposed to be ready and the time figured out when the first Express should arrive in Salt Lake City from the east, they thought that, on account of the level country to run over, that they would be able to make better time on the eastern division than on the western from Salt Lake to California. Therefore, the two riders that were to run between Salt Lake and Rush Valley were kept at the city.

Father alone of all the officers of the line thought his boys would make as good a record as the best and, if they did,

Pony Express; Indians after rider.
Pioneer of the telegraph line in the west.

there would be no rider at Rush Valley to carry the Express on to the city. So to be on the safe side Father went himself to Rush Valley. And sure enough his boys delivered the goods as he expected, and he started on his first ride. It was a stormy afternoon, but all went well with him till on the "home stretch."

The pony on this run was a very swift, fiery and fractious animal. The night was so dark that it was impossible to see the road, and there was a strong wind blowing from the north, carrying a sleet that cut the face while trying to look ahead. But as long as he could hear the pony's feet pounding the road, he sent him ahead at full speed.

All went well, but when he got to Mill Creek, that was

covered by a plank bridge, he heard the pony's feet strike the bridge and the next instant pony and rider landed in the creek, which wet Father above the knees, but the next instant, with one spring, the little brute was out and pounding the road again and very soon put the surprise on the knowing ones. And here let me say, it was a very long time before the regular riders came up to the time made on this first trip, if they ever did.''

This Pony Express continued in operation until the Overland Telegraph line was completed, October 18, 1861, from the east to Salt Lake, and October 24th from the west. All the fast messages, of course, went by telegraph, and there was no more need for the Pony Express, as there was at that time a daily mail coach, the Overland Mail, running regularly and continued for many years.

*Indian Raids.—The Indians attacked the mail station at Deep Creek, stole a band of horses, and shot a man May 28, 1860. They made a raid on Egan Canyon station August 12th, and the following day on Schell Creek. A company of soldiers came to the rescue and killed seventeen Indians.

The Overland Mail coach, with four passengers, was attacked by Indians at Eight Mile Station, near Deep Creek. The station men were killed, also Henry Harper, the driver, and one passenger wounded. Judge Mott, delegate to Congress from Nevada, climbed out of the stage, got the lines and made their escape to Deep Creek. (See details of this in later article, Indian Outbreak.) This was on March 22nd, 1863. Near Canyon Station, May 19th, the driver, W. R. Simson was shot while Father was riding by his side, who pulled him into the boot, got the reins, stopped the coach and ordered out the soldiers to return the fire, one of whom was shot between the toes. On the 8th of July, 1863, the Indians attacked Canyon Station near Deep Creek, killing four soldiers and Bill Riley, the water wagon driver, the latter of whom was thrown on the wood pile by the Indians and burned. One of the soldiers, being bald and having a heavy beard, the beard was cut off by the Indians instead of the scalp. This happened the day after we arrived at Deep Creek with our freight train, at the station we had passed, and I saw the dead soldiers who were brought down there for burial, and noted the bald soldier with his chin whiskers cut off.

The writer was then a boy of twelve and was traveling with Brother Erastus, who had charge of three six-mule teams. I and another boy were night herders and we were on our way with grain, freighting from Salt Lake for the mail stations and continued on to Carson, where we bought goods to stock Father's stores at Ruby Valley and Deep Creek. At this same time my brother Howard had charge of about ten big government wagons with four yoke of oxen to each wagon with freight for the stations, and he went as far as Dimond Springs with it. The mule and ox trains were owned by Father. Before we left Deep Creek with these trains, Eight Mile Station, next one west, was burned by Indians.

*35—DEEP CREEK.

Before the Deep Creek ranch was purchased by Father the old trail ran south from Willow Springs around Deep Creek (now called by its Indian name of I-ba-pah), but after that ranch was bought, it was made a station on the Overland Mail

eep Creek ranch and mail station. Left to right, H. R. Egan's residence, driver's sleeping rooms, the station with rest rooms and eating rooms,

Line and our principal home. Deep Creek was headquarters for many years, where Father and his sons were quite successful in raising hay and grain for the mail stations and in ranching. The home station eating house was also kept and the stations along the road supplied with beef and mutton. About twenty cows were kept for milking, which chore fell to the lot of the writer and brother Hyrum, as well as the cowboy job of riding the range for beef cattle, hunting horses and herding sheep, as well as helping on the farm, plowing, planting and irrigating, hauling hay, etc.

Father was superintendent on the Overland Mail Line and all these activities were carried on successfully until May 10th, 1869, when the railroad was completed on the northern route, north of Salt Lake, leaving Deep Creek almost entirely out of the general line of traffic, until of recent years the Lincoln Highway has been established and this old route now again becomes re-established, especially for auto travel, it being well selected for this purpose as it is the shortest and best route to the Pacific coast. We are proud to say that Father spent many a hard day and many a hard trip in searching it out

SEC. III.—STORIES OF WESTERN ROUTE, ETC.

36—GETTING RID OF AN INDIAN.

The articles and stories of thrilling experiences, to the end of the book, were written by Brother H. R. Egan and speak for themselves.

When Father was very busy trying to get things in shape to put a line of mail coaches on the Western Route across the desert to California, on one occasion I was his driver of a little spring wagon or ambulance. The pack trail at that time ran through Pleasant Valley, which is about thirty miles south of Deep Creek the present through route.

We were going west from the Pleasant Valley camp and had made about ten miles when we saw an Indian trotting along back of the wagon. When he noticed that we had seen him he ran alongside of the front wheel. Father stood this as long as his nerves could stand it, for he expected to see the man get tangled in the wheel at any moment, for he had to keep dodging around the sage brush and was doing this on the run, all the time looking at Father. So to get rid of him, Father asked me if I had any loose powder with me, a flask of which I always carried for pistol loading.

He held out his hand and I gave him a few loads; the Indian saw this and was all grinning with pleasure. The team at this time was trotting on a down grade, and in handing the powder out to the Buck's outstretched hand Father pretended to be jolted so, by the swaying of the wagon, that he missed the Indian's hand, and the powder fell to the ground in a scattered condition in dust and sage leaves. The Indian dropped like he had been shot, to his knees, and as far as we could see him, was working to pick up the powder.

Father said, "Well, I thought of that plan to get rid of him and I guess that will hold him back till we have time to bait the animals and get our supper in Spring Valley" (about eight miles further on). We lost no time, and arrived at our camp just before sundown, staked the team on good grass, and got our grub nearly ready to eat when Mr. Indian walked up to our fire. Father looked up to me as much as to say "fooled."

After a while Father said, "I should like to know how

much of that powder he saved." I said, "Every grain, or he would have been there yet." "Ask him," said Father. I did, and the Indian showed us that he had tied it up in one corner of his shirt tail, which was all the clothing he had on. The bunch looked to be about the bulk of clean powder that had been dropped for him. Father said he would like to see it. I told the Indian to untie it and let us see it; he did, and to our surprise we could not detect a particle of dirt. It was as clean as that in my flask. How did he do it?

I learned afterwards that he had taken off his shirt, spread it down near the powder, and was very careful to scoop up all the powder together with dirt dust and leaves, putting it all on the shirt. When this had been done he removed to another corner of the shirt all the coarse dirt and leaves which were there, searched and then cast it off. Then the process was simply to shake and blow out the dust and pick out gravel or lumps of dirt that would not crumble. We had traveled at about eight miles an hour. The Indian had appeared at our camp in less than one hour after we had stopped to feed. He must have done the job pretty quick and then run like a race horse every step of the way from where the powder was dropped to camp, yet he did not seem to be the least bit tired, not even sweating. Well, he earned his supper. and got it.

37—A RUN FOR LIFE.

Bolly and two others of the mail boys were building the first log cabin at Dry Creek, and had the logs laid up and the roof on, but the spaces between the logs had not yet been chinked or plastered. The road ran in front of the door, and just across it they had placed the covered top wagon-bed to serve as store room until the house was ready to use. The cooking stove had been put in place and the cook this morning had just started to make a fire to get breakfast.

Bolly had just crawled out of bed and gone back of the wagon, and was only partly dressed, but having his belt that carried his pistol, in his hand. The other man was still in 'he wagon ready to come out, when there was a gun shot, and the cook came running out of the house crying, "Indians! I am shot. Boys, run for your life! They are back of the house trying to shoot at us through the cracks."

The boys by this time were close together and soon saw that they must get farther from the wagon or be killed, without returning the compliment. So they ran down the road about one hundred yards, where they stopped to council as to their next move. Should they try to hunt up the team, or endeavor to stand the Indians off?

Each of the boys had his pistol and a pouch of ammunition on his belt. They did not get much time to consider, for the Indians showed up in a larger band than was expected and were trying to surround the boys to prevent any from escaping. Seeing this move, the boys agreed that their only chance for life was to run for the next station east, twenty-five or thirty miles away, and at once, as the Indians were almost abreast of them and had to be kept back by pointing revolvers at them.

The boys started on the run, when the cook told them to take his pistol and leave him and save themselves, as he could not run any more, and was dying anyhow. The boys would not consent to that, but one on each side took hold of him to help him along, but very soon he said, "If you won't leave me, give me my pistol so I can help to fight them."

They gave him the gun and as the Indians had to keep their heads out of sight while they were running down a crooked ravine, the boys could walk a few steps once in a while, and still keep ahead. They were doing this when the cook, who had fallen back two or three steps, shot his own brains out and fell in the middle of the road.

"We cannot help him now," said Bolly and, taking the pistol and belt off the man, the two went off on the run to keep out of the trap the Indians were trying to get them in. After going some three or four miles, the country was getting so smooth and level there was no chance for the Indians to spring a surprise on them, and the Indians were afraid to attack them on open ground.

So after they got well down in the valley to a place where they had a good view of the country for a few miles in all directions, they made a halt to rest and to deliberate as to what to do to get out of their scrape. The station they were going to had probably been treated the same as the one they had left, and no knowing how many more. How far would they have to travel before they could get a square meal?

They at last agreed to save their strength by traveling slowly so as to reach the station after dark, and from some other direction than the road and, if there were Indians there, to try a surprise on them, if there was any chance of success whatever. They approached the station at the time and, as agreed, pistols in hand. They tip-toed around the house to the door and listened for some signs of life before kicking at the door. Just then some one inside said, "I heard something outside, did you?" "Yes," yelled Bolly, "there is something out here and darn hungry, too. Open the door for the children," which was done at once, and when the boys had eaten their breakfast, dinner and supper and told their story, it was decided to hold the fort. As they expected the pack train with the mail at any old time, and then they would be strong enough to be the attacking party. They prepared for emergencies, and sure enough the next evening the mail arrived with three carriers, which made their force seven well armed men, who had no scare in their make-up and all ready for any skirmish that might turn up.

Their animals had to have a rest and feed, so it was decided to stay there till 10 or 12 o'clock that night before starting west, which they did, and arrived to where the dead man lay in the road, about 10 a. m. The Indians had stripped him of all clothing and then left him. He had been shot right through the body, and it is a wonder that he lived and traveled so far after being shot that way. They buried him just to one side of the road.

There had been left two men at the station, so there were five to go with the mail. They found that the Indians had burned up the wagon bed and tried to burn the house, but it was built of green logs and would not burn. The team that was left there was never recovered or even heard of. There had not been any other station on the line attacked at this time and Bolly was soon back on his old stamping ground.

38—"TRACKING STOLEN MULES."

It was while we were bringing back from Ruby Valley four mules we were to leave at Deep Creek. The "we" was my companion (Lafayette Ball, Bolly, as he was called for short) and myself. We had reached a point near the south end of Spring Valley, eight or ten miles east of Shell Creek, when there came up a violent rain storm, wetting our clothes through. So we concluded to camp for the night in a bunch of cedars that was close to the trail we were traveling. We staked two of the mules on good feed and let the two we had ridden all day run loose, thinking they would not ramble very far away. We made a good big fire, and stripping, dried our clothes and blankets, and went to bed.

Just as day was breaking, Bolly awoke and said, "You make a fire while I get the mules." The two not picketed were not in sight. He was gone till nearly sunrise—no mules. He said he had circled their tracks and found they were going in a southwest direction for Shell Creek mountains, and one going directly behind the other. He said, "They are stolen.

What shall we do?'' ''You say first.'' ''Well, I say, mules or hair.'' ''Good, the same here.'' We were not long in saddling up and getting to the place where Bolly had found the trail.

From this place to where the trail would reach the mountains, if it ran straight, would be about five or six miles. Where the trail was plain we would ride side by side as fast as possible, the trail between us. But when it was not plain and hard to locate, we would one of us keep to the trail going as fast as he could pick out the tracks, the other would rush ahead for half a mile or so in the direction the tracks were leading, and as soon as he saw the tracks would motion back to the other, who would then drop the trail and run as fast as possible up ahead of the other to find the trail.

So we were making pretty fast time and were not long in reaching the mountains, and here our really hard work was found, for the tracks led along the side of the mountain, over and across ledges of rock, where only a little iron mark was made by the mules' shoes. We were also careful not to fall into an ambush. But by one riding ahead as far as he could, yet keeping in sight of the other, we were still making pretty good time.

Bolly, in crossing one of these ledges could not find the trail, and therefore was circling back towards me, but below the rocks. He motioned that he was right; I was soon at his side. Here the trail was very plain, going in a southeast direction as if to cross the valley diagonally. When we got out of the timber line there was nothing to do but keep a watch ahead and follow the trail as fast as we could go.

After doing this for about three miles we came to within a hundred yards of a large, rocky knoll or mound covering about one acre, and about twenty-five feet high near the center. Bolly (who was ahead at this point) said ''Keep a watch on that hill, for the mules have been turned loose and the thieves may take a shot at us.'' We could tell by the way the tracks criss-crossed back and forth that the mules were left to ramble as they wished. Bolly said, ''Shall we get them, or the mules first?'' I said, ''We were hunting mules and I think we had better find them first, and then if we come across the thieves we can have a deal with them.''

Before we started on the trail again we circled that mound, keeping off at what we thought a safe distance, and far enough apart that one or the other could see the opposite side of the mound, but no Indian showed up. Still we were sure they were there yet, and if we half wanted them we would have found a way to get them.

The mules had turned west, going towards the foothills, which we soon reached, and when we sighted the mules, they were feeding along as they went up a ravine, probably hunting water. When we caught them we noticed that one of the mules had not been ridden, the other had carried both Indians. The one they had led still had the rope dragging from his neck. Bolly said that mule would not be ridden bare-back. All this compelled the Indians to travel more slowly.

As we started back on a straight line for where we had camped, we passed about half way between the timber line and the mound where the mules had been turned loose. "Shall we investigate?" said I. "No use," said Bolly, "for look there," pointing towards the timber. And sure enough, there they were, running at their best speed for taller ground We let them go.

A couple of years later I got the names of the two young bucks who did the stealing. Their excuse was that they thought us immigrants who had two animals apiece while they had none. But they began to be afraid they had made a mistake when they saw how they were being trailed, and when we were circling the mound, on which they were, one said, "If I get a chance I will take a shot at one." The other said, "Don't you shoot, for if you do we will both be killed, for don't you know who it is that wears that antelope skin shirt? He never misses. Lay down and maybe they won't bother us, for they surely know we are here."

We got to our camp about dark, this time picketing the four mules, and they were all right next morning, but we were one day late at our destination.

39. CHANGING A CAMP AFTER DARK.

In the times of Indian trouble we were very careful where we located our camp at night, but sometimes there was not much room to choose from. It so happened to a party of three. They had a choice of a camp up the flat a few rods, or down about the same distance, but stopped about the middle, picketed their horses on the best feed in sight, got their supper and made their bed down while yet light. One of the men noticed that across the hollow and about thirty yards distant was a ledge of rocks that made this a poor camping place for safety.

There was nothing doing till it got quite dark, then the animals were moved back down the hollow, and the camp moved down, and the bed remade, but no fire kindled. The first fire had been left burning. In the morning all was found to be all right and they started on their way up the hollow, and, as they were passing the place of their first camp fire, one of them saw an arrow sticking in the ground close to where their bed had first been laid down, and looking, found two or three more, and no two pointed alike, proving that there were three or four of the Indians that fired them from the ledge.

One of the boys said, ''A happy move; a miss is as good as a mile.'' An Indian generally has his own arrows all marked one way and all the same. This is done by small rings or stripes of different colors around the feathered end of the arrow, no dispute as to whose arrow killed the game, the arrow would show that.

Marked Arrows.

40. MY THREE DAYS' FAST.

It came about in this way. Ben Holladay, who had a large interest in the Overland Mail Line, was to make a quick trip across the continent, and Father, who was the boss of the road from Salt Lake to Carson City, made all preparations for a fast run. The time was set when Holladay should start from New York, and figured out by the road agents, as we called them, when he would arrive on their division.

Father, as I suppose—as did all the other agents—sent relays or stage teams back east of their station, half way to the next station, thus giving each driver a fresh team half way between stations, which would enable him to greatly increase his speed. This was carried out all along the line, but Father had merely said in his note: ''Send a relay back to such a point, and at such a time, and wait for me till I come.''

I was stationed at Butte and, on the date set, with L. Ball and the four mules, went back some eighteen or twenty miles to Egan Canyon, where we arrived about noon and had just got settled down to prepare our dinner when two of the Shell Creek boys came in and said they had lost the relay mules and had come this way in search of them. They were fourteen miles from their home station and as many more from their relay camp. They had started to get the mules at daylight and without any breakfast, had ridden a good many miles. They were hungry as wolves.

We had brought enough grub with us for three meals, dinner, supper and breakfast, if we needed it, for the stage was to come anywhere between sundown and midnight. So we all turned loose on the ''grub pile,'' and it was but a few minutes before all the eatables had vanished, also the mule hunters.

Bolly (as we called my chum) and I had no supper that night and, in fact, nothing till we reached our home station three days later. Well, the time dragged along slowly. The second day brought up the hunger to such a pitch that we held a joint debate as to whether we go back home or not, for we did not dare to separate and one go back for grub, as a band of strange Indians had come and made their camp less than a half mile from us. We decided to stay at our post at least another twenty-four hours.

That evening one of the Indians, a very big fellow, came to our fire. When I asked him what he wanted, he replied by asking if we were hungry. I told him no, and after looking all around to see how we were fixed, he pulled out from under his blanket a piece of fresh antelope meat about the size of your two hands, and said he wanted to trade that for powder and bullets. I asked him, ''How much?'' He said, ''Twenty charges powder, twenty bullets, twenty caps.'' I said to Bolly, ''What do you think about that?'' ''Well,'' said Bolly, ''if he gets that much from me I would not give much for his hide. It would be so full of holes as to be quite unsaleable.''

The Indian, after hearing my refusal to trade, and a gentle nod towards his camp, turned and went to his friends, who, we could see, were all watching what was going on at our camp. Just as dark set in we moved our saddles and traps to another place, but close to the road, changed the mules to another place on the opposite side of our camp from the Indians, and thus, by sleeping one at a time, we passed the night, and still no stage.

In the morning we found that the Indians had moved about a fourth of a mile further away. For what purpose we did not know or care much. About noon Bolly came to me, where I was on guard, and asked me for some smoking paper, as he had used up all the paper he had brought with him but had quite a bunch of tobacco. Well, I had used up the last slip of paper I could rake up about two hours before, intending to get some from Bolly. There we were, two smokers up against it, plenty of tobacco with no pipe or paper.

Bolly tried a cigarette made of tobacco and a piece of cotton shirt tail, but it was no good. We must find something better, but how and where? Bolly said if he could find some clay he could make a pipe and bake it in the fire, and started off to find the clay along the creek, and in the meantime I was hard at work splitting a small willow, cutting out the center and wrapping the two halves together to make a stem for the pipe. After he had made the pipe and cooked it a while, he removed it from the fire, when it broke and crumbled to fine dirt. "Good-bye," says Bolly, "for, like the 'Fox and the Grapes,' I don't want to smoke anyhow," so went back to his perch on the point of the rocks, close to the road and to the mules, and where he could view the Indian camp, also the road a short distance down the canyon in the direction the stage was to come from. While there he saw a half dozen Indian hunters return to their camp with two or three dead antelope they had run down and shot that forenoon.

After Bolly had made a mess of the pipe business I, merely to pass off the time some way, hunted along the creek for a willow large enough to be whittled into a pipe form. Not finding one, I returned to camp and sat down on the wire grass sod to await events. Seeing my crude pipe stem, I picked it up and had a new thought at the same time. I cut the grass off a small piece of ground and, after pounding it down to make it solid, I proceeded to cut down in it the shape of a pipe bowl, then a long slanting trench from the bottom of the bowl to the surface of the ground, about a foot from the bowl. Then I placed my pipe stem in this trench, tamping the dirt down over it, and when I had got through, I found I could blow through it, so I filled it with tobacco, put a coal of fire on, and had a very cool and pleasant smoke. I called to Bolly to come, and that I had made a pipe, but it was not portable. "Nothing doing," said Bolly, till I drew a long whiff of smoke from the pipe, then stood up and blew the smoke up in the air. That brought him on the run, and looking at the thing, he said, "By Heck! and how simple." I imagine I can see him now, laying down on his side, and one elbow on the ground (in a comfortable position) to reach the pipe stem, which stuck up about six inches. Well, no more trouble about smoking while there.

On the third day of our stay there, we had just put the mules on fresh grass, just as day was breaking in the east and while standing there at the side of the road, we heard the welcome rumble of the coach, and by the time we brought our saddles to the road, the stage, with Father and Holladay drew up, and immediately the team was unharnessed, and our fresh team put on. As the harness was taken off the wheelers, Father said, "You boys put your saddles on these, as they are not the least tired, and be ready to start as soon as the team is hitched up, and you keep close behind us, understand." We said, "Yes."

When he had got on the stage beside the driver, he reached under the seat and brought out some bread that had been baked in a skillet and was dry and very hard. Breaking the cake in two, he gave one part to Bolly and the other to me. Bolly looked towards the creek. Father saw him and said, "No, there is not time for that. Come and we'll start for the station." The boys that had lost their mules had reported to Father that they had eaten all of our grub, and that we must have gone back to our station, therefore he would not get the change of animals he had planned for.

"Who were the boys that were there?" said he. On being told that they were Bolly and Howard, he said, "Give me a loaf of bread for them, for I will find them at their post if alive." Well, when we got within sight of the station, about one-half mile from it, we got down to a walk, and when we arrived Father had already gone on his way, but had left directions to the cook how and what to prepare for us to eat, being afraid we might overfeed ourselves if we had our own way about it. He also knew that we could not eat much of the bread he had given us without water, which we did not have, and in fact did not get down more than a couple of bites on the whole sixteen miles to the station.

Here let me say at the very place and spot where I had invented the unportable pipe, were, a few years later, built by Judge Dougherty, a forty-stamp quartz mill, which was in operation the last time I visited the canyon.

41.—MAIL CARRIER.

Father was George Chorpening's agent, or partner, when he had the contract to carry the mail from Salt Lake to California. I don't know whether he had the contract to the east or not, but I know Father's division was from Salt Lake to Placerville, California, and, as the time came that money failed to come to pay off the men or other expenses, Father was forced to dig up and use every resource to keep the Mail going, expecting every day to receive the money that he had been told by letter from the boss had been sent by a trusty agent by way of California.

OFFICE OF THE ASSISTANT TREASURER
OVERLAND MAIL CO.

Salt Lake City, Utah Territory

July 1st 1862

To Agents
& Employees
of The Overland Mail Co.

Major Egan this day becomes Superintendent of the Overland Mail Line from Salt Lake City to Carson in place of Rowe resigned.

You will please regard his directions accordingly.

Fred Cook
Asst Treas O.M.Co.

Facsimile of Appointment as Mail Agent, Salt Lake to Carson,

Mail stage coach on Overland line. Prominent in Pioneering and the development of the great west.

*About the year 1856, after Father had selected the route for the mail line to California, Howard R. Egan, then sixteen years of age, drove the first mail coach from Salt Lake City to California. As the stations were not then stocked, it is probable that the same team and coach went clear through, camping on the way.

Father afterwards learned that this trusty agent was a connection of the boss, and when he arrived in San Francisco he was either robbed of the whole amount or had gambled it away. It was supposed it melted by the latter process. Chorpening had written that he would soon have another payment from the government and for Father to keep the mails running as long as possible, but after a few months there came a change of the contractors.

Ben Holliday and associates re-stocked the line with men, teams and coaches. I was at Willow Springs at the time and, not wishing to work as hostler, went to Ruby Valley, where Father and his partner, W. H. Sherman, had a good-sized supply store. Besides, they owned the station and were doing a good business, especially in the season when emigrants were traveling through. I had not received a dollar for thirteen months, and when I next saw Father he offered to give me an outfit and furnish the necessary supplies if I would go down the valley and pick out a good place and start a farm, and he would wait till I raised the grain to pay him back. That sounded good enough to me, so I went down about twenty miles and took up the first farm in Ruby Valley.

It was a fine location, a mountain stream coming out of a heavy timbered canyon ran through the land down to the lake in the valley below, with an immense strip of meadow land all around it. I built a log house and did some plowing, trying to get ready for fall planting, when I received word from Father to pull up stakes and come to Deep Creek and to start at once, not to wait another day, as he had learned through Dimmick Huntington that the Indians were going to make a raid on that country. I did not believe it, but then, Father must be obeyed. So as soon as the ox teams could travel there I arrived at Deep Creek.

It was understood I was to be a partner with Father and brother Erastus, but after some time something at Ruby Station did not suit Father so he had Erastus move out there and take charge of the business, with the understanding, as I take it, of being a partner with Father in that concern.

But after some time there seems to have been a different plan mapped out. For one day I received a list of animals, wagons, chains, plows, harrow teeth, milk pans, twelve cows, and in fact about everything that would be useful on a farm. The cat was out of the bag. My brother was going to farming the place I had started to. I don't remember how long he worked the farm before he received a notice that he was called on a mission to England. I know that he immediately stopped the plowing, made arrangements to lease or sell the farm, started for Bountiful, where he left his wife in the care of her people, and went on his mission.

*Although we are not giving a biography of each member of the family, it is considered advisable to add here to what Howard R. has said above: that Erastus, or R. E. Egan, became President of the Birmingham Conference in England during his mission, and after he returned he went again to the Ruby Farm for a short time, but sold out and moved to

**Richard Erastus Egan,
Pony Express Rider,
Bishop of South Bountiful.
Address, Byron, Wyo.**

Bountiful, where he was Bishop of South Bountiful for very many years. He was among the first Pony Express riders, riding from Salt Lake to Rush Valley. He took a special mission to hunt up the genealogy of the family. He went to the old home in Tulemore, Kings county, Ireland, which was built by our Great Grandfather Bernard Egan some time in the eighteenth century, for Grandfather Howard Egan was born in it in 1782 and Father, Major Howard Egan was born in it in 1815. (See page 10.) He obtained all he could of the genealogy of relatives there, finding that Bernard had two sons, Howard and William, and that all that was left of William's descendants was Edward, a bachelor living in the old home, as shown in the picture, as he stood in the doorway.

After returning from there he went to Montreal, Canada, where Grandfaher removed the family to, after the death of Grandmother Ann Meade Egan. There he found a considerable number of the family which he has faithfully recorded, but which we do not have access to at the present time. He also visited Massachusetts and New Hampshire and obtained a considerable genealogy of Mother's relations, the Parsleys and Caverlys, and has done what temple work could be done at that time for them. A few years ago he moved from Bountiful to Byron, Wyo., in the Big Horn Basin, where he now lives. His posterity is given in the Appendix. The family organization may some day give his biography more fully, as well as some other members of the family.

To show that Father was agent for the eastern division of the Overland Mail Line, in answer to Howard's inquiry in a preceding paragraph and to show the nature of some of his business we submit a couple of letters, as follows:

Superintendent's Office, Indian Affairs, Utah.

Great Salt Lake City. June 17, 1859.

Howard Egan, Esq., General Mail Agent,

Sir: Please inform me in writing, as soon as convenient, of Indian depredations committed on the United States mail property under your charge, as communicated to me verbally this day. I remain,

Very respectfully your obt. servant,

(Signed) J. FOURNEY. Supt. Ind. Affairs, U. T.

Salt Lake City, March 14, 1861.

Col. Benj'n. Davis, Supt. Indian Affairs, U. T.

Dear Sir: Mr. W. H. Shearman informed me that during an interview with you yesterday, you stated that you had information of foul play having been used towards an Indian who was missing at Willow Springs, on the C. & S. L. M. Line, by one or more of the employees of said line. As I have no knowledge whatever of any person or persons, in my employ, having been engaged in any such nefarious transaction, you will confer a favor upon me by referring me to your informant.

My position, sir, entitles me to demand this information, or else that the subject be never again mentioned either in private or public connection with my name.

You will oblige me by replying at your earliest convenience. Very respectfully,

(Signed)   HOWARD EGAN,
          Agent Eastern Division, C. & S. L. Mail Line.

42.—FATHER'S INDIAN DOCTOR.

While Father was out west on the mail line one hot spring-like day before the snow had melted, he had his eyes burned so bad that he was completely blinded and could not stand the least bit of light, and although he kept them bandaged with dead tea leaves, they did not seem to get any better.

After a couple of days of misery, two Indians came to the station where he was. One of them asked one of the men, ''Egan sick?'' The man said, ''Yes, eye sick. No see. Snow no good.'' ''Me see Egan.''

The man told Father that there was an Indian there that wanted to see him. ''Well, let him come in.'' He did so. The Buck came up close to Father and said, ''Big sick?'' Father said, pointing to his eyes, ''Eyes big sick; you savey fix them.'' He had hardly got the words out of his mouth when the Indian jumped and caught Father's head in both hands, and at the same time pushing the bandage out of the way, placed his mouth over one eye and set to sucking with all his strength.

Father said he thought the buck would suck his eye out, if not his brains too. He tried his best to push the Indian off, but he only stayed and sucked the faster. But just before Father had made up his mind to choke him off, the Indian stepped back a little and spit up as much or more than a tablespoonful of blood. After a little rest he said, ''Fix more?'' Father said, ''Fix little, eye big sick.'' ''Alright, little fix.'' But when he got fastened to the other eye he worked just as hard as before, with the same result, Father trying to push him off, but no go, he was after the blood and he would not let go till he got it.

After about one hour the buck said, "A little more fix eye?" Father said as his eyes felt to be considerable better, he thought he could stand a small dose of the same medicine, and told the fellow, "Fix little bit." Well, he did, but with just about the same force. When he got through he said, "Big Chief see all right two days," which proved true. In two days after the operation Father joined the pack train and went to Salt Lake, his eyes perfectly cured of snow blindness. He says he would sooner stand the Indian treatment than to suffer any length of time without it. There was no pain after the dose, but plenty and very severe before.

43.—A TRIP TO RUBY WITH BEEF CATTLE.

In the fall of 1862, Father wanted to send fifty or sixty head of beef cattle from Salt Lake to Ruby Valley, and as I was at home on a furlough, he did not ask me if I would drive them out, but said, "I want you to take these animals out to Ruby, and you must start tomorrow, for they need them there now. Everything is ready, a wagon loaded with about a ton of supplies, three yoke of broken oxen, two ponies for the two Indian night herders, and an ox driver or teamster." Myself and riding pony made up the whole outfit. I was told to make as good time as I could, but get the beef through in the best shape possible, and keep a good watch on the animals, as there was a good deal of stealing going on about that time.

All went well, although there was a sleet storm when we started from a ranch just south of the city, where the cattle had been pastured while the outfit was got ready. The second day out we had, by noon, crossed the Jordan and made our dinner camp on the west side of the divide that separates Utah and Cedar valleys. While we were eating dinner, Lot Huntington rode into camp, ate dinner with us, and during the conversation I learned that he was going out west and might join us later on, and travel with us as far as Ruby Valley. . That was the last I ever saw of Lot.

The next night we camped in Rush Valley about ten or twelve miles east of the Faust Mail Station. We were camped close to the road and in the night heard a stage, going west, pass by. I thought it strange, for it was not a mail day, as they were only running tri-weekly at that time. And I was more puzzled when, next morning, as we were about to move camp, another stage came from the west and stopped opposite our camp fire and Porter Rockwell, the sheriff, or deputy, sang out: "Hello kids, all right?" "Yes, all right so far." "Good! Your Father told me to tell you—whose ox is that?" (pointing to an animal standing a couple of rods away). "You had better ask Father when you see him. These cattle at present are every one of them mine. What did Father say?" "Oh, all right. He said for you to be very careful and keep a good watch on the cattle and guard them well."

I noticed that those on the coach, I could see, were all heavily armed. I supposed there had been a rabbit hunt, as there were on frequent occasions in the fall. When we reached Faust Station we found there had been a hunt, not a rabbit hunt, but a man hunt, and the men that were hunted were in that stage coach with the sheriff. One, Lot Huntington, being dead, and the other a prisoner. The latter was killed while trying to escape after arriving in Salt Lake City.

I could give more details of the affair as I heard it at the station but, as I did not see it, will only say that it was afterwards reported that a certain gang had planned to capture my herd of beef before I could get them to Ruby, drive them south to the Simpson's, and trail them west to California, where they would sell for a hundred dollars a head. Quite a tempting bate for the speculating trio of saloon bums. Well, they could have taken the whole outfit very easily by coming and joining us and taking their choice of time and place for the coup, as I was well acquainted with them and supposed they were good friends, although I never had any deal with them, or played with them as boys. Though some were neighbors, they were a class older than my chums or I. If there was a plot laid for me, old Porter burst the bubble and I got through safe.

When we arrived at Simpson Springs the pony rider told us we could not cross the river bed (seven miles west) until the road was repaired, as there had been a big flood that had torn the whole bottom out, road and all. The rider on the previous trip, going west, as he started down the bank, heard a sound like a very heavy wind among trees. He stopped to listen; the sound was coming from the east and increasing rapidly. He put spurs to the pony and, just as he made the opposite side of the bed, he could see a wall of water, brush and other debris, twelve or fifteen feet high, spread from bank to bank, rolling down the bed at race horse speed. If he had been one-fourth of the distance back across the bed, when he first saw the flood, he could not have escaped with his life.

When we arrived there, by a little exploring and zig-zaging, we made across with not much loss of time. But what a wreck of country! The whole bottom of the old river bed had been covered with a thick growth of very large sagebrush; all had been torn out root and branch, and the level bottom that had been, was now gulled and gouged in a terrible fashion. There had been no storm at this place, but there had been seen, that morning, a heavy storm on the mountains about seven or eight miles to the east, and there was perhaps a cloudburst, for a common rain over a sandy country could not have done the job.

That river bed was no place for a station, but they built one there and dug a well that furnished very good, but a little brackish, water, which they hauled to the Dugway Station, where there were three men and a change of horses for the mail coach. One man tended the horses and acted as cook. The other two were digging a well for water. I was let down that well when they had reached a depth of one hundred and thirteen feet. I have never seen anything like that before or since. The surface soil at this place is a white clay that is very sticky when wet. The walls of this well are of the same material from top to bottom and about the same dampness from three feet down to the bottom, where I cut my name in the side about two feet above. The wall was very smooth and plumb, no need of curbing and no danger of ever caving in. Some time after men were put to work boring with a well auger in the bottom. They bored some forty feet and found no change. Then the job of trying more to find water there was given up and it made a nice place to dump the stable cleanings.

When I reached the desert just east of Fish Springs, the road was very bad, mud hub deep, and my work oxen gave out when I was about four or five miles from the Springs and could not budge the wagon another foot. I had the driver unhitch from the wagon, take some grub for himself and the Indians, who had gone ahead with the cattle, and also take my pony and drive the team to water and feed, and come back next morning with one of the Indians to help get the wagon over to hard ground.

When they came back next day we moved the wagon about one-half a mile, where the road was still worse than before. There were three empty coaches stuck in the mud within a half mile of us. Well, I simply had to get out of there some way. There was a part of the load I must not leave alone. So this is the way I managed it: We had a double cover on the wagon. We took them off and spread them out on the mud alongside the wagon and loaded the most of the valuables on it and folded the sides and ends tight over all, hitched the oxen to the end and away we went as easy as pulling a sleigh over a good snow road.

It was easy after that. All was over but the wagon by night. Next day I sent the driver and one Indian back to get the wagon if they had to take it all apart and haul it on the wagon cover, which did not appear to be damaged at all after about ten miles' drag with a load over the creamy alkali, sand-less but sticky mud. The inside of the wagon wheels had the appearance of an old-fashioned wooden butter bowl, in this case turned by contact with the bolster of the wagon. On the out-side there would be no hub or spoke in sight, and mud would pile on till of its own weight a portion would fall off, but at next turn of the wheel would be on the job again.

Well, we made it across all right and had no more trouble till we passed Butte Station about a mile, where there is a very steep pull going west and, as the snow had drifted very heavily over the crest, our team gave out just about a couple of rods below the summit and, as there was not expected a mail stage for at least ten or twelve hours, we left the wagon right in the center of the road where there was no passing around it with a wagon or sleigh. So when the stage that night came up to that point, the driver unhitched his leaders, hooked on the back of our wagon and dragged it back down the hill to near the bottom. This we did not know till next morning, when the driver and one of the Indians went back after the wagon, as we were camped some distance off the road and had not heard the Mail pass. My driver made some bad talk, so the Indian said, when he found the wagon down at the bottom, but he hooked on and did not have the least bit of trouble getting over, and when he came to camp was in good spirits and seemed to think it had all worked out for the best.

I haven't the time or space to tell of how we lassoed and snubbed up and yoked up a couple of the beef steers just before we got to Mountain Springs, the last station between us and Ruby. The road through this little valley was all staked out as the snow was very deep and only traveled by sleighs, but thanks to our extra team and with frequent digging out, we got through the beef helping to break the road. Ruby, at last, but beef not as fat as when we started, but all there.

44.—SHORT LINE CUT OFF.

I was at Rush Valley Station (H. J. Faust, station keeper). This was the end of the first express ride from Salt

Lake City. The next ride was from here to Willow Springs across the desert. The stations at this time were only half as many as they were later, being some twenty-five or thirty miles apart and at some places more than that. Well, the express came in from the east, the next rider was not well and was afraid he could not stand the ride. I volunteered to go in his place, and arrived at Simpson Springs at the edge of the desert all right.

From here the road runs in a southwesterly direction seven miles, to River Bed, then keeping the same direction to the Dug-way, then over the mountain, taking many turns to the salt wells, then west around the point of mountain where the road ran nearly west across the worst part of the desert. Nothing but mud grows there and that seems to get taller the more you sink in it, and the harder it is to get out. It then goes north past Fish Springs, around the point of the mountain and back to the south, about opposite of Fish Springs to where Boyd Station was afterwards built. From here the road ran in a westerly straight line to the Willow Spring Station, thus making a large semi-circle, the points of which were many miles closer together straight across than by the road.

After leaving Simpson's about three miles I thought (as I had many times thought before), it was a shame we had to go so many miles around to get a little ways to the west. At any rate, boy fashion, I left the road and took a straight line for Willow Springs. The first half of the distance I was able to make very good time, then the desert began to get softer as I went till finally about one inch of water was standing all over the surface as far as I could see in any direction. The pony sank to his fetlocks in the mud, that made it slow traveling.

After about five miles of this kind I came to a little higher ground where I could make better time. In looking back I could see the little knobs of mud sticking up above the water. It seemed to me I could see them for miles. Well, I made Willow Springs all right and had saved a good many hours' time. I expected to get considerable praise for this exploit, but nix.

This is what I got: The next time I saw Father it was for only a few moments; he asked me what kind of traveling I found it to be across the way I took with that express. After telling him, he said, "Well, don't ever do anything like that again without orders." That was all, and plenty. I never did, for that was a cold bath for me. I would like to cross that route again and measure it.

45.—IRRIGATION.

When Father and his partner (Mr. Severe) had got some land cleared, plowed and seeded to wheat on their new location at Deep Creek, Mr. Severe running the place while Father tended to his mail business, Father, in passing that way, stopped over long enough to ride over the place with the boss to see what had been done and lay plans for the future.

In going along a small field of grain Father said, ''This looks fine, but don't it need irrigating?'' ''Yes,'' said the boss, ''I sent a couple of hands early this morning with their dinners to turn the creek and water it. I wonder where they are.'' This was about the middle of the afternoon.

In going around a clump of willows they found the two men lying on their backs, on the west side of the willows, both sound asleep, paying no heed to the sting of flies or mosquitos. After they had been awakened Father said, ''Boys, if you had wanted to take a little rest why didn't you get in the shade?'' ''Why,'' said one, ''it was shady here when we laid down.'' They must have been very tired, for they had lain there at least six or eight hours.

Live Irrigating Machine.—It was this same field, a few years later, I sent a couple of green hands to work putting a dam in a creek to turn the water and irrigate. They were gone about half a day, came back and said ''there could not be a dam made there without lumber.'' ''I'll see about that and prove different.''

Calling my Indian (Ned) I told him what I wanted done and sent one of the men with him to help him put in the dam and irrigate that field. Just before sundown the white man came back and said the Indian had motioned for him to leave. He didn't know what for. I told him I would know when the Indian came in. The Indian said, ''Keep that white man out of the wheat or he will dig it all up,'' so I let Ned have his way about it.

Next day I was going to take a ride down the valley, and told Mr. Muncey, the operator, if he wanted to go there was a horse in the stable that he could ride. Much pleased, he accepted the invitation, and enjoyed a long ride. In returning, I thought I would see how Ned was getting along with the irrigating, so we came up through the fields that way. We came to where Ned was at work. He had stuck his shovel where he could see it, and with pants and shoes off was stooping over and with his fingers spread out, was going backwards, making little drills for the water to reach the dry places. When Muncey saw that, he said, "Well, I'll be d—d if that ain't the first live irrigating machine I ever saw," and it did look comical.

Coyote in Chicken House.—At Deep Creek we had a large chicken house built of logs, the door of which faced the kitchen door, and about forty feet from it, and on the west side of the yard that was formed, which was about sixty feet square. The stables were on the south side, the bunk-house on the east, the row of buildings (double row), the whole length of the north line. The west room was the telegraph office, and in which the operator slept. About sixteen feet west of the office was the northeast corner of a field, and in this corner was our garden fenced off along the road, and from the corner down back of the hen house.

It was just at dusk as Father came out of the stable, he saw a coyote enter the hen house, the door of which had not yet been closed for the night. He ran as fast as he could and pulled the door shut; he then ran to the telegraph office for the shotgun that most always could be found there. "Ed (the operator's name), hand me the shotgun, quick!" "What is it?" "Oh, only a coyote in the hen house."

In place of handing out the gun he came out with it, and excited, ran for the hen house, but seeing the door shut, he said, "Where is the coyote?" "Inside," said Father; "give me the gun and I will get him." "No, let me shoot him. Open the door." The door was opened, but it was so dark inside that they could not see very plain. But finally Ed said, "I see him" and he fired. There was a terrible commotion in that hen house, for there were about one hundred chickens and a coyote very badly scared.

The coyote was trying to escape by way of the roosts, knocking the chickens to the floor, but it was not chicken he wanted just then. Father said, "No use to shoot again till we get a lantern so we can see the thief. Stay in the door till I get a light." "Alright, hurry up." When a light was finally turned into that house, there squatted the coyote in one corner watching for a chance to spring out of the door, and the chickens fairly climbing all over him.

After getting the light in the best position to show up the coyote, Ed fired again, causing another outburst of squacks and cacklings. When the smoke cleared away, Father dragged the coyote outside and then picked up five or six large chickens that Ed had shot. He said, "See here, young man, what you have done, and on purpose, too, I believe."

The next morning Father was up early. He took the coyote that had frozen stiff during the night and set it up about thirty yards from the house in the garden and propped it up with some sticks to appear as if alive. Then going to the office, he called Ed to hand out the gun. "What for?" "A coyote in the garden—the gun quick before he goes." The gun comes and Ed with it. "Where is he?" and turning around the corner of the house, said, "I see him; that's my hide," and he fired. The coyote seemed to squat a little. Father said, "You missed him." Ed fired again. This time the coyote fell down.

"I got him this time," he said, and stood the gun up against the house while he climbed over the fence to get the coyote to place beside the one he killed last night. When he took hold of it he found that it was frozen stiff. He then knew that he had been sold, and turning around to accuse Father, he found that there was no Father to be seen, for he was in the messroom telling the boys how Ed had killed a dead coyote, and when breakfast was called, every one Ed met had a grin on his face.

At dinner when all were seated around the table, the cook brought in the final dish, which was the cooked chickens. Placing it on the table he looked at Ed and nodded. Ed said, "Is this the chickens the coyote killed?" "I guess so, for they were plumb full of shot." Then the "Ha! Ha! Ha!" all around.

While we are talking of coyotes, and just to prove that there were a few out there, let me tell you that one night one of the men that slept in the bunk-house went outside and left the door open, and the blacksmith, whose bunk faced the door, saw a coyote come into the room. He kept still till the men came back, then he said, "Close the door quick! There is a coyote in here."

The man was frightened and feared the coyote would bite his bare legs, and attempted to go out again, when the blacksmith said, "Stand still a minute while I light the candle. Then we can get him." The man obeyed, and when the light was made, there in one corner, and under the bunks crouched the coyote, which was soon made ready for skinning.

Another dark evening one of the men was passing along by the hog pen with a lantern. He heard the old sow making a terrible fuss. He went to the side of the pen and swung the lantern over into the pen, then he could see the old sow backed up in a corner with her six or eight young pigs behind her, her bristles sticking straight up and her mouth open. In the opposite corner crouched the cause of all that commotion, a large coyote, who was either after a young pig or a supper out of the hog trough. Well, his hide was worth one dollar.

PART IV.

THRILLING EXPERIENCES OF PRE-FRONTIER LIFE, INDIAN CUSTOMS AND LEGENDS.

SEC. I.—INDIAN PRACTICE.

46.—A LITTLE SURPRISE

To a Small Band of Indians, and This Is How It Came About.

The express rider at Shell Creek was too sick to undertake the ride, and I volunteered to take his place. The ride at that time was from Shell to Butte, there being no station at Egan Canyon at that time. Therefore the one pony had to go about thirty-two miles, fourteen of them being to Egan. I started just at dark and made pretty good time, but being careful to not overdo the pony, but give him frequent breathing spells, at which times I would let him go on the walk, and was doing so when I was about in the middle of Egan Canyon and, just before turning a sharp point ahead of me, I could see the next turn of that, and on the side of the hill towards me the light of a fire was shining. These two turns were about seventy-five or a hundred yards apart, but the curve the creek took between the points made it some further. As it did not run close to the side left quite a large flat, which was smooth and level.

In going very carefully along and keeping a sharp lookout for a sentinel, I reached the point where I could see the camp. They were on both sides of the road and about in the center of the bend. Well, I had to make up my mind very quickly as to what I should do. Should I turn back and go north to another canyon about six or eight miles, where there might be another party of Indians, if they had planned to catch the express rider? I could not wait long, as their dogs might scent me and give the alarm.

Well, I soon decided to go straight, so, taking my pistol in my hand, I rode on as close as I dared, then striking in the spurs and giving an awful yell, a few jumps of the pony brought me to about the middle of the camp, when my gun began to

talk, though pointed up in the air, and my yells accompanied
each shot. I got a glimpse of several Indians who were doing
their best to make themselves scarce, not knowing but there
might be a large party of whites after them.

When I made the next turn, I was out in the little valley
at the head of Egan Canyon and had two trails that I could
take to finish. I chose the shortest but the roughest and got
home all right. Three days later I came back through the canyon with a companion. We saw where they had had their
camp-fires, and where they had fastened a lariat across the
road, but I did not see one that night and don't know how
I passed it.

Later I got it from some friendly Indians that there had
been a trap set to catch an express rider for the purpose of
seeing what he carried to make him travel so fast. They had
placed a party in each of the canyons used, when suspicious of
the other. They had planned it pretty good, but it did not
work and they never tried it again there, but if I had turned
back and tried the other canyon, probably there would have
been one "Express" lost.

47.—LASSO PRACTICE: WHERE I GOT LEFT.

It was while I was building the new Butte station that I
took a jaunt to the north along the range of mountains, in
hopes of locating a log big enough and long enough to make
a ridge pole for the rock house. It needed to be thirty feet
long. After going ten or twelve miles and not finding one, I
was just swinging around to go back on another route when I
came to a family camp of Indians. Most of them I knew, and
the father was a good friend of mine.

After joining the circle that was sitting around a small
fire, we had our peace smoke and I told them what I was
hunting. The old man said he thought I could find what I
wanted across the valley east in the next range and pointed
out the canyon, where afterwards I found what I wanted. I
had been dragging my rawhide lasso. We do this to keep them
more pliable. When I was ready to start back, I thought I
would coil the rope up and tie it to the saddle in the usual
way, but, boy fashion, I must have some fun. So getting on
my pony I made a large loop, and before they knew what was
coming, I threw it over four or five of them, which caused
much laughter. And the old man said, "That would be a good
way to catch a Squaw."

I said, "Yes, I will try it on your girl." So I tried. She
was very good at dodging, but at the third throw I caught her
tight, which seemed to plague her considerably, for she said I
could not catch her again so easily.

When about to start home, I swung the rope in the usual way, and looking at the girl, said "Run!" She was off in an instant, but instead of running around the camp she dodged among the trees. After some chasing I was about to throw the loop when she ran around a large tree. My pony being a good lasso animal gave a quick jump aside to head her off and ran under a low limb of a tree which caught under the rim of my saddle, breaking the cinch, and I was on the ground.

The old man was the first to reach me and, finding that I had not been hurt, said, "Shall we try to catch your horse?" I said there was no use unless they had something that could run faster than he could, but I would give any of them five cups of flour that would carry my saddle to the station and I would walk back. "Alright," said the old man, and, pointing to the saddle, said, "You take it" (to the girl). She got the things together and started off. Going about fifty yards she stopped until I got through talking to the old man and got started, when she turned and went ahead.

That was as close to her as I could get; the faster I would go the faster she would. When I reached the station she was standing beside the door, saddle still on her back. I asked her if she was tired and wanted to stay all night. "No, flour." I said, "Soon dark; aren't you afraid to go now?" "No afraid to go; afraid to stay here." So I gave her the flour and a chunk of cold bread. She asked for a drink of water and after getting it she started down the hill on the run for their camp.

About a year after, she came to the station with a band of Indians and camped near. She was married. When I went to their camp I saw that she had a fire, by which she and her man sat. I said, "I see that a man did catch you." "Yes, but he did not have a horse and saddle," and seemed to think the joke was on me. I guess it was, but I don't like to own it.

48.— EATING ANTS.

When I lived at Deep Creek I had occasion to send some men and teams south to what we called "Fifteen Mile Canyon" to get some saw logs down to the loading place. They were to stay there till Saturday, then come home with a couple of loads. When they had been gone a couple of days I thought I would go up and see how they were getting along. I got there just before dinner time, while the rest were piling the logs that had been brought out of the canyon.

There were five or six Squaws sitting around, and when I unsaddled my pony I noticed that there was a great many very large ant-hills all around the place. I had heard that the Indians often eat them, so I thought I would see for myself.

So, pointing to a large hill, I asked one of the Squaws if Indians eat them. She said, "Yes." "Are they good?" "Yes." "Well, I am very hungry. Hurry up and get some and cook them just the same as Indians like them. Hurry up."

She gave her Papoose to another Squaw and, taking a large flat basket arrangement, pushed the top of the hill to one side and then scooped up about a peck of ants, gravel, dirt and all. Taking it to one side she spread on the ground a piece of flour sack, then taking the pan or basket in her hands, gave it an up and down motion at the side opposite from her. You ought to see those ants roll over the side and fall on the cloth! But not a bit of gravel or speck of dirt went with them. I have often seen the Squaws cleaning grass seed or wheat the same way, only the wheat or seed was left on the pan, and the chaff and dirt went over the edge.

After she had gone to the hill two or three times, she had collected about a quart of ants and eggs, and as I acted like I was very hungry, she asked for a kettle to cook them in. I asked the boys for the loan of their wash bucket. She took the bucket and went to the creek, got what water she wanted, piled the ants in and put it on the fire.

Then she asked me for some salt. I said, "Indians don't use salt." She said, "No, but they like it but don't have it." I gave her a handful of salt, as I did not care how she seasoned the mess. She would put in a little, stir it up well with a stick, then taste, put in a little more, then taste, and so on till she was satisfied that the right amount was used, then she brought the balance of the salt to me. I told her to keep it, pleasing her very much.

Then she asked me for a little flour. I asked her if Indians used flour when they cooked ants. She smiled and said they would if they had it, but she was cooking for a "Boss White Man" and wanted it to taste good. She got about one-half pint of flour. After that was all stirred in, she asked me for some of that black stuff the white men shake on their food. That was pepper, of course. I gave her a small amount, and when that was added she gave it a final stir, set it off the fire and said, "Now you can eat."

I got a tin plate and tablespoon and told her to put some on that. She did so. "Now, let me see you eat it," I said. She laughed, so did the rest of them. Just then the cook said dinner. I told the woman that they might eat it all, as my dinner was ready. Well, they soon cleaned up the whole mess, besides some bread and potatoes we had to spare.

49.--INDIAN CRICKET DRIVE.

I was on a three days' horseback trip in the wilderness, and had for a companion the Indian called "Egan Jack," a trusty, intelligent buck of about thirty years of age. We were on a prospecting or exploring trip to the northwest of Deep Creek, or Ibapah as the Indians called it. At one place, as we came out of a canyon onto the bench land, we saw quite a number of Indians that were quite busy, some digging trenches and some gathering arms full of the tall wheat grass that grew on the flat in the bottom of the canyon. I asked Jack what they were doing. He said, "Catching crickets for bread." "Well, we will go and see how they do it." We went, and saw that they had dug quite a number of trenches about a foot wide and a foot deep and about thirty or forty feet long, and around like a new moon with the horns uphill.

They had been a number of days at the work, but were now ready for their cricket drive, having five or six of the trenches strung across the bench, the end of each trench joined, or was very close to the end of another. They covered these with a thin layer of stiff wheat grass straw, for what purpose I did not know then, but I thought they were making a mistake, for the crickets could crawl over the ditch on it, but I must wait and see.

As it was getting the hottest time of the day, and therefore the best time for the drive, they were soon ready, and probably hurried their best to show their visitors how they done it, and at the same time get a little help. Well, there was a few crickets scattered all around, but were more of them above the trenches and near the foothills. But I thought they were going to a great deal of trouble for a few crickets, why not catch them by hand, we will see.

These trenches ran in a north and south direction, the land sloping to the west. The Indians, men, women and children, divided into two parties, one going to the north end and the other to the south end, all carrying a bunch of grass in each hand. They went single file towards the foothills, and making the distance between the parties wider than the length of the trenches. When they had gone what they thought far enough, as judged by the scarcity of grass left by the black insects, the party closed in and, walking back and forth swinging their grass bunches they gradually worked down toward the trenches.

We followed them on horseback and I noticed that there were but very few crickets left behind. As they went down, the line of crickets grew thicker and thicker till the ground ahead of the drivers was as black as coal with the excited, tumbling mass of crickets.

A cricket when disturbed can jump about one foot down hill at a jump and but half that distance up hill, but will never jump up hill if it has any show to avoid it. Well, as we neared the trenches I noticed the Indians were going down slower. Jack said this was to give the crickets time to crawl through the grass into the trenches.

When all had been driven in the Indians set fire to the grass they had in their hands and scattered it along on top of that they had over the trenches, causing a big blaze and smoke, which soon left the crickets powerless to crawl out, if any were left alive when the grass had all burned up, which did not take many minutes. I rode along the line and in some places the trenches were over half full of the dead and legless crickets. I went down below the trenches and I venture to say there were not one out of a thousand crickets that passed those trenches.

They are a scary and excitable, but a clumsy insect, that hardly ever when excited land on their feet, but roll over, then turn their head down hill and jump again. If not molested they seldom ever jump, but travel by crawling. Now the bucks and children had done their part and were sitting around in groups. The squaws were busy gathering up the game.

They had large conical shaped baskets; some of them would hold over two bushels. These the women carry on their backs, held in place by a flat band either over their foreheads or about the shoulders. Now here is what I saw a squaw doing that had a small baby strapped to a board or a willow frame, which she carried on her back with a strap over her forehead:

When at work she would stand or lay the frame and kid where she could see it at any time. She soon had a large basket as full as she could crowd with crickets. Laying it down near the kid, she took a smaller basket and filled it. I should judge she had over four bushels of the catch. But wait, the Indians were leaving for their camp about three or four miles away. This squaw sat down beside the larger basket, put the band over her shoulders, got on her feet with it, then took the strapped kid and placed him on top, face up, picked up the other basket and followed her lord and master, who tramped ahead with nothing to carry except his own lazy carcass. There were bushels of crickets left in the trenches, which I suppose they would gather later in the day.

Having seen enough there we rode on across a narrow valley, and in the foothills came to a large camp of Indians, the chief of whom I was well acquainted with, and we decided to stay all night with them, as we did not know and they could not inform us as to the exact location of the band we wanted to visit. We were also getting hungry. We had no provisions of our own left, except a couple of rabbits I had killed on the way.

They treated us fine and we had a good time telling and hearing the news. Jack took one of the rabbits and put it to roast on the fire, the other he gave to the chief. When the rabbit was done to his liking, Jack asked the chief if he had any bread; he nodded and called in a low voice the name of his squaw, who came into the tent at once. When told to bring some bread she went out, but returned immediately with a cake of black bread about two inches thick and ten inches in diameter, which she handed to me. I thought it looked too black for pine nut bread, for the latter has a yellow cast and this was decidedly black. Holding the bread in one hand and pointing to it with the other, I asked her if there was pine nuts in it. "Yes," she said unconcernedly, "is there crikets in it?" "Yes, yes," smilingly, "sure." Well, I handed the cake to Jack to divide and told the squaw that I would like some pine nuts. She soon brought in some that were all mashed up. These I refused and asked for the "whole" pine nuts. These were soon brought in and I commenced my supper.

The chief noticed that I was slow at shelling the nuts, so he called a young squaw that came in with a basin of water, setting it down near the door, washed her hands in the basin and brought in a flat stone about one foot in diameter and one-half inch thick and another about eight inches long and a couple of inches in diameter. Seating herself between Jack and me, she proceeded to put the mill in motion. She placed a couple of hands full of nuts on the flat stone and taking the other in both hands, gave it a rolling motion over the nuts which cracked the shells so they fell off the kernels, which she rolled off on a piece of sack as clean and plump as I could shell them one at a time. She simply shelled them much faster than both of us could eat them. Well, we had a good supper and breakfast, but Jack ate my share of the bread.

When the crickets are dried the squaws grind them, feathers and all, on the same mill they grind the pine nuts or grass seed, making a fine flour that will keep a long time, if kept dry. Jack says the crickets make the bread good, the same as sugar used by the white woman in her cakes. Well, I am willing to take his word for it, as otherwise I might squirm a little.

50.— TRAPPING A COYOTE.

We were on our way for Carson City with a train of four wagons with three yoke of oxen each and teams of six mules and wagons loaded with produce to sell on the way and bring back a threshing machine and other farm machinery, also dry goods, etc., to supply our little store at Deep Creek. Our first camp was at Antelope Springs, where we arrived just before dark. After watering and taking care of the animals, the next job was to get supper. We had quite a variety of foodstuff along and we soon had the meal ready, consisting of fried bacon, boiled potatoes, pancakes, mollasses, coffee, plenty of sugar, a few pounds of fresh butter, but no milk or cream for the coffee.

One of the boys said that butter was a good substitute for cream to put in the coffee, and proceeded to stir some in his cup of coffee. One of the other boys cut a good size lump and stirred it in the large coffee pot, so we all had to take our coffee that way or go without it. Well, no one went without his coffee, but after that, when the butter was all gone we missed it much. Well, after supper was over the plates, cups, knives and forks and spoons were all pushed back of each boy, thus making a circle around the fire, as we had sat that way to eat our supper. The frying pans, coffee pots and skillets were left close to the fire, where they had been used. Not a thing was washed or taken care of and you can safely bet that every single piece of the cooking and eating utensils were as greasy as grease could make them.

After supper we sat around the fire talking chaff till late, and as each became sleepy went to bed; but first, during the evening, we appointed one of the boys to tend to the cooking for one week. This one was the first to crawl out and very soon found out that the whole lot of cooking and eating utensils had taken wings or had been stolen by the Indians. He called the boys and at the same time was looking for tracks of the thief. He soon found a tin plate, then a spoon, or cup, then we were all on the hunt in a circle from the fire, when one of the boys that had gone about one hundred yards from camp yelled out that he had found one of the thieves. We all ran to where he was and this is what we saw: A coyote with his head in our largest coffee pot and the bail over his head back of his ears, fast enough, but still trying to get away. He was bumping against the brush at every step. He could make no progress.

Well to make a long story short, as they say, we had lots of fun with that coyote and the next day his hide was tacked on one of the wagon beds. When we had finished our search, back from the fire about one hundred and fifty yards, we took count of the recovered articles and found that we were out a couple of forks and a spoon. That was a cheap tariff for leaving dirty dishes where the coyotes could get to them and a lesson I venture none of us will ever forget.

Pioneer cottage.   Several families working together.

SEC. II.—HUNTING AND HARVESTING.

51.— A RABBIT DRIVE.

One afternoon, while visiting the Indians, I heard them talking of rabbits and, asking them what it was all about, the chief said a rabbit hunt. I said I would like to go along to see how they done it. He seemed pleased at me taking so much interest and said, ''Good! Come tomorrow before noon, as we want to start the drive about noon and it is quite a distance to the place. You had better come on horseback.''

About the middle of the forenoon next day I was at their camp. Most of the hunters had already started. Going about three or four miles, we came to the place selected for the drive—a piece of sage and rabbit brush land about a mile in diameter. The party I was with stopped, when we saw a fire about a half mile to our right and soon another about the same distance to the left, and then we could see the smoke rising a mile ahead of us. My party soon had their torches at work and the drive was on.

Working all around the circle and towards the center was a continuous ring of fire and smoke, which was gradually closing in and the rabbits were being crowded together thicker and thicker. Each Indian, squaw and pappose had a stick about four feet long, the only weapon they carried. A small boy or girl was just as good as a man, and oh, the fun of it—all laughing and hollering and making as much noise as possible. The rabbits got so dazed by the fire, smoke and tumult that they simply could not run. They would jump a few jumps and sit up trying to see a way out. I saw dozens of them stop within reach of the sticks and many of them were picked up that had not been hit. When a rabbit was seen to pass out of the human ring, someone would follow him in the smoke and put his body in one of the piles of rabbits they had made as they proceeded towards the center, for they could not carry much of the game and do their work at the same time.

When the drive was over the field was a black, fire-swept, but still smoking patch of ground. Talk about rabbits, I am sure there were more caught on that drive than could be packed in a large wagon bed. It seems that the black-tailed rabbits gather in herds or colonies and these places are noted by the Indians. I learned afterwards that they had intended to attack a smaller colony, but the chief wanted his white friends to see a good, big drive, and he did, and I was well pleased to be present, but thought it was taking too much the advantage of poor Mr. Rabbit, who had no chance to save his life.

The Indians do not like to use fire for a drive, as it takes years for the brush to grow up again. . I have seen a drive where no fire was used, but grass nets about two and one-half feet high and two inches or even smaller mesh. A sharp pointed stick a few inches longer than the width of the net was fastened across six or eight feet apart, to act as fence posts, when the sharp end was pressed into the earth. One buck could easily carry a role of one hundred fifty to two hundred yards of the small twisted grass twine nets. Each large family usually have such a role and at times, when living apart from other families, can use them either as traps or to drive; but then, these are only small catches.

The drive I witnessed was when there was six or eight of these nets together. When they had decided just where to run the nets, two of the Indians put the end sticks of their nets together and commenced to unroll their nets, going in opposite directions, sticking each cross stick firmly in the ground as they unrolled, making a rabbit-proof fence. When the first two had placed their nets, two more Indians commenced where they ended and continued the line in the desired direction.

I noticed that when they were through stringing their nets in a kind of semicircle form, there was part of a roll of nets not unrolled at each end. These ends, when they were ready to drive, were strung out, but not in a circle, but flaring straight out from the opening, making a long V-shaped mouth to the field. When the Indians swung across this mouth they began coming in slowly. But every rabbit that was started went into the pen and kept running back and forth to find a place to get through. Vain search, for they were trapped. When the men had reached the opening of the circle the two ends of the net was brought in and strung across the opening, this making a complete enclosure. Then the fun began. All the Indians were inside with sticks, or bows and arrows, picking up the game. Sometimes I could see at one glance five or six rabbits that were entangled in the netting. If the Indians were engaged at on place getting the ones caught, the others were getting into trouble at another place.

It seemed a little strange to me that when a rabbit running along the fence would see a man ahead of him he would turn and run across the circle till he came to the fence, then run along it till he saw someone ahead, then either make a dive at the fence and get tangled, or take another run across lots, but never stopping or trying to hide in the brush in the center, but seemed to know they were trapped.

It took the Indians over a half day to get as many as they wanted. There were many left when they took up the nets and were none the worse off by their little scare.

I have seen the black-tailed rabbits in bands so thick they could not all get in the shade of the sagebrush and I have seen coyotes where there seemed to be dozens and dozens of them in the middle of the day, standing and sitting or laying down, and when approached too close, moving off just fast enough to keep at a safe distance, all of them with full bellies and acted very sleepy. I asked Jack what they were about, he said, "Them coyotes had a rabbit drive last night and now they are resting up and sleeping." I said, "Jack, do you want to see them run?" (Taking my pistol.) "They won't run far," said he. At the crack of the gun one tumbled down, the others that were near jumped to their feet, some trotted off a little distance, others merely glanced around and walked off a little way and squat down again.

52.—MOUNTAIN RAT, FOOD FOR INDIANS.

On one of my days out I came across an old Indian going home with his day's catch of rats. He had a large sheet iron camp kettie nearly filled with them. They had all been caught the night before by dead falls, as we call them, which consists of two sticks about three and a half or four inches long fastened together at their centers by a string that will allow them to spread apart about four or five inches in the shape of the letter "H." One of these, with any convenient flat rock heavy enough to smash and kill a rat, is one dead fall. This Indian had over a hundred of the triggers that he hadn't used, but said he had set the most of them.

His plan was to go up one side of the canyon, setting the traps wherever he saw the sign of rats, and the same down the other side. The next day, taking the same route, gathering the catch and resetting the traps. The rats the Indian had were six to eight inches long, two and a half inches wide and half an inch thick. They were packed as close as he could pack them in the kettle and were quite heavy for the old man to pack to camp, so I carried them for him. At his camp was where I first saw the squaws making rabbit skin robes. This is how it was done:

They had a lot of twine, that had been made of some fiberous bark or grass, and a pile of rabbit skins that had been dried and then rubbed pliable. But it must have been done with care, for a rabbit skin is very tender. These squaws were not making a new robe, but patching up and making an old one larger. The robes are of length to reach from the neck to about the middle of the thighs, say about three or four feet long, and wide enough to reach around the body at the shoulders.

One of the squaws was twisting the strips of skin around a twine that was stretched to two stakes, placed a little past the length of the robe, and as she proceeded the other was following her up and tying that fir rope thus made and laid alongside the previous one close together at about every four inches. They worked back and forth in this fashion till the skins were all used up. There was a strip about two feet wide of new robe attached to the old one. I examined it and found that the tie strings were placed in a straight line across the robe, with the ends of the ties left to attach more robe or to be used to tie the robe together as wanted.

When hung around the neck the person so clothed can stand in a hard rain or snow storm and not one drop of wet will pass through the robe. They are wind and rain proof and almost cold proof. There is no right or wrong side, as both sides are just the same—one solid piece of fir that will stand the wear of years, used as a mattress or bed covering or wind brake. In fact, they never completely wear out.

When the fur at any place gets worn off it is replaced with a few strands of new. This makes an old robe look striped and of different colors. The squaws while at work seemed as happy as a party of white women at a quilting and were talking and laughing just as fast. After spending some time chatting and smoking with the old man, he gave me the location of another family. I gave him a little tobacco and left them much pleased with my visit.

53.— THE ANTELOPE HUNT OR DRIVE.

I had sent word to the old chief (White Horse) that I would make him a visit in a few days, and to make it interesting to me he planned an antelope catch. For a few days before I came the squaws and bucks were busy repairing and extending the flanking arms of the old corral, or trap pen, which was located near the north end of antelope valley and about twenty miles northwest of Deep Creek. It was pretty cold weather, but no snow on the ground. The Indians thought it a good time and expected a good catch.

After they had all come in from their work a great deal of talking and planning was on and each knew just what part and place he or she was to take. By daylight all were ready for the start and, in fact, a number of the young men had left early in the evening before to go to the extreme south end of the ground to be covered and about twenty miles from the pen. They were to spread apart across the valley, travel in open order back to the north, being careful that not one of the antelope jumped would run, except in a northerly direction.

This valley has a good many hills or knolls along the base of the mountains and a few of them scattered more to the center of the level ground in the middle of the valley. An antelope, when started up, will always run directly for one of these, that lay opposite from where he gets his scare from, and they run from hill to hill. They see no one ahead of them but the party behind being constantly increased, and if they undertake to pass around the drivers a buck or squaw is sure to raise to his feet, and that sends them off to the center again.

Thus it goes till they come to the line between the outer ends of the arms, which, there, are about four miles apart, but gradually closing in as they get nearer the pen. The arms or leads are started at the extreme ends by simply prying or pulling up a large sagebrush and standing it roots up on the top of another brush, thus making a tall, black object visible for miles. The standing of these brush were at first some ten to twenty feet apart, but were placed more and more near together the nearer towards the pen, and when the two lines came to about one hundred yards apart they were built so the buts of the brush were as close as the tops would allow them to be joined and by this time both wings had swung to the east side of the valley, where there were many ravines to cross and plenty of cedar and pine to use for fencing.

There were many turns to the lane thus formed, but was getting narrower and stronger till finally, around a sharp turn through a large, thick bunch of cedars, the game were in the corral, which was about two hundred feet in diameter and built strong and high enough to withstand the charges of a herd of buffalo. The pine and cedar trees had not been removed from the inside of the pen, and not many from the runway, for a mile back.

Well, White Horse and myself rode the only two horses in the drive and we went to about half the distance to the ends

of the arms and were soon back as fast as possible on the
outside to take advantage of the bends and turns and to try
and keep abreast of the drivers, who were all on a fast run,
yelling like a pack of coyotes. The drive came to an end with
a rush and everyone working desperately closing up the entrance, a few small children appearing on the wall at different points around the pen. By the time we had tied our horses
and climbed to the top of the wall the entrance had been closed.

Then began the killing of as many as were wanted that
day, the killing was done with arrow and seldom missed pierc-
ing the heart. The catch was about twenty-five, mostly all
bucks or does, there being only five or six yearlings in the
bunch. There were five or six bucks killed that day and one of
which had tried to jump the fence, but got entangled in the
fence and was killed by having his throat cut with a knife.
The reason they were not all killed in one day was to give
the squaws time to cut up in thin strips the flesh and dry it on
a rack built over a small fire, thus curing it so it would keep
for a long time if kept dry.

The next morning I went to the pen with some of the Indians and found that there had been left three or four young
men to guard the place and see that none of the animals broke
through. The antelope had run themselves down and were hud-
dled in the center of the enclosure, most all laying down. The
Indians soon picked out five or six of the largest, which were
killed and soon on the way to camp to be made into jerked
meat, as it was called. The brains are seldom eaten, but carefully preserved to tan the hide with, by spreading them all
over the flesh side of the skin, after the hair has been removed,
rolling them up and leaving them this way for a few days,
when the skins may be washed clean and rung as dry as possible, then stretched and pulled and rubbed till dry, when they
are soft, white and pliable. Then they are ready for trade
or use.

The Indians told me that the last drive, before this one
at this place, was nearly twelve years ago and the old men
never expected to see another at this place, for it would take
many years for the animals to increase in sufficient numbers to
make it pay to drive. These drives are mostly in the desert
valleys, where the poor horseless natives live.

I have been with a number of hunting parties where most
of the hunters had horses. The last one was a few miles south
of where the drive I have just told about. There were ten on
horses and five or six foot men. When they arrived at the
edge of the hunting ground they divided into parties, one

going to the right and the other to the left and occasionally leaving a man, and so spacing them apart that when the two ends of the line swung around they formed a very large circle.

We could see where the antelope were running and the plan was to keep them in the circle and on the run all the time and not allow them to rest. When any of them attempted to pass out they were headed off and turned back or around the circle. We could not see an antelope halfway across the circle, but could see the dust they raised and the direction they were traveling.

When, after they had been kept running back and forth till they were very tired, a man would chase one on a fast run and as he neared another man would stop to rest his horse and watch for another run. The second man could run his horse alongside the antelope easily, which I did, and wished I had brought my lariat, as I could have caught him easily, but I shot him when at a distance of about eight or ten feet. There were only three killed and Jack was in high glee, for he said to the other Indians, "You see, it takes a chief to get the antelope." One was killed by him, one by "Antelope Jake," as he was called, a young chief, and one by myself.

54.— PINE-NUT HARVEST.

Jack and I were taking a scouting trip high up in the Shell Creek range of mountains, when we came across an Indian who, with his squaw and children, were busily engaged gathering pine-nuts. The man had a long pole with a strong hook fastened to one end. He would reach up in the tree to the pine cones, hook the crook around the branch on which they hung and pull branch and all down, the squaw and children carrying them to a place and piling them up in a heap. When they had collected as many as they wanted that day, the buck had finished his part of the work and could pass the rest of the time sleeping or hunting squirrels just as he pleased.

The squaws and children gathered a little dry brush, which was thrown loosely over the pile of cones and set fire to. The cones are thickly covered all over with pitch, for this reason they make a hot fire, the squaw watching and stirring it up as needed to keep the nuts from burning, as all she wants is to burn the pitch off. When this is done she rakes them back from the fire as a man would do when drawing charcoal.

When the pitch was all burned off the burs, or cones, the squaw spreads a blanket down close to the pile, then taking up one cone at a time, would press them end ways between

her hands, which opens the leaves, under which there were two
nuts to every leaf. Then shaking the cone over the blanket the
nuts would all fall out as clean as you please.

We stayed with them to see the finish, which was not so
very long. When the nuts had all been cleaned from the cones
they were put in a large basket that would hold over two
bushels and was nearly full, the squaw carrying that on her
back to a place where they were to be cached and left till
wanted. These caches were placed all through the pine-nut
grove to save carrying them too far and save time, for the
harvest does not last long, for a heavy frost will cause the
cones to open and the nuts drop to the ground, where the squirrels and coyotes feast on them.

A pine-nut cone looks like a green pineapple, but some
smaller and covered with pitch, that protects them from insects and squirrels. The Indians put them in caches holding
about ten bushels or less.

Once on a time when Jack and I were passing along a
range where there were a good many pine-nut trees, and as
we were getting hungry I asked him if he thought there was
any nuts cached there. He said he didn't think they were all
cleaned out and would look around. He was not long in locating one, and pushing the large stick of wood aside that
was placed on top of the small raise in which the nuts were
to be found, he moved off about six inches of dirt and found
a tight layer of cedar bark about two inches thick. He dug a
hole through this big enough to pass his arm through, which
he did, and pulled out a handful of very fine nuts, as fresh
as when first put in.

Well, we took about two gallons, covered and left the
cache as we found it, minus the few nuts taken.

55.— HUNTING FOR WATER.

In traveling through Go-Shute Valley (later called Flower
Lake Valley), we were getting very thirsty, having been traveling five or six hours from the last water hole and it being
a dry hot and sultry day I and the horses needed water.
The nearest I knew of was about twelve miles distance and
that not in the direction of our travel, and our one canteen
being empty, I thought we would have to change our course
to get water. I asked Jack, "How far to water this way,"
pointing the way I wanted to go. He said, "I do not know,
maybe no water. Well, are you thirsty?" "Yes." "Well
then, think fast and locate water or Indian no better than
white man."

We were about the middle of the valley, facing southeasterly, and were among the sand-dunes, which spread a few miles in width and many miles in length through the valley. We had not gone far after this talk when Jack said, "Wait," and pointing to some rat or gopher holes in the side of the sand-dunes, said, "They must have water, I see." Dismounting, he picked a place between the dunes and with his hands scraped off the loose sand to a depth of about six or eight inches to water. He then made the hole nearly a foot deeper and a foot wide, which quickly filled to the water level. Waiting for it to settle, we then tasted it and found it to be a little brackish, but still nice and cool and quite drinkable. Having drank what we wanted, filling the canteen, we let the horses have their turn. They got some, but soon caved the sand in and made the water so riley they would drink no more.

Jack filled the hole up and leveled the sand over it as it was before and said if he did not do it there could not be any more water ever found anywhere near there (Superstition), and I think he actually believed what he said.

Towards evening we were traveling along the foothills, going in the direction of where we knew there was a water hole five or six miles distance. Where we were the limestone formation lay very flat and in some places was washed clean of all soil for large areas and but few cracks or breaks all along the lower edge of these limestone beds.

I noticed that the grass and brush was thicker and stronger than farther down. I asked Jack if he thought we could get water near the edge by digging. "No," he said, "too deep; but wait, see the coyote tracks. They get water somewhere close to here." So hunting around a while I got off my horse and sat on a little raise watching Jack. He zig-zagged around till he had worked off about one hundred yards from me. I went to where he was standing and said, "Did you find water?" he said, smiling; "Come and see," leading the way to the bottom of a large saucer shaped swag, and what I saw was an oblong hole about four feet across the narrowest way and about twelve feet deep. There was eight or nine feet of water in it and so clear that we could see the bottom and sides very plainly and all the walls were solid limestone.

The water was cold and not a bit brackish, so I proposed to camp there that night. Jack said, "Yes," for he was very tired; but said, "We must go a little way off so the wild animals can come and drink." How were we to water the horses here? They could not reach it and if one fell in, it would be good-by, as we could never get him out, except in pieces. Well, we watered the horses and gave them all they wanted by using my hat for a bucket.

I noticed that all around the hole the surface was slanting towards it, except at one point where, when the hole was full and more rain or snow water came to it, it could flow on down to the sand valley below.

The next day we, having crossed the summit of the desert range of mountains, about noon, as we were riding along the base of the mountain or about half a mile above the white alkali desert (the most desolate and dreary country I ever saw) seeing a poor, pretty near hairless coyote, I asked Jack what he was doing so far from water. "Maybe not far," he said. "We will try and find his drinking hole." So in riding along he pointed up the mountain a little way and farther along our way to where the limestone ledges dipped at a very steep angle into the mountains, he said, "We will go along that way."

We came to a place where a thick ledge about thirty feet high hung over a thinner one that was about eight or ten feet high and from two to six feet from the higher one, that hung completely over it. Jack went to one end of the ledge, or to where he could get on top of the smaller ledge, gave a whoop and said, "Plenty of water." I was soon at his side and saw a pool of clear water (no scum or dirt) that extended from ledge to ledge and some thirty feet long. At the ends the bottom sloped toward the center, at which place there was no way to judge the depth, as the bottom could be seen only a few feet from the ends, but there was thousands of gallons of water held there, as good, too, as any you ever tasted. But let me tell you, a person might ride or walk within six feet of it and still think it was miles, and hot ones, to the nearest water. A tenderfoot would die of thirst leaning his back against the four-foot wall that separated him from enough water to supply an army. One could not see the least sign of water, every spot all around being sunburned and browned.

We, of course, camped a little way beyond after watering the horses the same as before (in my hat). I would depend on finding water at this place any time of the year, as there was now plenty, and it was in the fall that we were there and there could not be much lost by evaporation, and it was replenished by every rainstorm, the water draining in at the ends. The hole or crevasse would contain a good many thousands of gallons more before running over, so I think it safe to say that there was always plenty of water there.

When we were traveling in the direction of the sink of Deep Creek—that was about fifteen miles away—I knew of no water nearer in that direction, but knew of a small spring off to the right some five or six miles out of our way. Jack asked me for a drink out of the canteen. "There is only about half a pint in it," I said, shaking it, "we had better wait as long as we can before drinking it all." He said he had waited a long time and thought the water was better now than it would be when it got warmer, so it soon vanished.

After going a few miles farther and still thirsty I asked Jack if he was afoot and very thirsty which way he would go for water, trying to have him judge which way lay the closest. He stopped, and looking around, said his mother, when he was a little boy, had camped somewhere near where we were and when she went for water it was to one of the mounds that we could see scattered in the edge of the desert. So selecting a rather large one, about half a mile to one side, we rode to it. Jack got off his horse and made a complete circuit of it and said, "No water, but plenty coyote signs." I said, "You did not go over the top of the hill?" "No," he said, "wait, I go." He had not reached the top when he gave a yell and I knew he had found a water hole.

On going up I found it to be about two by six and about eight or nine feet deep, with about three feet of clear water in it, but hard to get at without a rope and bucket, but we managed to sink the canteen in it by tying a small stone to one side. We had a good drink and with a refilled canteen went on our journey.

56.—"SQUAWS CATCHING GROUND MOLES."

The ground squirrel, or large white bellied mole or gopher, are very numerous in some places on the bench lands along the mountains. One day, while taking a little exercise with Mr. Muncey, the telegraph operator, we rode along the foothills. When we came to the edge of fifteen-mile Creek Hollow and were going down to the creek we came to a ditch about eighteen inches wide and six or seven inches of water running, with a good ripple, to our right, the mountains being to the left. Muncey said, "Who in h—l done this. This water is running up hill." And so it appeared to be. "Well, let us follow it and see where it goes to."

We followed along the ditch until it came out onto the flat, where there was a division, making two streams. A little lower they were again divided. Then we could see about eight or ten squaws very busy, each with a stout stick, digging a trench and leading the water to a gopher hole. The gopher would soon make his appearance in a half-drowned state, get a rap on the head, then put in the sack at the back of the squaw, who would then turn the water into the next nearest hole, with the same result.

All of the squaws were hard at work the same way, making a very clean job of it, and very few would be left for a future drowning out. Muncey said he was going to time that young squaw. We saw her divide her part of the water in two streams, thus running it in two holes at the same time. Sometimes she would have three or four streams and then again but one, and according to Muncey's time she had caught between twenty-five and thirty in the half hour.

When we left them some of the squaws had over a half bushel in their sacks and quite a large field to go over yet. It would take a number of days to finish the job.

These rodents are skinned, gutter, then dried the same as beef, only they are dried whole, no bones being removed. Of course, they are also eaten fresh and stewed with Indian potatos and segos. I most fancy I could stomach to eat one. It's all in the way we were brought up. But I don't think I would starve to death if I could find a place where there was water and plenty of gophers, or any other animal I could drowned out, even a pole cat would save a man's life for a week or more. But I don't want to be caught wanting to try either.

Making Fire With a Stick.—On one of my trips with a comrade we camped for the night just before sundown and soon found out that we had no matches that were dry enough to light a fire with. That did not put us out much and we did not worry a bit, for we could soon make fire with our pistols, but just before we were ready to do it an Indian came up and squat down close to the little pile of wood we had collected.

Then the thought struck me that I would see if an Indian was always prepared to make a fire, so I said to him, "Make a good fire and I will give you something to eat." He jumped up and said, "Give me white fire stick." (Matches.) I told him, "No, they are all wet and no account, and Indian no good either if he could not make fire." He gave a grunt and proceeded to get busy.

He took a stick about eighteen inches long and the thickness of an arrow out of the quiver he carried his arrows in and another flat stick about six inches long, one-half inch thick and three-quarters to one inch wide, there being four or five counter-sunk holes in the flat piece about one-fourth inch deep. After rubbing some dry cedar bark with his hands till it was very fine, he placed the flat stick on the ground and one end of the long stick, which was at one end a little smaller, and putting the largest end in one of the counter-sunk holes, placed his hands together around the top of the stick, which he made to turn around back and forth very fast. As he worked his hands this way, at the same time pressing down all he could, it caused his hands to work down on the stick and he had to place them at the top very often. In about twelve or fifteen minutes he had a few tiny sparks of fire he had made with the sticks, burning the fine ground bark.

After that it was easy, but when the fire was lighted Mr. Indian was in a very sweaty condition. We did not begrudge him his supper, as we thought he had earned it and he seemed pleased to get it that way. I have seen an Indian make fire by simply rubbing two sticks together. This plan takes longer and harder work.

SEC. III—HARD EXPERIENCES.

57.—SAVED BY A RABBIT.

This was told me by one of the Pony Express riders whose ride was from Salt Lake City to Rush Valley. He passed the point of the mountain eighteen or twenty miles south of Salt Lake City, but as there was a heavy snowstorm raging he could not tell which way he was traveling. He knew that he had gone far enough to bring him to the river, if he had kept the right road. He went on till himself and pony were both about give out, then seeing no signs of a break in the storm, got off the pony to give both of them a little rest. The snow was quite deep and drifting.

Curling up beside a sagebrush he soon was sound asleep. He did not know just how long he had slept, but he did know that some animal had jumped across his face, that instantly brought him to his senses, and scrambling to his feet saw the rabbit that had awakened him.

He found that he was very numb and cold and had a time in getting blood circulation through arms and legs. His pony was standing with his head down and back to the storm, shivering like a man with the ague. He finally started again and after some time found a light. Going up to it he found that it shown out of the window of a farmhouse, the owner of which had just got up and started the morning fire.

Calling the man to the door, he inquired the way he should go to get on the right trail again. The man said, "Straight ahead." "Well, if I should go straight ahead I would ride through your door and as I have been riding all night I am very cold and would like to get warm by your fire and have a cup of coffee."

Well, after getting both and feed for the pony he went on and got through all right. The place where he found himself to be was close in the northeast corner of Utah Valley and if it had not been for the rabbit he was satisfied he would have gone to his last sleep.

58.—LOST AND FOUND, OR RIDING IN A CIRCLE.

Another pony express rider on the Salt Lake ride to Rush Valley made Cedar Fort (Fort Crittenden), in Cedar Valley.

It was snowing to beat the band. He got his next pony and started up the long slope toward Rush Valley, his home station. It was still snowing and blowing and it was impossible to see the road or any object to get his location, but finally it seemed that he was going down hill. He thought he had passed the summit and was now in Rush Valley, so hurried up the pony a little faster, but after a couple of hours of this he could not discover any familiar ground, so then he came to the conclusion that he was lost, not even knowing in which valley he was.

It was too cold to stop; he must keep moving. Which way? Why go straight ahead for sure? It would take him somewhere, so he kept going supposedly in a straight line. Just about daylight he discovered a light. Going towards it he soon saw plenty of lights and then some buildings that he recognized as belonging to Cedar Fort, the place he had left the evening before. He had made a complete circle around the valley. After eating a lunch and taking a fresh pony he made it through all right, for the storm had passed.

59.—AROUND A BUSH ALL NIGHT.

I left Ruby Valley station after breakfast. I was traveling west and with no companion except my pony. All went well and I arrived at Diamond Springs about 4 p. m., where I rested. Just after sundown I thought I would go to the next station, about twenty-five miles distance, from which I could next day finish my west trip and get back to Diamond Springs.

I had not traveled more than a couple of miles before it began to snow, and so fast that I could not see twenty-five yards in any direction, and soon the snow was so deep and it was so dark that every direction from where I was seemed to be up hill. After going far enough to take me across the valley I came to the conclusion that I was off the right trail and no need to go further till I could see some landmark to go by.

It had turned very cold and I was quite wet, there was nothing to make a fire of. I was somewhere in Moon Shine Valley, as it is called, on account of its white soil and very short shad-scale greece wood brush, which makes it appear as if the moon or sun was shining upon it when there is no moon or sun visible.

I needed rest, so did the pony, but how could I get rest and not freeze. I got off the pony, made a loop in the end of my riding rope, put this around the stoutest bush I could find, took hold of the pony's tail, driving him round and round.

When I would get a little warmer by this exercise I would squat down a few minutes, but the cold would soon set the pony to shivering (me, too), and then round and round again. Oh! What a night and would it ever end? I had hard work to keep from laying down and going to sleep. Well, if I had— but I didn't.

Just about daylight I saw a little blue sky right up in the center of my circle and after a little while a number of clear places. I was now on the pony riding around the bush, but watching at all points for a view of the mountains. Finally, just before sunrise I located east by the light and of course I then knew which way to look for the mountains.

Very soon after this the clouds broke away and I had a full view of the range on the west side and found that I was some five miles to the south of the trail and two or three from the west side of the valley. The first thing to do was to get to the trail, which I did by a straight line to the foot of the mountains. I could not see the road here, but that did not worry me, I knew the mountains.

A few years after that I was crossing this same valley with a few others, when one of them said, "See that lone young mountain way out there in the middle of the valley, I would like to go on top of it to see what it is made of." And he said, "Did you ever visit it?" I said, "I may have rode around it, but I certainly did not go to the top." "Well, if you rode around it you certainly know if it is a limestone or granite knob." "No." I told him of my night around a bush. That explained why I did not know.

SEC. IV.—INDIAN CRUELTIES IN PEACE AND WAR.

60.—THE OLD MAN LEFT TO DIE.

There is a little spring of very brackish and warm water about a mile north of Fish Spring station and a few rods below the road. Between this spring and the road the Indians had selected as the place to leave a very old man to die. He was totally blind and very poor, hardly any flesh on his bones. He was clad with only a very old and small strip of rabbit skin robe hung about his neck.

The Indians had gathered some sagebrush and made a small semi-circle about two feet high. He was led to the spring and back to the circle and left to die of starvation. Father heard of this from one of the stage drivers and the first time he passed that way was prepared to supply the old man with food and blankets. He told the driver to drive out of the road to the old man's camp.

When they arrived there the old man was down to the spring with his hands down in the water, which was literally alive with fish that were about two inches in length. When he could feel one of them touch the inside of his hands he would grab them and immediately eat them. That was the only way of keeping himself alive.

Father raised him from the spring and tried to make him understand that he would give him something to eat and a blanket to keep him warm. But he soon found that the old man was very deaf and did not seem to understand a word. Father got him back to his camp, gave him enough food to last several days, also a gallon can of water, placed a good new blanket around him and left the old man eating very sparingly of the food, as if to make it last as long as possible.

Father went on his way west, but left word with the stage driver to bring food for him after that every time he passed that way. On his return trip, when he met the driver he asked him about the old man. He said, "He is still alive, but the blanket, water can and grub was gone the first time I passed there. I have left him food every trip. He seems to be some stronger than when we first saw him.

Father got another blanket, more food and a water can, and when he arrived at that place found the old man sound asleep, curled up about as a dog would for a nap, and getting him awake and placing the bread in one hand and the other on the can of water with the blanket around him left him to himself again.

Father was planning to have the old man moved near the station, where he could be fed at regular times and provided with more shelter and clothing and with means of having a fire when necessary, as the weather was getting quite cold. Too late, for on his next trip out he learned that the old Indian had been taken away and everything that had been given him and even the small semi-circle wind-brake had been burned.

Father's generosity had not been appreciated by the old man's relatives, or the band of Indians that he belonged to, so they made it impossible for him to prolong the life of the old man, who ought to die, and would very soon if let alone.

61.—HOW A YOUNG BUCK GOT HIS WIFE.

It was Willow Spring Bill, as he was called, as he had been working here for some time as chore boy. The band of Indians he belonged to lived in the country around Fish Springs. He was very saving of what little money or clothing he got and finally traded for a small bore Kentucky rifle, that had the tube or nipple broken off, therefore useless to the Indian he got it from.

He brought it to me, knowing that I usually had a few extra tubes on hand. He asked me if I would put on one for one antelope skin. That was the usual price.) "Let me see the skin." "No. I can't get it till you fix my gun so I can shoot antelope." Well, I fixed the gun without taking his note.

About two weeks after I got the skin and traded for a couple more that he had, giving him a few rounds of ammunition, a shirt and a red handkerchief, which he said he wanted to catch a squaw with. He had quit the station. He was now past chore boy. He was a man.

I did not see him again for two or three months, when I chanced to be at Willow Springs. Bill came to the station, a young and good looking squaw at his heels. "Hello, Bill, you catch squaw?" "Yes." "Where you catch him?" "Me catch squaw over to Shell Creek." "When you catch him?" "Two sleeps me catch him. Me go home, Fish Spring."

The young squaw seemed to be very bashful. I asked her if she loved Bill. "Yes," she said, "him very good man, very much like him." And she acted as if she did and I have no doubts but she did. But, oh! the difference between white and red people!

I afterwards learned from other Indians just how Bill proceeded to get his wife. She lived in the Shell Creek country with her father, there being no more of the family or relatives left. The father had lost one eye. He was getting old and feeble, so the young girl had a hard time of it gathering enough food for both. There had been many a young buck that wanted her for a wife, but the old man had always driven them off. Well, one day the young Indian Bill made his appearance at the old man's camp and commenced to lay siege to the girl's heart. He made that camp his home and helped out the food supply with game. This went on a month or more. The old man still said no one should take the girl from him. But Bill soon solved the problem. There is no way of finding out just what agreement was made between the boy and girl, but this is what happened:

One afternoon, after coming in from hunting, Bill took his gun all apart and cleaned and oiled it up in fine shape. Then he loaded it ready for work. The girl was busy shelling nuts, the old man sound asleep on the sunny side of the camp, with his face towards Bill, who aimed his gun at the old man's good eye and fired. The ball passed through the eye and the brain, too, killing the old man instantly.

The marriage ceremony was completely over. Bill coolly reloaded his gun, turned to the girl and said, "Come," and the girl picked up her blanket and followed her lord and master and was willing to do so as long as life lasted.

It was two days later that I had seen them at Willow Springs on their wedding tour, apparently as happy as a couple of love-sick millionaires could be and live. All they owned on earth they had on, or carried in their hands. Not much to start married life with, but then they were Indians, whose wants are few.

62.—THE CROSS INDIAN.

Our pack train, of half a dozen mules and three men, camped for the night near a small spring that was in the west side of the valley. We had got the mules all picketed on the best grass we could find about there and that was not very good. I was just starting a fire when there appeared three Indians coming towards us at a lively walk. "See boys," said I, "we are going to have visitors and they seem to be in a hurry to arrive before supper time."

They came along in single file, the leader, the biggest buck of the three, coming to within about eight feet of me before stopping or saying a word, or making a sign. They were well armed with bows and arrows, which they seemed to want us to see and probably fear when we saw them, but the fear didn't come from our side. Then straightening up high as possible and with a very important pose, pointed with one hand to a blanket that was thrown over a saddle, then slapped his own breast.

I knew what he wanted, but I asked him (in Indian) what he wanted He took a good look at me as if suprised at my Indian talk, but said, "I want a blanket, and shirt, and flour, and (looking around) meat, and coffee, and sugar, and matches, and powder, and bullets."

I let him get through with his wants and as he had not mentioned saddles or mules I asked him if he did not want them, too. After taking another good look at me, he said, "No white man wants them." I said, "Why do you want all this you have spoken about?" "White man steal Indian water, burn Indian wood, steal Indian grass (swinging his hand around), all mine. Hurry give me blanket." "Wait, who gave you that water, that grass?" He answered, "I always had it."

I said, "Now you lie, for that grass grows every year." "I don't lie, for all this land with the game and water is mine and I don't lie." "Well, what little water and grass we get would not do you any good, for the water would run away and the grass all dry up." "It ain't that way now, give me blan——"

"Stop your talk and if you want more than bullets sit right down there and wait a little while." Sigh. "White man mad." "No, but why did you ask for so much for nothing?" "Indian hungry." "Why didn't you say so the first thing." "I didn't know you would understand."

"Well, I don't know if you will understand me when I say to you that you cannot scare any of these white men and you had better sit down and wait till they have a mind to give you something to eat." He gave a grunt and sat down with the others where I had pointed.

I told the boys that if they would get supper that I would take care of the natives, as we wanted no trouble if it could be avoided. After they had seated themselves so they could watch every move in the camp,, I heard one of them say, "These men are mad." I said, "Yes you talk to much snake." (Meaning forked tongue or lieing).

After awhile I filled and lighted my pipe then handed it to the nearest Indian, who passed it to the one next, who drawed three or four whiffs of smoke, then passed it back to me. I took my share and the pipe passed back to the other end of the line and came as before and was repeated till the tobacco was all burned, when one of the Indians cleaned all the ashes out and passed the pipe back to me and said, "Good."

After we had eaten our supper there was enough left (intentionally) to give the bucks a good fill. After the pipe had done its work again, as it was getting late, I told the boys I would go and change my mules to better feed and when I came back they could tend to their animals.

Making the change, I started back and up jumped a rabbit not over twenty feet from me. He sat up quite straight, his side toward me, a good mark. I could not resist the temptation of a try at the bright eye. I fired and as luck would have it (I was noted for being lucky), almost centered that eye, and as the other eye was almost directly opposite it was not my fault that it went in the same direction. I took the rabbit to camp and threw it down by the Indians. "There, I will give you my rabbit. You may take it to your camp and eat it in the morning."

I then reloaded my pistol, the Indians watching every move, They took the rabbit up and held it side ways to see how it must have stood to get both eyes knocked out at the same time. One of them said, "Good shoot, and he could shoot more with his little gun without loading again."

When the Indians were ready to go home I gave them a little piece of tobacco, a dozen matches and a cup of flour apiece, and said, "This is for friends and not to pay Indians for water or grass that belong to anyone that can use it, understand?" "Yes, chief talk heap good. Me big friend, good chief. Me come back (pointing to where the sun would be at about 7 o'clock next morning). Have more big talk."

Well, we moved early next morning and I did not see the Indian again for over a year, but when I did see him was when all the Indians had collected to get their annuities the Indian agent was expected to give them. When all were ready for the pow-wow, or big talk, I sat on a pile of logs with a number of Indians that I was well acquainted with, when a large buck came up to me, held out his hand and said "Good friend." "Yes," I said, "but I don't remember you, for I don't see you much." Then one of my friends said, "This is the man that tried to scare you to give him blankets." "How do you know?" "All Indians know." "He told it himself." "What did he say?" "He said he did not know you was Big Chief's son, but soon found out that you would not scare and made him much afraid, but as soon as he could understand that you could talk some Indian he remembered that he had heard of you, and when you shot that rabbit through the eyes he was sure you was a chief and the Indian's big friend."

63.—THE INDIAN OUTBREAK.

This was, as I afterwards learned from the Indians that were left alive when peace was declared. General Conner had given a band of Sho-sho-nee Indians a good example of bravery by attacking a large party of them that were fortified at Battle Creek, southern Idaho.

He came near getting the whole bunch, but there was some eighteen or twenty that made their escape and, of course, wanted

**Howard Ransom Egan,
as he appeared shortly after these
experiences.**

revenge. They got the idea of attacking the enemy by a flank movement, which they proceeded to carry out by traveling around the north end of Great Salt Lake to the Go-Shute country and scaring them by bragging of the large number of their tribe that would come out there and clean them all out, as well as the whites.

I did not hear of this till all was over. I was out two or three days with Egan Jack, an Indian friend of mine, on a prospecting trip. He was not much of a rider, having never owned a horse, and I used to jibe him about his horsemanship. And at one time, while we were crossing a nice, level piece of ground, I let him see how a rope that was being dragged by a running horse could be picked up by a man on another horse without stopping or dismounting. Also how some Indians that were used to horses could ride on the horses' side so that only one hand or foot could be seen from the other side.

These demonstrations so pleased Jack that at every level piece of ground he wanted to see it again, but did not attempt it himself. When we arrived at the Indian camp about sundown and about one mile from our destination I learned during the evening that there were some Sho-sho-nee Indians that had their camp adjoining the Go-Shute camp. All were in a thick grove of pine timber.

After the squaws had watered and hobbled our horses on good feed, in plain sight of us, and we had eaten our supper and with a few of the leading men were sitting around the camp fire smoking and talking, I said, "Why don't your Sho-sho-nee friends come and talk and smoke?" "Maybe my friends won't come." Well I said, "Tell them I want to talk to them."

They sent a boy to tell them that the white man wanted to talk with them. The boy returned and said, "They said, 'if white man wanted to talk, to talk to their dogs.'" I told the boy to go to them again and tell them, "I was no Sho-sho-nee, and did not talk dog talk, but would see them in the morning." The boy went, but soon came back with the news that the Sho-sho-nee said that they would steal our horses that night.

Jack asked me what I was going to do about it, for he said he thought they would try to get the horses. "What would you do, Jack?" said I. "Go home tonight," he said. "Are you afraid of them?" "No, they would not hurt me, but no friends of white men." "Well, call the boy once more." Now, boy, go tell them Indians just what I say, that there is my horses (pointing to them) and if they want to steal them to go ahead, but they must take them through the air, so as to leave no tracks, or I would get my horses and them, too."

After the boy had gone I asked Jack if he would stick by me. He said, "Yes, my friend, talk good." I soon noticed a couple of young bucks sitting on the hillside quite close to our horses. I asked Jack what they were there for. He said to shoot Indian if he came to steal horses. "They won't come," I said. "I don't know," he said. "I do," said I, "for that kind of talk with a split tongue is no good and they are cowards, you will see." And sure enough when morning came we found that they had left during the night.

After visiting the prospect we went home. I heard nothing more of the Sho-sho-nee for about two weeks, when one evening our chore boy, Dan, said that there was nine or ten Indians at the Indian Camp, which was about one thousand yards south-east of the station, Deep Creek, and he wanted to go and hear what they had to say. He asked me if he might take the wagon cover he usually used for a bed in one corner of the kitchen. I told him no, but he could go and hear and then come back and sleep in the kitchen, for he must have a very early breakfast as we were going to have a cattle drive tomorrow and must start early. "Me bring cover back early," said Dan. I looked at him sternly and said, "Dan, I don't like anyone to lie to me and I do not like your actions a little bit. He went and that was the last time I ever saw Dan.

Well, as the Indian riders that I had engaged to help in the drive did not come for their supper that was promised them I felt very suspicious that something was brewing at the Indian Camp and I immediately made the round of the station to size up the situation. I found the telegraph operator sitting by the instrument facing the window, his lamp shining on him so as to make him a good mark to shoot at a hundred yards distance. I guess he was some scared when I told him this and I also asked him if he had any shooting irons and if they were loaded. "Good Lord, no. I forgot to load up after cleaning my gun. Why, what is the matter?" "Maybe nothing, but I don't like the way the Indians are acting. You had better hang a blanket up at that window or work in the dark. And you might as well tell other stations that the Indians here are having a pow-wow with some strange Indians that are not friendly to the whites."

Then I went back to the house. There was two six-light windows on either side of the kitchen door. In looking through there the cook or anyone else in the kitchen could be seen plainly by anyone on the outside. No blinds at the windows and two large lamps burning inside, making the whole interior show up plainer than by daylight.

After seeing that every thing was understood and set right here I went to the bunkhouse. Here I found it some better for there was a curtain up at the window, as there was most always a driver slept there in the day time. There were three guns none of them loaded, but plenty of ammunition for them. They were soon ready for use and placed in a handy position. The next place was the blacksmith shop, about fifty yards east of the station, where the smith usually slept when the weather was warm. He was soon on his way to the sitting room or our parlor that was between my room and the dining room. I had blinds up at every window.

I set a guard to watch the Indian camp, for I knew that if they meant any mischief they would first send their squaws and children away. I told the boys to keep a good watch on the camp and if they saw a single tent go down to let me know at once, for there would soon be trouble. I stayed up myself till a little while before daylight. I needed some rest and sleep, so laid down on the floor in front of the fireplace and with my clothes on, as did some of the other boys, for most all were together.

About the first break of day the smith gave me a gentle touch and said, "The Indian's tents are going down." I jumped up and said, "Someone of you run to the stable and saddle my horse and bring him out, and you may as well saddle up the whole bunch, to save them from being burned in the stable.

I told the boys, "H—l was cut loose, but if they would stand out there a little way apart I would ride over to the nearest group and try to find out what was in the breeze and why the ones that were going to help us drive had not come. And if I should fire or any of the Indians did, to turn loose and see how many they could get before they got out of range.

I rode straight towards the middle of their camp ground, but seeing a couple of bucks about fifteen feet apart and a little to the left of my line of traveling, I turned to the left to bring them on my righthand side, which I considered was the handiest in case of trouble.

I did not stop till I reached a point about sixteen feet from the two and as near to one as the other. I recognized the right-handed one was Jack, although he was dressed for traveling. The other I knew to be a Pa-Van-Ute named Tung-a-Shump, whose country was south of Provo, Utah. I did not know he was here at this time. He carried a large bore, buffalo gun, which I could see below his short blanket, his right side toward me. He faced Jack, who faced him, and his left side toward me. Jack's rifle laid across his left arm, in position for immediate use if necessary.

I asked Jack where the boys were that was going to help me drive the cattle. No answer. I said, "What is the matter here?" still no answer. I rode a few steps past the Pa-Van-Ute, when Jack said, "Where are you going?" I stopped my horse and said, "After the cattle, but why don't you talk?" Still no answer.

Well, I tell you by this time I was thinking pretty fast and wishing I was back with the boys. I started again, turning in my saddle so as to watch both Indians, and not let them get the start of me if there was going to be fun, and I thought there was. As I started Jack spoke again and said, "Where going?" I said, "Home." Not stopping this time, Jack said, "Ride side horse fast."

I knew what he meant for me to do, so after going in that direction as far as I could without going farther away from home I suddenly turned and dropping to the right side of my horse, went as fast as I could to the station.

I told the boys, "It is all off with the Indians and we will have to do the driving ourselves if we can find any stock to drive, which I doubt." While we were laying plans for our next move we saw nine or ten bucks in single file go over the bluff in the direction of eight-mile station.

"No more danger here at present," I said, "so now who will go with me to see if we can find any animals left on the range?"

Jerome Kenney and another boy volunteered to go. I left word for the rest to keep their eyes open and not be surprised or caught asleep, for I felt sure we might be attacked yet. The three of us had not gone over three-quarters of a mile when we came to the place in the road where the Indians the night before had bunched all our loose horses, twenty-four, and one mule, to catch what they wanted to ride and had taken the direction that would take them between our station and Eight-Mile station.

After seeing this we rode on, zig-zagging this way and that way so as not to run into a trap, if any was laid to catch us. In this way we proceeded for about eight miles, not seeing a single animal till we came to a deep ravine that was wide and flat at the bottom. As soon as we came to the edge, where we could see the bottom, there, just below us, laid a freshly killed animal. The top side had been skinned and the front and hind legs cut off, all the rest left as the animal had fallen shot. They must have placed a guard, that saw us coming and left in time to keep out off sight, for we did not even get a glimpse of an Indian. If we had, there might have been something doing.

While we were holding council as to our next move one of the boys noticed a big smoke just rising in the west. "Look there, what does that mean?" "It means dead men and burnt station." I said, "for that is about where Eight-mile is and now I know what to do, for the Indians have driven off every animal they could find, so we will go home at once, but by another route, and we may find some animals they missed."

We went on our way back, frequently changing the direction and at last coming in sight of home, we could see that every man there was out watching for our return, and when we rode up to the station there laid the stage driver dead, stretched out in the dooryard, and one of his passengers in the sitting room. He had been shot in the head, but was still alive. There had been four passengers—two men and two boys—sons of the wounded man, who had been riding outside with the driver.

When the coach came within sight of Eight-Mile they could see a bunch of Indians standing around the door, not an unusual sight, so the driver did not hesitate in driving, as usual, until he had come to about twenty-five yards of the house. Then he saw a white man lying in the doorway as if dead. He immediately plied his whip and turned his team so as to get no closer to the house, but to strike the road some distance beyond.

The Indians seeing this move, opened fire at once and the first shot to take effect hit the passenger in the head and he slid down into the boot. The next moment the driver was shot through the body. He fell on top of the other man. He had not lost grip on the lines, but used the ends of them for a whip to keep the horses running as fast as they could go, at the same time calling the other passengers to crawl out and drive, as he was shot and could not guide the team.

The passenger said afterwards that he did not know how he got to the driver's seat, but he did, and taking the lines from the driver's hands, told him he would drive." "Well, make them go as fast as you can, for they are following us on horseback." Those were his last words. The man could not see anyone following, for they had given up the chase.

When he arrived at the end of the lane, about half a mile west of Deep Creek, he stopped the team, for he could see a small bunch of people in front of the house and he was afraid they were

Indians. After considering the matter over he drove on up and stopped in front of the door and commenced telling the boys of his experience, when one of the little passenger boys called for help to get his father from under that big man that was crushing him down so he could not get out.

They got the dead driver out and laid him beside the door, where he was when we got back. The other man, when they saw that he was still alive, they carried into the house. This man lived and when well enough to travel went east to his home and friends, although he had lost about a tablespoonful of his brains. The driver, to go east, had started about one hour before we got home, as the operator said, Fish Springs was all right, there seemed to be no danger that way.

It now being late in the afternoon, we decided to waite till morning to further investigate affairs. Next morning very early three or four of us went up to Eight Mile and the sight I saw there made me "D——n an Indian, anyhow," and I said, "I would not try to learn another word or even speak another word of their lingo without it was in case of an emergency," and I have tried to keep my word ever since.

Eight Mile Station was built of adobes, two rooms about sixteen feet square and sixteen feet apart. The space between the rooms was covered the same as the rooms. The doors of these rooms opened in the center of this space. The north room was the kitchen and bunk room. The south room was the granary and full of sacked grain at this time.

The stables were east of the house about fifteen feet, parallel to them and of the same length. They were joined to the house by a wall at each end about six feet high. The swayle in which ran the creek was close back of these buildings.

The cook was lying just outside of the space between the rooms, stripped, scalped and cut all over his body. They had even cut his tongue out before, or after, death, I don't know which, but I think it was before, because they had dobbed his face with blood and then covered that over with flour to make him a white man again.

We had some trouble in finding Mr. Wood, who was the Overland Mail hay-stacker, in haying time, and hustler the rest of the year—a good steady young man. After about one hour hunting around, we found him. He laid about seventy-five yards north of the house and about thirty yards west of the road in the rabbit brush. They had taken off every stitch of clothing and left him as naked as he was when born. They had not cut and slashed his body as they had the other man's, probably because they had killed him before they got him. There were three or four broken arrows left near his body. They had been pulled out of him so as to get his clothes off.

Some of the boys said they had been shot into him after he fell. "No, I said, "he must have been shot with arrows at the first break, but they did not prevent him from running, and when he had got this far away from them he received the fatal shot."

There was a very large wound in the center of his breast. We turned him on one side to look at his back, and there, square in the center, between the shoulder blades was a large hole. It was some smaller than the one in the breast, but yet so large it must have been made with an ounce ball. "D—n that Pah-Van-Ute," I said, "he did this with his big bore buffalo gun, and I would bet all I have that I am right in my suspicions.

He was a good shot, so I had heard, but that he had any cause for revenge on the white man I did not know at that time, and of course did not hear till some time after peace was made. And here I will tell what I afterwards learned from the Indians.

When they saw me coming from the station and alone, the Pah-Van-Ute jumped up and said, "White man coming. I will kill him!" Jack had then jumped up and got in the position as I found them and said, "All right, you kill him, I kill you." Jack said afterwards, that he would not have waited till I was killed but as the Indian made no move to raise his gun, he did not want to shoot him. Well, if he had made a move to raise his gun it would have been useless for Jack to have wasted his ammunition, or, if he had made a move to change the position of his gun, I would not have answered for the consequences, but when Jack finally spoke, I knew I did not have him to deal with.

Well, we had now seen enough and rode back to the station. On the way back we took a different route, and came to the place where the Indians had crossed the creek with our horses. Here laid one that they had shot, probably because he would not carry bare-back, and would most always buck when the saddle was put on, but after his little jumping was over he was a splendid little riding pony and was as tough as a knot.

That evening a party took tools and went up to Eight Mile and buried the men just where the cook was found, in front of the house. The driver was buried just as he was dressed when shot. He lies about one-half mile east of Deep Creek Station.

After about a week's time we had hunted and found two or three cows with young calves. We had in the corral at the time of the break, twelve milch cows and calves. When hunting the range we had seen five or six of our Spanish beef cattle. These were all that was left out of fifty, and they were so wild we left them to roam where they pleased, for no Indian or white man could come in sight of them on foot without being attacked and gored, unless he laid flat down and then he might be rolled a little, but if he laid still they would go away. They had never been handled in any other way than by horsemen, and took a person afoot for a wild animal.

I remember of a strange Indian one day coming to the station in a very mad state of mind and demanding a blanket, a shirt and ammunition to pay him for being pounded, and his shirt and blanket torn by one of them as he was coming down the valley. "Well, had you ever heard that they would not hurt if you would lie down and keep still?" "No, and I don't believe it, for he kept trying to get his horns through me, and I tried to shoot him, but my gun had lost its cap and I could not shoot, and when I tried to crawl away he would come at me again."

Well, I gave him a shirt and told him to keep out of the way of the cattle, for if they killed him I would not give him anything more. He was satisfied, and said, "All right."

64.—BURNING OF CANYON STATION.

After the California volunteers had been placed along the mail line to guard the station from being attacked by the Indians, a small squad was scouting around government springs and about fifteen or twenty miles south of Simpson Springs, and in the same range of mountains. They ran onto an Indian camp and killed all that were in camp, men, women and children, leaving none to tell the tale.

When Peah-namp (the old Pah-Van-Chief), came home in the evening, he found that the soldiers had been to his camp and killed his wife and papoose and all the rest that had been left in the camp, and he had thought the whites were friendly as he was. This was too much to overlook, so he took his few men and went west to his wife's country (she was a Go-Shute), and hunted up her relations and planned for revenge.

After holding a council it was decided to attack either Willow Spring or Canyon Station, and as Canyon Station was in the mountains, and also as was reported, more men were there, it was decided to do what they could to leave it in a worse condition than the Pah-Van camp had been left. So, making their camp about three miles south, they sent two men to size up the situation. They were to go as close as they could without being seen. They did, and back they came and reported that there were five or six men there that slept in the barn where the four horses were, but the men went to the house in the ground to eat their food, and do not take their guns with them.

They had reported the situation just as it was, and the next morning before day-light they were all around the station and within easy gun shot of it. On one side there was a small ravine, not more than fifteen yards away, and on the other side another larger one a little further off.

The barn was nearest the small ravine, where they prepared their fire arrows, to shoot into the canvass roof, which they done as soon as the first gun was fired on the other side. The Indians waited till the men had been called to breakfast in the dug-out, and were all down in the hole without their guns, all except the hostler, William Riley, who was currying a horse just outside the north door of the stable at the time of the first alarm, and he was shot through the ankle and the bone broken short off. He started down the canyon on the run, but did not get far before he was caught and killed.

The men at breakfast were mostly all killed as they came out of the dug-out to reach their arms that were stacked in the south end of the barn. Not one of them ever reached his gun. One man, though wounded, tried to escape by running down the canyon as Riley did. He got further away, but was caught and killed, and, as he was some bald on the top of his head, and a good growth of whiskers on his chin, they scalped that and left him where he fell. Riley they dragged back to the wood pile, threw him on and set fire to it. When the boys went up there they gathered his bones that were left, put them in a small soap box, and buried them where they had found them.

The Indians got four head of horses, as much of the harness as suited them, all the guns and ammunition that was there, also all the provisions and cooking utensils that they thought worth carrying away, and every thing else they burned. They took the clothes off of every man and left them just where they fell all this had been done without a shot being fired by the whitemen. A most complete surprise and massacre.

65.—JESSE EARL'S DEATH.

The Indians had run off a band of horses from the Deep Creek range that belonged to a man named Kennedy. Father was in Salt Lake when he received a telegram of what had been done. He was not long in picking up a few of the range boys around the saloons that were supposed to be brave fighters, and some others, among the latter Mr. Earl. They started west, all on horse back except Mr. Earl and Father, who rode in a covered spring wagon. They lost no time and were traveling by forced marches. Father and Earl took turns at driving the two mule team, the horse-men usually riding behind the wagon.

All went along all right till they arrived at a point a little ways down the canyon and east of where afterwards Canyon Station was burned. Father and Earl had just changed positions. The back curtain was loose and sometimes it was raised by the wind so as to give a good view inside to those that were riding behind.

This was the case at the point named, when a man, nicknamed Buffalo Bill (I have forgotten his name), so called after the famous scout of the early days, rode up close to the wagon and, as the curtain flapped up he shot Mr. Earl in the back, killing him instantly. The other riders had fallen back and did not see the shooting or know what had been done till they came up, which they soon did after hearing the shot, and when they saw what had occured they were in for killing Bill on the spot.

Father asked him if he had not made a mistake and killed the wrong man, He said, "It was an accident." He was examining his pistol to see if it was in good working order when his thumb slipped off the hammer. He did not intend to shoot at all." Well, there was a doubt, and they gave him the benefit of it; but he was closely watched after that with the intention of giving him over to the officers on their return to Salt Lake.

On the return trip he disappeared in the night at Simpson Springs. He was afterwards killed by a sheriff's posse near Fort Bridger, who wanted him for horse stealing and murder. He held the posse at bay with his two large revolvers, threatening to shoot the sheriff if he made a move towards him. The sheriff told his men to fire but they were afraid Bill would kill them, so held their fire till he had backed off a considerable distance when the bunch raised their guns and fired all at the same time. Bill dropped to the ground and in doing so lost his pistols.

When they came up to him he was feeling around for them for he had been shot blind but would have found them if they had not been kicked out of his way. He soon died, his last words were, "By h—l, I will have a lead mine of my own when I get to H—l." Every shot fired at him had taken effect. Jesse Earl was taken down to Deep Creek and buried there.

The Kennedy horses were never recovered, but one of the men in the party, that was sent to try and get them, shot one of his arms off while trailing his gun through the brush in the canyon where the horses had been driven through. This satisfied Father of the value of a "City Rough" in an Indian country, for he said, "He would not give a half dozen of his mail boys for a hundred saloon bred Roughs." He never hired any more of that sort, but instead, it was the farm boy that he wanted, and he generally got what he wanted.

66.—THE INDIAN, NO LEGS.

On my way to Fish Springs with supplies for the station I staid over night at Simpson's Springs. It was there that I first heard of the "Indian no legs." The boys said, he had left there yesterday morning to cross the desert to Dug Way Mountains, and said they did not believe he could make it and would die on the desert of thirst.

I was traveling alone, I had two mules and an ambulance, or mud-wagon, as we called it, and had quite a heavy load. The roads were dry and dusty and it was very warm during the middle of the day. I started about six in the morning and by eight o'clock was some eight or ten miles from Simpson's, when I discovered something moving some distance ahead and keeping to one side of the road and bobbing up and down apparently in the same place.

On looking down at the road for tracks I saw what might have been made by setting down a flat bottom basket in the dust and repeating the operation on every foot of the distance along the road. Of course when I saw this I knew what it was that I could see ahead, and hurried up my team and was soon along side of the man, who had turned just out of the road to let me pass.

I stopped, and asked him, where he was going? He said he was going to the Indian camp over to that mountain, (Pointing to a place about fifteen miles away). I asked him how long it would take him to go there. He said, " One day and one half day. You got water?" He asked me. I said, "Yes. have you?" "Just a little bit, will you give me some?" "Yes, have you anything to eat?" He had a small piece of bread that the boys had given him. "Are you tired?" "Yes, Indian all the time tired."

I said, "I would give you a ride if I could get you up there" (pointing to a place back of my seat.) "Me go alright," he said. How he did it I do not know, but he got to the place I had pointed to as quick as I could have done it, and as I started along he seemed as tickled as a little child on his first ride, and would watch the brush go by as fast as it did before he lost his legs, which was some fifteen years before.

He told me that he lost his legs by having them frozen, when he was caught in a blizzard, and a doctor had to cut them off to save his life. I thought it would have been better for him if the doctor had not cut them off for then he would have saved a good deal of suffering. I asked him if the Indians ever helped him to travel. He said, "No they have no horses and can't carry me every where they go." "Do they give you food?" "Yes when I am at their camp, but not at any other time." How do you carry food and water enough across a place like this we are crossing?" "See I carry water in this, (holding towards me a willow water jug that would hold about one gallon).

Just think of that, crossing a twenty-five or thirty mile desert, one foot at a jump and in the hottest weather, with only one gallon of water and that as hot as the weather. What little food he left the camp with he made to last as long as possible by catching mice or the chipmunks that he could reach with his stick or dig out of their holes when he saw them go in. What a life! No, thank you, not for me.

I had went about ten miles from where I had caught up with the Indian when he asked me to stop as he wanted to go that way (pointing off to the right to a place about five miles away). As I could drive no nearer I stopped the team and before I could get to help him he had taken hold of the side of the wagon and swung his body over the side and dropped to the ground all smiles and talking as fast as he could make his tongue travel and that was not slow.

I gave him his bottle full of water, and all of my dinner, a hand full of matches and my big red cotton handkerchief. He seemed a very proud Indian. I asked him when he would get to camp. He said, "Sun-rise tomorrow."

Now when he started off I noticed that he twisted his body at every jump, placing one end of his stout stick on the ground by his side, and by force of his arms, lift his body, and at the same time shove it ahead about one foot or less. This he could repeat very fast which made it look to me as if his body was moving ahead all the time.

He had a raw-hide sack arrangement which was made to fit around his body fastened around him above the hips. The sole or bottom of this sack was made of the thickest hide, I do not know if he had any soft material in the bottom or not, but I presume he had, or how could he stand the shock of jumping out of the wagon? or the continual bump, bump, while traveling I heard of him several times after that but never saw him again.

67.—PLAYFUL GOATS.

We were on our way from deep Creek to Salt Lake City and on going through E. T. City, the first settlement in Tooele Valley, this is what we saw. There was but one Street running through the place and that was nearly east and west. In front of the south row of houses and about ten feet from them there was an irrigating ditch, about eight feet wide and two feet deep, with ten or twelve inches of water running with a slow current and so clear that the bebbles on the bottom could plainly be seen.

Right in front of the doors a plank was laid across the canal to serve as a foot bridge to the road, which we were traveling.

"Oh! look there," said my pardner, "See that little girl on that plank playing in the water with a short stick." She was about three years old. She was standing on the plank over the water with her back towards the door of the house and leaning over to reach the water. "Look there," said my pardner, "there is going to be something doing".

What I saw was a Billy Goat coming up the side walk, a few rods down stream. He would come a little ways, stop and look, then come again. In this way he soon reached the plank and sizing up the situation, backed away a few steps, then made a jump striking the little girl in the back so hard that she went sprawling face down in the water.

The goat then turned and ran down the side walk as fast as he could for about fifty yards where he turned and looking back seemed to be enjoying the sport and wagging his tail and chewing gum.

My pardner jumped out of the wagon and ran to rescue the girl, but before he got to her ,the door of the house opened and out ran a woman crying, "Oh my daugther why did you fall

into the water." "Madam" said my pardner who was now close
to the plank. "She did not fall in but was knocked in." "What
do you mean by that?" "I mean that I saw the goat butt her
in." What goat?" "That fellow that is down there on the sidewalk laughing at the fun." "Oh that is father's goat and I told
him he must kill him for he is always butting someone, and
now if he don't kill him I will. Oh my poor child might have
been drowned just on account of that beast. My child often
crosses here, but never before fell in." "Not her fault now."

68.—WAGON GOING WITHOUT THE TEAM.

I sent a couple of our best Indian teamsters to Eight Mile
Canyon to get a load of logs. It generally took two or three
days to make the trip with oxen, which was the kind of team
they had. The second day the two men came back without
wagon or oxen. When I asked them what was the matter, it
was a long time before they could tell me for laughing. But
I finally thought I had it. So I gave them some more grub and
told them to go back, and early next morning I would ride up
there and see what they had done to make the wagon start for
home and leave the drivers and team behind.

Next day I was up there about 8 a. m. and found the men
there and still laughing at what they seemed to think a good
joke. The men had cut and dragged to the wagon three good
sized logs that would make a good load. They rolled two of
them on the wagon, and in trying to get the other on top,
had started the wagon on the down grade. It was in the road
which it kept for a hundred yards to where a small ravine crossed
the road, where there was quite a steep bank on the lower side.
Here is where I found the wagon with the tongue buried two
thirds of its length in the lower bank. I asked the Indian what
they were going to do about it. They said they could not get
the wagon but could drive the team home. I said "Here you fellows are going to take this wagon, logs and team home and
start very soon too.

I had not got off my horse, and did not till they started
home. "You fellows bring the oxen here," which they soon did
for they thought I was getting mad, "Now fasten a chain around
the back axle-tree, hitch the oxen on and pull the wagon back
till the tongue is out of the ground and if it is not broken you
will soon be on your way home.

The first pull brought it out all right, "Now hitch the oxen
on the wagon and take it to where I say." This done. "Now
take the oxen and drag down the other log." Of course I went
with them to see if they did it right. When the log was beside
the wagon, now, I said, "get the skids used in loading." When
these were properly placed I told them how to place the chains
so as to load the log with the oxen, which was soon done.
"Now bind your load as you have been told." This was done,

"Now water your oxen and then start for home and the next time don't act like babies." Well they were proud to think they had done it alone.

69.—THE DOG POMPEY.

The dog was a large St. Bernard, very stout built with thick black curly hair. He had a very intelligent look and a kind disposition. He had been taught to carry things in his mouth. He could carry a common water bucket full of water without spilling any, but of course with such a load he had to travel slow, there not being much room to step ahead.

When we were repairing our little Saw Mill at Deep Creek we had a carpenter named Dick Pettit, who was very fond of Pompy and used to let him carry the large dinner basket that held the dinner for the four men.

The mill where they were to work was over a half mile below the Station, and the trail or path crossed the creek on top of the dam at the head of the canal that led the water down at the mill. The dam made a large and quite deep pond where the boys used to have much fun bathing and always took Pompy with them as he was very fond of swimming and playing with them while in the pond.

One day as they were going down in single file, Pompy in the center with the dinner basket, one of the men that was in the lead had a stick in his hand, and as he was passing about the middle of the dam threw the stick out about eight or ten feet in the pond. It no sooner struck the water than Pompy made a jump for it still holding the basket, and finding he could not swim and hold it out of the water managed to turn around and tried to push it out to the bank. The men, some swearing, some laughing, tried to help the dog land the basket, which they finally did. But oh! what a sad looking mess that dinner was in, not a bite fit to eat, except baked beef.

Some of the men were so mad they wanted to whip the dog for that dirty trick, and others were just as willing to fight to protect him, especially Dick, who said, you darn fools, the fault is with the man who threw that stick in the pond, not the dog, and I will thrash any one that trys to whip him for it, and duck them in the pond afterwards.

Another time all the ranch hands were eating their supper in the large dinning room when the cook came to the kitchen door and said, "Dick, where is that dinner basket?" "Why didn't Pompy bring it to you?" "No, and I told you if that basket was not brought back I would not put up any more dinners for you and I wont." Well said Dick, "It ain't my fault for I gave the basket to Pompy and told him to take it to you."

Just then one of the men said, "there stands the awful brute that is the cause of all our trouble." Dick looked around and seeing the dog, said "Pompy you darn scamp where is that dinner basket? If you have lost it you get no supper (talking crossly). Go get the basket at once, git." The dog seemed to know what was wanted for he turned and went out.

Some of the men left the table to watch the dog, who went down the road on the trot for about fifty yards to where a couple of wagons had been left just to one side of the road and opposite a dwelling house. The people kept three or four dogs, who had intercepted Pompy as he was coming home with the basket, and in order to defend himself had set the basket down under the wagons, and after the scrap was over had forgotten the basket, but now he picked it up and brought it to the dinning room door and stood there holding it in his mouth until Dick called the cook to come and get it, which he did and patted the dog's head and told him to go around to the kitchen door and he would give him his supper. This he seemed to understand for he went at once as told.

Another time the boys had caught a coyote late in the evening, and concluded to not kill it till morning, so tied the trap chain around a post and left it for the night. Father, when he got up for his early morning ride saw the coyote and made up his mind to see a little sport. So after saddling his horse and calling his dog, he turned the coyote loose and the chase was on. The coyotes leg that had been held in the trap all night was so sore and stiff that he could not keep out of Pompy's reach only by dodging one way and another, but always working towards the west creek about half a mile from the starting place. When he reached this creek and attempted to jump across it, Pompy jumped at the same time and both landed in the water clinched, and struggled to keep on top.

The creek at this place was very deep, but only about four feet wide, with perpendicular banks. Father dismounted to help the dog if necessary.

The coyote had the dog by the side of his neck. The dog kept his body over the coyote and turning his head sideways was trying to keep the coyote's head under water to drown him loose, which he did, and then with Father's help got out of the creek, and then reaching back pulled the coyote out with Father's help. He was not dead but Pomp soon made him like sausage.

I had loaned by plastering trowel to a man who lived a couple of miles down the valley from Deep Creek Station, and as he had not returned it, I thought I would ride down to his place and get it. While I was saddling my horse I noticed that Pomp was watching me as if he wanted to go with me, so when I got on my horse I said, all right Pomp, come on. He ran a noseing around till he found a small stick which he picked up and seemed pleased for the privilege of going for an airing

Most of the road was dry and dusty, but at one place the creek ran close to the road, and was about eight feet wide and a foot deep, with a gravely bottom that made it a nice place to water teams or cattle. When I arrived at the man's place and found him at home, after getting the trowel I still sat on my horse, talking to the man and tapping the trowel on the horn of my saddle.

Pompy had a number of times placed his front feet as high on the saddle as he could reach, trying to call my attention to him. He wanted to carry that towel, so I placed the handle of it in his mouth and after getting through talking with the man, I looked around for Pomp. There he was lying down, with the trowel between his paws. As soon as he saw me start he picked up the trowel and followed, keeping close behind the horse. I occasionaly looked back to see if still had the trowel. I had done this just before we got back to the creek bend, and not again till most home, and as I did I saw that the dog had dropped the trowel.

Well I could not blame him much, for, it was a very hot day. As I turned around Pomp stopped and turned back, but would not go unless I did, and keep him only about two rods ahead of me. I was jawing and promising him a good thrashing if he had lost that trowel and could not find it. This went on till we arrived at the creek bend, when the dog left the road wadeing out into the creek and stood still, but kept sticking his nose in the water.

I then knew where the trowel was, and how he had lost it by letting it fall out of his mouth while he got a drink, and the current had carried it a little down stream. I got off my horse and picked up a small stick to fish for the trowel. Pomp saw the stick and thinking it was for him he jumped to the further side of the creek, turned and kept sticking his nose in the water up to his eyes. After searching for some time I located the trowel about four feet down from where the dog was hunting for it. He seemed to know where he had dropped it, but did not allow for the current. It was some time before I could coax him far enough to see what I was pointing at, with the stick, and I was also afraid I would hit him with it.

But finally as I was about to give up trying to make him understand where the trowel was, he caught a sight of shineing mettle and then there was something doing. The water there was eighteen inches deep. The dog made a lunge and landed both front feet on the trowel, as if it would try to get away, then under went his head. Gee but he made the wtaer fly. But he came up with the handle of the trowel in his mouth and stood in the road till I was ready to go. Then he kept the lead till we got home, where some of the boys tried to get the trowel from him, but no, he had got it from me, and I was the one to get it back.

As I rode up I called to him to come and give me that trowel before he lost it again. He came and placing his feet the same as when I first handed it to him allowed me to take the trowel. Then seemed to think all was off and went to the side of the house to lie in the shade.

70.—WILD PETS.

I will now have to tell you of a few Pole Cat incidents. First I was out prospecting with a Mr. Shell we had located a claim and built a small log cabin, and were sinking a shaft some five or six rods up the hill from the cabin. One noon Shell went down to start dinner while I stayed to load the drilled holes for blastsing. He soon came running back all excited, and said, "Come quick and help me catch the prettiest little animal I ever saw in all my life, I want to catch it alive, it will make such a fine pet.

Don't get excited I said I think I know what your pet is, and you had better give him plenty of room, but Shell fairly pulled me down to the cabin, where on looking through the logs we could see the pet gnawing at our bacon sack that laid on the floor, not having been hung up in its proper place, "Don't make a noise" he said, "How are we to catch him alive?"

This was a well educated man who came from New York City and did not know a skunk when he saw it. Stand back, I said, "that is a pole cat and if he is a mind to he can make the cabin uninhabitable." Well if you know it why don't you shoot it, there is a good view of him from here. "Yes but don't you know that if I did shoot it in there we would have to move out. Can't I make you understand that that animal has a supply of scent that would clean out the whole of New York City. "Well what are you going to do wait till he eats up the whole of that bacon?" "No, you come to this side of the house and I will see if I can get him to leave.

I took some small pebbles, rolled them towards the cat, at the same time kicking at the logs, the cat got alarmed, crawled under the logs and started up the hill towards the shaft, as soon as it was out of the house, Shell said, "Now shoot him." "Not me, he is too close yet."

About half way between house and shaft, the ledge cropped out with a large crevice or crack in it, the cat went into this. "Now I am going to get him without you shooting him." Never fear, I wont shoot him that close to the trail, and you had better leave him alone.

No, he must have his own way, so he took our largest drill and by leaning over the crevice, drill and arm straight down he was able to reach the cat. I saw him make two or three fierce lunges and then leaving the drill in the crevice, raised his hands and came running down to where I was standing, and said "Oh, my, What a smell." I said "You are very lucky if you haven't got some of it on your clothes." "Well," he said, I must seem like a d——d idiot to you and I guess I am.

For two weeks after our trail to the shaft was in the shape of a semicircle. When we were about to leave I could not get Shell to fish out the drill he had killed the cat with, and said he would sooner pay for half a dozen like it than get it. And if I would agree to say nothing about the d——d pet, when we got

to a place where there was liquor I could have as much as I
wanted. Well I wanted much.

At another time much later, and in Cache Valley I had traded
for a saw mill in High Creek Canyon where I run a custom
shingle mill. We had a log cabin in which the hired men slept.
There were six double bunks and at times they were all occupied,
and in stormy weather the floor space would have a few beds
spread down for the night. This floor was of rough lumber with
many large cracks and not-holes. There was a large open fire-
place in one end of the room that was usually kept full of burning logs in cold weather.

I had a young Scotchman hired to work in the mill, he occupied one of the lower bunks facing the fire-place. While laying in his bed he could easily reach the floor with his hand. One
night when all had retired Johnny lay awake and saw a pole cat
running around the room picking up the crumbs and scraps
that had been left by those who had eaten their supper by the
fire. He watched the cat till it had cleaned up all it could find,
even going under the lower bunks. He saw the animal crawl
through one of the cracks in the floor.

He said nothing of this to any one, but the next evening he
left a few bacon scraps on the floor beside his bunk, swept the
floor and left the fire to give a little light. After all had been
quiet for a while the cat made its appearance again, coming up
through the same crack as before and exploring the room, found
the crumbs, and ate them all before going the crack route for
home.

This was kept up for a few nights in succession and finally,
the boy ventured to touch the cat's back. It seemed to understand that there was no harm intended, and the boy after a few
days got braver, and would stroke the cat's back as long as he
was eating the crumbs. The cat also seemed to enjoy the pet-
ting, and now would come straight from the crack to the bunk
side, and not do any hunting about the room.

This went on for a long time. The boy saying nothing to
anyone. When there was to be company in the cabin he had a
piece of board that he would place over the crack, after dropping a few crumbs through for his pet.

One stormy night all the bunks were occupied, and a bed
for two spread on the floor, with the foot towards the fire. The
boy had forgot to place the board over the crack. He was very
tired and was soon asleep. There had been a good big fire, but
was now a bed of live coals. After all was quiet the cat came up
and finding no food in the usual place, proceeded to search for
something to eat. In doing so it crawled across one of the men's
legs. The weight of the animal awaked him and not knowing
what it was, drew both his legs up as far as he could, and then
kicked them back as hard as he could kick. Well he had done
it in fine shape, for he sent the cat plunging into the fire, at
same time saying, "What in H—— is in here?"

"Darn your eyes," said Johnny, you have done it. Now you

can pick up your bed and get out of here. And that is just what all hands did too, and lost no time in doing it. They had to make temporary shelter for the night, as it was raining. We got the hose to work and give the house a good drenching, and afterwards a good coat of lime whitewash. But it was over two months before we could use that room to sleep in again. Johnny and the man that done the kicking, were never good friends again.

71.—THE SAND HILL CRANES.

I had been on a trail where there was quite a number of horse tracks all leading to the north. I had satisfied myself that they were made by Indian ponys passing that way, all of a week before and possible longer. So had left the trail and was crossing a desert valley of about twelve or fifteen miles in width.

I was about in the middle of this valley when I noticed to the north of me and about a mile distance what appeared to be a couple of horsemen that were up to some game, for they would go this way, then that way, crossing each other, then sometimes dropping most out of sight. This getting out of sight I thought was by them going through a swayle or low place. The other, or crossing, I thought might be by their coming along a crooked trail that would make it appear to me that they were crossing first one way and the other.

But there was something else that I saw that set me to thinking pretty hard, and that was every little while one or both of the horsemen would hold their blankets by two corners and raise them above their heads and work their arms back and forth like wings. What was this? If not to call my attention to them, while probably another party was sneaking up from some other direction to spring a surprise on me. But I could see no signs of danger in any such direction, so going slowly to save my horse for a fast run, if it should be necessary, I kept good watch of the two horsemen. They did not seem to get any nearer to me but kept up their antics.

I was some puzzled over the affair, as I had never seen or even heard of anything like this, and as to what would happen next I did not know, but was determined to not be caught asleep, every foot of the country I was to travel over I seached well with my eyes before venturing toward it, but there was no place for miles in any direction where there could be laid an ambush without digging and common sense told me that an Indian would not do that for how could they tell which way I would come or go. I did not know myself. It was all according to circumstances.

I knew that I had about fifteen miles to go to get to my home station, and, if headed off in that direction I could reach another station by going to the right about twenty miles. It was now past noon and I was just going to travel faster, when a cloud came over the sun and put an end to the Mirage. It was nothing more than two sandhill cranes feeding and exercising themselves by stretching their wings.

72.—THE INDIAN STORY OF A GREAT CAVE.

I first got this from a young buck and just enough to cause me to want to hear all there was to it, and I told the young man so. He said there were some old men that knew all about it, and he would tell me who they were as soon as he could. Some time later I was at the Indian camp that was near the station taking lessons in their dialect. When the young man came in and said there was an òld man over there in another wig-wam, that could tell me about the big cave. I was soon over there and after a friendly smoke. This is what he said as near as I can remember:

"There was camped at the very south end of the Schell Creek range of mountains a large band of Indians, and a little ways from the camp was a large knowl. In the side of it was a cave that no one had ever been to the end of, and in fact none would try to explore it, on account of it being said that the bad spirit lived there, and killed all who entered very far inside.

The chief of this band of Indians had two squaws, one was quite old and cross, the other was very young and gentle and good looking, but the two squaws were most always quarreling, and the chief had frequently given the old one a good thrashing, thinking she was to be blamed for being so cross but the time came when he thought he would try whipping the young one, but first asked her why she could not get along with out quarreling with the old lady. She said the other woman was always scolding her for not working harder and thereby making it lighter work for her and if he didn't make her stop her growling, she would run away as she was tired of living this way.

That kind of talk made the Chief very mad so he gave the young squaw a very hard whipping, using his horse whip and holding her by the hair of her head while he laid the whip on till the blood had started out most all over her, then throwing her to one side said now let us have peace or there will be something worse coming.

That night the sore little squaw took some dried meat and a few pine nuts and went to the cave determined to go as far in as the bad spirit would allow her to go, and, if she did not see him, to go as far as she had strength to crawl as she never wanted to go back or have the Indians find her body if they tried to do so.

For some distance the floor of the cave was covered with sand that laid in small wave like ridges and on the whole nearly level, but further on took a steep grade down for a long way, then a nearly level stretch, then again down grade, this kept on she did not know how long, for when she got tired she would lie down and sleep, and when she woke up would continue feeling her way down.

She had no idea how far she was from the mouth of the cave when she stepped into a pool of water that came nearly up to her knees and was cold as ice. She felt around and found there was quite a stream that was running out of the spring on the opposite side and she could hear a small waterfall a little farther down. She soon made her way to this fall and over it and down the creek.

This went on for a long time, her food had all been eaten and she expected to soon have to give up and die, but what was this under her feet so soft? It was grass. She tried to eat some of it but it did not taste good, so went on and when tired out laid down beside the creek to sleep, and lying on her back opened her eyes and saw that there was stars above her and in watching these discovered there were clouds up there to and this kept her awake for a long time, but she did sleep again and then was awakened by some thing running by her.

She found it was day light and the sun was coming up over the hills and she could now hear birds singing, and she saw numerous wild animals the like of which she had never seen before. Every where she looked the ground was covered all over with grass, bushes, and trees. Any where else in her life, she had not seen such a beautiful country not even in small patches, having lived in a desert country.

Hunger caused her to look around to see if she could find any berries or roots that she could eat. Going on down the creek she found there was plenty of berries and many kinds that she had never seen before, some very large, and others very small. She eat of them such as tasted good until satisfied. Then went on still following the winding brook.

She had not traveled over a half a sun when she saw a large herd of very white animals feeding on a large open space where there was nothing but fine grass. She had never seen any animals like these. They were not as tall as an antelope, nor as little as a coyote. They were covered all over with long curley hair, and as she drew near to them they raised their heads and looked at her, then went on with their feeding, and seemed to know that she was not dangerous. While watching these animals, she saw something else that gave her quite a scare. It was a man and, as he had seen her and was coming towards her there was no use in running away, so she stood still but watching to see if he was freindly or not. He came up pretty close and stopped then spoke to her in a language she had never heard and could not understand.

After some time he seemed to know that she was of some other people, and was lost, and was probably hungry, so putting one hand on his stomach and the other pointing to his mouth then pointing down the brook motioned for her to follow him, which she did as he seemed very friendly.

After going some distance they came to where a broad trail led to the door of a big house that had four or five other houses inside of it, and in the sides of all of them were big holes that had something over them that kept the wind and rain out, but you could see outside through them. In every house the ground was covered with wood and the whole houses seemed to be made of wood with different kinds and colors of paint. There were places to sit on, places to eat on, and places to sleep on, all very beautiful to look at.

The man went to one of the walls and opened a door that did not open clear through the wall and brought out some meat that was cooked and some very white bread and some yellow grease, and a pan of berries, a cup of sugar and put these on the place to eat on, then got some water in a cup you could see through. Then motioned for her to sit there, and he sat opposite, all the time talking in a kind voice.

He would point to some thing and say one word, and keep saying it till she would repeat it, when he would laugh and seemed much pleased. She knew that he was trying to teach her to talk his language and she was anxious to learn, and it was not long before she was able to ask questions and understand the answers. She slept in one of the inside houses and the man in another. The man done all the cooking for a long time, or until she had learned to talk well, and also how the cooking was done. Then she took hold of that part, which left the man more time to attend to his flocks and herds of which he had a good many. Some days he would take her out with him to get the fresh air and view the country, and at such times she could see scattered around at quite a distance numerous houses like the one where she lived and could also see many herds of different kinds of animals. When she asked the man if friendly people lived there he said yes. It is a very big country and all over it just like it is as far as you can see.

One day the man dressed himself in finer clothes and told the girl he was going away, but would come back by sundown. He was back by the time, called the girl to come and see what he had brought for her. It proved to be a dress that would reach from neck to ankles, and cover the arms too. It was covered most all over with different colored beads which were put on so as to show trees, birds, etc. and was very beautiful to look at. There were some leggings and shoes all finished off with beads like the dress. She was much pleased with the present as her own clothes were badly worn. The man told her to put them on and wear them every day, and after a while would get her another and better outfit.

One day he called her to set down, and as she could talk good enough to make him understand, to tell him her story of where she came from and how and all about her people, as he was satisfied she was not of his country. So she commenced her story form the time she could first remember, up to the time her husband had whipped her, which seemed to make the man very mad.

He frequently asked her questions as she was telling her story. Then when she was telling of her running away and entering the cave to die he was all excited as there was an old story in his country that the cave had another opening far in the mountains that led to a bad country.

Well, she ended her story, after telling all that happened to her up to the time she met him. He knew the rest. One day he took her out to the side of the great trees, where he sat down and said three years ago I had a wife, she died and is laying there pointing to a small mound near him and two years more must pass, before I can marry again, as that is our custom here. Then maybe I will talk to you about it.

One day some time later he found the girl sitting out in the shade she was crying and sobbing like her heart would break. After a good deal of coaxing she told him she was thinking about her husband and her boy, and wanted to see them again at least her boy that was one year old when she left them. The man seemed very much depressed but said, your husband is no good I wouldn't cry for him, but I do not blame you for wanting to see your boy, and if there was any way to help you get him I would, but there is no way, so try and forget them. And soon she was crying most of the time, till at last she told the man if he would let her go she would try and go back the way she had come, and get her boy.

The man tried to make her understand that it would be impossible for her to find her way back. But she was determined to make the attempt. So seeing that he could not persuade her to his views, he told her that if she was bound to take the chance of getting back through that awful hole, he would help her all he could but would not go one step inside of the cave to save his own life or her's either. So as she wanted to start at once they both began getting together such articles as they thought would help her to make the journey through the cave.

The man got a small bundle of grease tourches any one of which would burn a whole day, and advised the girl to use as few as possible while she had the creek to follow, and after leaving the spring at the head of the creek might be able to trace her steps back if she had light enough. Well, one day when they could think of nothing that would help her, the man went with her to where the creek came out of the mountains tried again to have her give up such an awful undertaking, but as she would go, made her promise that if she could not find her way out at the other end, or did get through and found her boy she would come back to him and he would wait two years for her.

So they parted, the man to his peaceful home, the girl to the dismal cave, where, after a very long time, and her provisions were about all used up, and the torches all burned out, she came to the light of day, and about noon. She climbed a small hill where she could view the country around her at least some distance away discovered a smoke that showed her where there was a camp of Indians.

She went to it and found it to be her husband's band who was all very much surprised to see her again and alive, and dressed so fine and looking as pretty as ever, only tired out, and whiter than when she left them. The old woman had died while she was gone. Her husband said he would never whip her again and she must come and live with him and the boy, which she did."

There is another Indian story about that same cave, of how a small band of Indians lived near it, and was attacked by a large band of strange and hostile Indians, that was determined to kill all of the men and children and keep the squaws for servants. They had a running fight and all that were not killed took refuge in this cave. Their enemy placed a guard near the entrance to prevent any from escaping and they were determined to kill or capture the whole band. But after keeping their guards there for a whole moon, and not seeing or hearing of any one that had went in they came to the conclusion that all had starved to death. So they went in to investigate, and could plainly see the tracks of the fleeing party all pointing further in, not one had turned back. This was enough, all had gone to their heaven or their hell.

Now a white man story about this same cave. We had a number of men hired for haying season, and among them were some that had lived in the settlements south of Utah Lake. I had been telling a bunch of them some of What the Indians had told me about this cave, when one of the men said there must be something in it, for I heared a man down south say he was acquainted with some of the party that done some exploring there.

The party were returning from California and making a cut off across the desert, when they camped near and discovered the cave. Some of the party went in quite a long ways, but had to retreat as their light gave out. Then they made a number of torches and with what lighting material they had, attempted to again reach the far end of the cave. There were many leads off to the sides but only one led down, kept one general direction. By following this, and just as they were about to back out going any further, they came to a spring of nice clear and pure water. The stream from which ran on down into the cave. There seemed to be plenty of room to follow it but they could not at that time.

All said they would go to the settlements and provide themselves with the means of finding the end of that cave if it took them six months to do it. I know that a good many men have been willing at any time to go and explore it. But there was always lacking a leader that would go ahead and organize a party for that purpose.

73.—A PONY EXPRESS RIDER'S EXPERIENCE IN 1860.

Richard Erastus Egan better known in boyhood days as "Ras" Egan, born in Salem Mass. March 29th 1842, was employed in April 1860 to ride Pony Express between Salt Lake City and Rush Valley station, a distance of seventy five miles. He made the first trip on the west bound express on the famous and beautiful sorrel mare "Miss Lightning" making the first station twenty two miles in one hour and five minutes.

The scheduled time for the seventy five miles was five and one-half hours though it was made once in four hours and five minutes when the President's message was going through called by the boys the "Lightening Express." At first the ride seemed long and a tiresome one but after becoming accustomed to that kind of riding it seemed only play, but there were times when it didn't seem so very playful. For instance. I was married January 1st 1861, and of course naturally wanted a short furlough, but was only permited to substitute a rider for one trip, and the poor fellow thought that was plenty.

I had warned him about the horse he would start with from "Rush" on his return trip telling him that he would either "back" or fall over backwards when he got on him. "Oh!" said he, "I am used to that kind of business. "But" said I "Bucking Bally is a whole team and a horse to let and a little dog under the wagon, be careful. So as a precaution after he had tightned the saddle on he led him out about a quarter of a mile from the station and got on, when the horse true to his habit got busy, and the next thing the rider knew he was hanging by the back of his overcoat on a high stake of a stake and rider fence with his feet about five feet from the ground.

He could not reach behind him to unhitch himself. He could not unbutton his coat so as to crawl out of it, but he could get his hands in his pockets for his knife to cut the buttons off and release himself, after which was a search for the horse on the dark night. He finally found him and made the trip, getting "a black eye" for loss of time. He said to the boys, "No more 'Bucking Bally' for me."

74.—A RATHER UNPLEASANT EXPERIENCE.

Shortly after my marriage in the winter the time of arrival of the Pony Express from St. Joseph was uncertain on account of deep snow in the Rockies. So one night when I was supposed to remain in the office waiting, the hostler through sympathy said you go home to your new wife and if the express comes I will jump on a horse and come after you. Of course I accepted. Oh! what luck! About midnight here comes the pesky fellow and I had to jump out of a snug warm bed and start of in a howling blizzard to ride seventy five miles.

The cold was almost unbearable, but, through the kindness of a friend who took me in for an hour and warmed up my almost freezing body I pulled through O. K.

On another accasion I rode from Salt Lake City to Fort Crittenden, a distance of fifty miles, then started at sun down for Rush Valley in a very heavy snow storm, and the snow knee deep to my horse. I could see no road, so that, as soon as darkness came on, I had to depend entirely on the wind. It was striking on my right cheek, so I kept it there, but, unfortunately for me, the wind changed and led me off my course, and instead of going westward I went southward and rode all night on a high trot, and arrived at the place I had left at sundown the evening before with both myself and horse very tired.

Now the only thing to do was to jump on to the horse I had rode in the evening before and proceed on twenty five miles further. Then, instead of having a night's rest at my home station, I was riding all night, in consequence of which I met the "Pony" from Sacramento and was compelled to start immediately on my eastward trip to Salt Lake City. This made my continuous ride 150 miles besides all night in deep snow.

Just one more incident. My brother-in-law was riding west from me and had a sweetheart in Salt Lake City whom he desired to see, but could get no leave of absence to go see her and I naturally had sympathy for him, so we got our heads together and agreed to accidently (on purpose) pass each other in the night and he would have to ride his route and continue on mine. But he had all night in Salt Lake to rest or spark as he choose and return the double route next trip.

But with me it was different for after I had rode the double route, 165 miles I met the "Pony" from west and had to turn around without any rest and ride over the double route again, making a continuous ride of 330 miles and again I was tired.

On this same route the Indians had attacked the stage, killed the driver and a passenger, rifled the U. S. Mail and took the four horses and when I came along, one lone Indian with rifle and bow and arrows started after me. But I thought I had the best horse, so played along just out of easy gun shot from him. Finally I thought I would play a bluff on him, which worked as I thought it would.

I turned and run at him full speed, swinging my pistol and yelling at the top of my voice. He immediately left the road kicking and whipping his pony and kept it up as far as I could see him.

The agent, to encourage the boys to make good time, said to them, "Boys if you kill a horse by riding fast we will buy a better one.

One trip I was riding a lovely rangey bay, $300.00 horse at a 20 mile an hour clip, when the poor animal missed his footing and fell, breaking his neck and almost sent me to St. Joseph. When I gathered myself up and found my horse dead, I had to walk about five miles and carry my saddle and express matter and so registered another tired. —R. E. Egan.

75.—*CONCLUSION.

We realize that so far this book does not contain a complete Biography of either Major or Howard R. Egan; but we are very desirous to preserve in type these writings as far as they go, and as the limits of the book are very near to a close we can only add in conclusion a few words to show some completness to it.

Will say first that Howard R. Egan, the principal writer and publisher of the forgoing had some matters to write about that has not yet been submitted, and many things should be said yet. In brief we will state: that in 1870 he closed up business with Father and the Deep Creek branch and left there, going to Richmond, Cache County, Utah. Near there he and I took up a quarter section each of land. He bought a saw mill in High Creek Canyon and run it for a number of years, also other saw mills afterwards and he died in March 1916. Many of his activities there must await some later date to be made known.

A small brief has been made of R. Erastus Egan on page 214 and we will now give a statement of the conclusion of Mother's family, Ira E. Egan, who was the last born, Feb. 5th 1861, in Salt Lake City and lived through his early life there, got his schooling and was messenger boy for the Telegraph Company. He married and raised a family (See Appendix) and is now living near Smithfield, Cache County where he has a home.

Mother's Children were six in number, one died a baby, and Hoarce died in Salt Lake City at the age of fifteen. The rest are alive Howard R., R. Erastus, William, and Ira (See Appendix

Nancy, the second wife had two daughters, Helen J. who married and raised a large family, Vilate L., who died some time after Horace and they were both buried in the Salt Lake City Cemetery where Father had the lot fenced with cut stone and an Iron fence hammered out of old wagon tire by R. B. Margets.

Hyrum W. Egan was a son of Mary, the third wife. He married at Deep Creek and raised a family, (See Appendix). He moved to Goose Creek or Basin, Idaho, and died there. His wife and family are now living at Burley, Idaho and have quite a posterity.

When the immigrants came in with trains each season and also with the hand cart companies there was much suffering for want of the necessaries of life which they were entirely deficient of, during the early years after first ones began to arrive. This would have been much greater but for the benevolence of those that were here who were able to help them. Father was doing well during this period with his beef trade in California and Mother had means to use and being naturally very benevolent she helped them a great deal. We were situated close to the Union Square on which they could get some better quarters.

I remember Mother saying that she kept an account one season and found that she had purchased $1500 worth of provisions which she had given emmigrants of the hand cart companies and others that were in need. She told Father about it and the only comment he made was "That is right Mother and you shall be blessed for your good heart."

After the completion of the railroad from the east to the west across the continent, the route having been chosen north of the Salt Lake, there was no more use for the Mail Line and there was not much left at Deep Creek for activity except in connection with the mines that had been discovered during the many years that the ranch had been in operation, so Father turned his attention to them. He seemed to be quite successful in developing some good properties in partnership with two other men and could have sold out for $50,000 which Father wanted to do, but his partners wanted more and they got nothing, as all the railroad projects failed to reach there, and as the ore was low grade it would not pay to ship. The mines failed to reimburse him for the means he had expended in them, which was the substance of the entire Deep Creek Ranch farm land etc.

While Father was working the mining property he was also engaged in missionary work among the Indians, who were induced through his influence to settle down to civilzed life, and have since became quite successful in farming, for they had been used as farm and hay hands many years on the Deep Creek property and now they were shown how to work for themselves. He also aided much in teaching them and also imparting to them a knowledge of the Gospel, as well as in good habits of honesty and industry. June 2, 1874, one hundred Goshute Indians were baptised and there was a general religious movement among them.

Having exhausted all his resources at Deep Creek Father came to Salt Lake about 1875 and lived at the old home with his family, (what were left at home.) He became one of the Salt Lake Police and also Deputy Sheriff both of which appointments we now have in our possession.

He also became a special guard for Pres. Brigham Young at the Lion House and Church Offices before and at the time of Pres. Brigham Young's last illness and acted as special nurse, in which capacity he had many times acted before in various cases, and was often called doctor. Brigham Young would tell him to get him a pitcher of cold water and pump it full forty times. Many other little attentions he would render for him. After the death of Pres. Young Father was the special guard at his grave, and a building was erected so that he could look out on the grave any time of night, without getting out of bed, by the light that was kept burning.

Pres. Young died Aug. 29th, 1877, and in March 1878 Father got his feet wet one dark night and took sick, which resulted in inflamation of the bowels, and died at the age of sixty-three.

Mother lived till March 31st, 1905, and Father's papers were kept until then, but after that many of them were destroyed.

If all his life work were written it would take many volumes to contain it. The Pioneer Monument was erected to the honor of the band of Pioneers of which He was a member and his name appears with the rest upon it.

This year, 1915, the great Capitol of the State of Utah, has been finished, as if in memory of the one hundreth anniversary of the birth of Major Howard Egan, but at least representing the grand advancement of the great commonwealth of which with other Pioneers he played so prominent a part in laying the foundation; and it. was on this anniversary of his birth we commenced to publish this volume, and expect in the near future to build a monument in honor of his name.

Eagle Gate, Beehive House, Church Offices and Lion House, Where Brigham Young Lived and Where He Died.

APPENDIX

GENEALOGY

From Adam to the Stem of the Egan Family. Of this line are the Kings and rulers of Judah, of Spain, Ireland, England, Scotland, Wales and others.

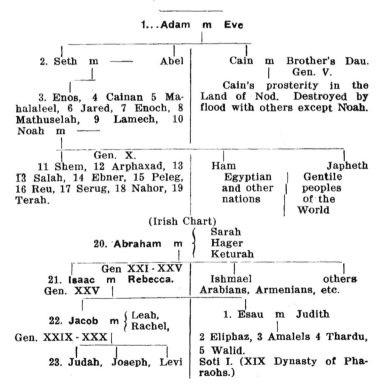

1...Adam   m   Eve

2. Seth   m   ——   Abel

Cain   m   Brother's Dau.
Gen. V.

Cain's prosperity in the Land of Nod. Destroyed by flood with others except Noah.

3. Enos, 4 Cainan 5 Mahalaleel, 6 Jared, 7 Enoch, 8 Mathuselah, 9 Lamech, 10 Noah   m   ——

Gen. X.
11 Shem, 12 Arphaxad, 13 13 Salah, 14 Ebner, 15 Peleg, 16 Reu, 17 Serug, 18 Nahor, 19 Terah.

Ham
Egyptian and other nations

Japheth
Gentile peoples of the World

(Irish Chart)

20. Abraham   m   { Sarah / Hager / Keturah

Gen XXI - XXV
21. Isaac   m   Rebecca.
Gen. XXV

Ishmael   others
Arabians, Armenians, etc.

22. Jacob   m   { Leah, / Rachel,
Gen. XXIX - XXX

23. Judah,   Joseph,   Levi

1. Esau   m   Judith

2 Eliphaz, 3 Amalels 4 Thardu, 5 Walid.
Soti I. (XIX Dynasty of Pharaohs.)

23. Judah m Tamar.

24. Zarah (or Tara) 25 Ethan, (King of Scythia) 26 Tuahol or Phonensis Farsaidh (inventor of letters)
27. Gadhol m Scota

(Friend of Moses and founder of Port Gathelas or Portugal)
28. Asruth, 29 Gruth, 30 Heber Scutt, 31 Beouman, 32 Oggoman, 33 Lamfionn, 34 Heber Glunfionn, 35 Agnan, Fion, 36 Febric Glas, 37 Mennall, 38 Nuadhas, 39 Alladh, 40 Aroadh, 41 Dreag, 42 Brath, 43 Breogan, 44 Bile

45. Mileaus m { 1st d. of no. 25
{ 2nd Scota
{ 3rd Meriam

46 Herman, six others, Heber Mileseus, King of Spain or Gallam the conqueror of Ireland and hero of 1000 battles had eight sons. Three of them reigned through their descendants in the 183 Milesian Kings from whom all Milesian families are descended.

Herman Eochaidk (crowned horsemen) youngest son of Mileseus a prince of Dan, through his mother, Meriam and his grand father McGreeme (last Tuatha de Danaan King, see Irish History) as well as a prince of Judah, a knight of the "Red Branch, two fold simbolized in coat of arms by two Red Lions. He was born in Spain, educated in Ireland and wore a seven colored kilt.

24 Pharez, 25 Easru, 26 Aram, 27 Amimadob, 28 Nashour, 29 Salsmon, 30 Boaz, 31 Obed, 32 Jesse, 33 David, 34 Solomon, 35 Rehoboam, 36 Obijah, 37 Ada, 38 Jehosaphat, 40 Ahazieh, 42 Jotham, 44 Amajiah, 45 Hezekiah, 46 Manasseh, 47 Amon, 48 Joshiah, 49 Zedekiah— his sons were slain, 50 * Tea Tephi "Tender twig of prophecy" youngest daughter of King Zedekiah escaped the Balylonian capitivity with her great Grandfather the prophet Jeremiah. His palace was Teamor the Palace of Tahpamhes in Egypt unearthed by Petree Contanis. A tradition of Kings daughter says: "The stone on which Jacob slept they carried with them. On that she was crowned, the 50*th from Adam, Queen Victoria 150th, Queen Victoria of Spain 153rd, the last of great fishes in the net, finishing up times of Gentiles."

Jacob's stone went to Scotland in the time of Pergno. It is now the Cornation stone of Westminister Abbey, carried there from Scotland. She had met Herman years before in Egypt and when with her great grand father the prophet, she landed in Ireland, with Druedic ceremonial she and Herman were married.

These two lines of Judah joined together by this marriage in the year of the world 3434 A. M. constitute the "Royal Arch Degree" of Free Masonry, which the prophet Jeremiah founded.

He also placed in the mound of Tara Northwest of Dublin, the Ark of the Covenant and England's Title deeds to the Holy Land. It is now the property of England and being approached from all sides. "Britham" is the land of the Covenant, "Mount Ephriam, the land of Dan or "Pridian."

The only child of this marriage of Hermon and Tea Tephi in 562 B. C. was Irial the prophet, the ancestor of the Cobb family of America and many others.

MILESIAN KINGS—LINE OF HEREMON.

46 Herman m Tea Tephi, 47 Ireal Faidh X. 48 Eithrial, 49 Foll-aigh, 50 Tigernmas, 51 Eubotha, 52 Smiorughall, 53 Fiacha Labhrainn XVIII, 54 AEneas Almucach XX, 55 Main, 56 Rothactach 57 Dein, 58 Siorna, 59 Olioll Aolchevin, 60 Gialchadh XXX VII, 61 Nudahas Fionnfail, 62 Aedan Glas, 63 Sioman Breac XLIV, 64 Muredach Bolgrach LV, 65 Fiocha Tolgrach, 66 Duach Lodrach, 67 Eochaidh Buadhach 68 Cobthach Caol Bhreagh LXIX, 69 Melg Molblhach LXXI, 70 Coula Caomh LXXIV, 71 Oliohh Cas Fiaclach LXXVII, 72 Eochaldh Alt Leatham, 73 AEneas LXXXI, 74 Enna, 75 Assaman, 76 Eochlaidh Feidioch XCIII, 77 Lughaidh XCVIII, 78 Crumthann C, A. D. 79 Feredach, 80 Fiacha, 81 Tuathal CVI, 82 Fedhlimidh, 83 Conn CIX, 84 Art, 85 Cormac Ulfhada, 86 Cairbre, 87 Eochardh Dubhlen.

88 Colla da Chrioch founder of the Kingdom of Orgiall, O'Carroll, of Oriel and O'Kelly (P. 365 O'Hart) families of Nester and princes of Hy Maine, Kings of Orgiall to 12th century. 89 Iomchadh, 90 Domhmall, 91 Eochaidh, 92 Main Mor, 93 Breasal, 94 Dallan, 95 Lughach, 96 Fearach, 97 Cairbre Crom Ris, 98 Cormac, 99 Eoghan Foinn, 100 Dithchiollach 101 Denitheach, 102 Fiacalach.

103 Coscrach, head of the stem of the Egan Family heireditary Brehons or Lawyers 104 Flaithghead, 105 Anluan, 106 Flaitheam or Felin, 107 Gosda, 108 Aedhaghan (eye Kindle-Anglisized Egan) 109 Flann, 110 Murtach, 111 Donach Mor. 112 Donoch Oge, 113 Simeon, 114 Justin, 115 Maloliosa, 116 Flann, 117 Finghan, 118 Owen McEgan, 119 Teige, 120 Conor, 121 Teige (2d). 122 Melachlin Egan.

No. 1 to No. 20 is taken from the Bible —From No. 20 Abraham to No. 83 Conn is quoted from the Chart from "Regal Roll," "Annals of Four Fasters," showing the descent of the Carrolls, Egans and other families of Ireland, England, Scotland and Wales. This is also corroborated in most part by O'Hart's "Pedigree of the Irish Nation" from which the balance is quoted except the serial numbers. It so happens that No. 50 * Tea Tephi from Adam corroborates the statements made in the Chart that she was 50th from Adam.

I copy the following words from a Patriarchal Blessing given Howard Egan Sept. 24th, 1842 at Nauvoo, Ill, by Hyrum Smith:- "I place a blessing on you consonant with your lineage and right unto the Priesthood for behold I say unto you Howard, you are the lineage of David and of the Tribe of Judah........you shall have an inheritance in Mt. Zion and your house or your posterity that cometh after you."

Family tree, original 3 x4 feet. Reduction not readable, but is printed in type below. Right hand lower branch represents family No. 17, left branch, No. 18, and so on up. The limbs represent grandchildren of Howard Egan. (Enlarged photos can be had from R. D. Johnson, photographer, 118 S. 11th East, Salt Lake City.)

PEDIGREE OF HOWARD EGAN FROM HIS GRAND FATHER AND HIS POSTERITY TO THE PRESENT TIME

1. Benard Egan born about 1760, married Betty Egan b. a. 1762. **Chil. 3.** * Howard b. a. 1782, 4. * William b. a. 1784, all of Tullimore Kings Co. Ireland.

3. Howard Egan b. a. 1782 md. 1805, 5 Ann Meade b. a. 1784, d. 1822. **Chil: 6** Eliza b. 1806. **7** Mary b. 1807, 8. Catherine b. 1808, 9. Bernard b. a. 1810, 10. John b. a. 1813, 11. *Howard b. 15 June 1815 (author of the Diary of this book) 12. Ann b. a. 1817, 13. Richard b. 1820, 14 Evelina b. 1822, 15. Margaret b. 1822, in Tullimore, Kings Co., Ireland.

FATHER   **MOTHER**

11. Howard Egan, md 1 Dec. 1836, 16. Tamson Parshley b. 27, July 1825. **Chil: 17.** * Howard Ransom b. 12 Apr. 1840, 18. * Richard Erastus b. 29 Mar. 1842, 19. Charles John b. 1844 d. 1845. 20 Horace Adelbert b. 12 Aug. 1847, d. 24 Mar. 1862, 21. *William M. b. 13 June 1851, 22. *Ira Ernest b. 5 Feb. 1861, 23. Nancy Redding Egan (2nd wife) md. 1846 at Nauvoo d. 3 Apr. 1892 **Chil: 24.** *Helen J. b. 25 Aug. 1847, 25. Vilate L. b. 13 Oct. 1849, d. 1866. 26. Mrs. Mary Egan

(3rd wife) md. 1849. Chil: 27. *Hyrum Wm. b. 24 July 1850 in Utah No. 17 and 18 in Salem, Mass. 19 in Nauvoo 20 and 24 in Winter Quarters 21, 22 and 25 in Salt Lake City.

Four sons of Howard and Tamson Egan, all living. Standing: Eldest son Howard R., and youngest son Ira E. Sitting, on the right: R. Erastus, left, Wm. M. Egan. Following is the descendants.

17. Howard Rausom Egan, md. 10 Oct. 1864, 28. Amanda Andrus b. 19 Nov. 1847. Chil. Annie T. b. 1 Aug. 1864, d. 1908, 30.. *Julia J. b. 22 Aug. 1866, d. 1888, 31. *Howard M. b. 28 Nov. 1868, 32. *Mary b. 28 June 1871, d. 1914, 33. * William J. b. 24 Aug. 1873, 34. *John R. b. 22 July 1875, 35 Linnie J. b. 9 Dec. 1877, 36 * Charles E. b. 23 June 1880, 37. * George E. b. 9 July 1883, 38. * H. Walter b. 27 August 1885, 39. * James A. b. 16 Feb. 1888, 40. * Inis P.

b. 7 Mar. 1890. No. 29 and 30 Born in Salt Lake No. 31 at Deep Creek, the rest at Richmond, Cache Co.

18. Richard Erastus Egan, md. 1861, 41. Mary Minnie Fisher b. 1844 d. 1887. Chil: 42. *Tamson M. b. 2 Mar. 1863, 43 * Erastus H. 10 Sept. 1864, 44. Harry O. b. 2 Oct. 1866 d. 1879, 45. Hoarce F. 2 Nov. 1867, 46. * John L. b. 4 Oct 1870, 47. William F. b. 5 Apr. 1872, 48. Willard R. b. 5 Apr. 1872, 49 Joe. R. b. 7 Sept. 1874, 50. * Ira I. b. Sept. 1875, 51 *Linnie J. b. 25 Feb. 1878, 52. * Mary b. 5 Feb. 1880, 53. * Charles M. b. 27 Aug. 1881, 54. * David b. 13 July 1884. No. 42 born in Salt Lake City Nos. 43, 44, 46, 47, 48, 49, and 50 born in Ruby Valley, 51, 52, 53 and 54 born in Bountiful, Davis County. 55, Mary Beatrice Noble Egan, (2nd wife) md. 1889 b. 10 Nov. 1864. Chil: 56. Harold E. b. 23 May 1890, 57. *Ora May b. 16 Feb. 1892, 58. * Nellie L. b. 25 Apr. 1894, 59. Erma A. b. 19 Oct. 1896, 60. Byron Noble b. 26 May 1900. 61 How-

Ira Ernest Egan,
Youngest son of Howard Egan.
Smithfield, Utah

Hyrum Wm. Egan,
son of Howard and Mary Egan. His
widow's address, Berley, Ida.

ard N. b. Nov. 1904. 62. Richard N. b. 8 Apr. 1907. The first six born in Bountiful, last in Byron, Wyoming.

21. William M. Egan, md. 1886, 63. Ruth Nichols b. 7 Feb. 1840. Chil: her's six. She was born in Chatham, Kent Eng.

22 Ira Ernest Egan md. 1882, 64. Emma Moss, b. in Australia Chil. 65. * Effie J. b. 1883, 66 * Emma Myrtle b. 1886, 67. Ernest L. b. 1888, d. yg. 68. Ira E. b. 14 July 1889, 69. Jeanne T. b. 1893, d. yg. All born in Salt Lake City.

24. Helen Jenet Egan md. 1886, 70. John K. Irvine b. 3 Jan. 1844 Chil: John b. 7 Feb. 1867, Howard G. b. 23 Mar. 1869, Helen N. b. 21 Nov. 1871. Wm. E. b. .12 Jan. 1874, Clarence E. b. 10 Dec. 1877, Maud M. b. 29 Oct. 1880, Luella. A. b. 9 Sept, 1883, Robert L. b. 19 Sept. 1886. All born in Salt Lake City.

27. Hyrum William Egan, md. 1871, 71. Mary Salome Preator b. 18 May 1851. Chil: Hyrum L. L. b. 30 Nov. 1872, 73 * Theresa E. b. 21 Jan. 1875. 74. Mary E. b. 8 Nov. 1883. 75. Vida V. b. 14 Feb. 1886. First two born in Deep Creek, last two in Bason, Idaho.

FIRST BRANCH; FAMILY OF NO. 17 THEIR MARRIAGES AND CHILDREN.

29. Annie Tamson Egan, md. 1884, 76. Freeman Burnham. Chil Nora T. b. 14 Mar. 1885, Afton b. 22 Mar. 1887, Ada, b. 26 Sep. 1888, Pauline b 8 Apr. 1891. Howard A. b. 4 Apr. 1893, Mildred 22 Apr. 1895, Walace F. b. 26 Jan. 1897, Donald J. b. 12 Nov. 1899, Arthur H. b. 7 Sept. 1900, Mourice L. b. 11 Sept. 1903 Harold L. b. 14 July 1906, Wayne E. b. 27 June 1908. First three at Richmond next two at Ogden, the rest at Salt Lake City.

30. Julia Jane Egan, md. 1883, 76. W. R. Tripp b. in Salt Lake City. Chil: Effie P. b. 7 Feb. 1884, Julia A. b. 26 May 1887, d. Inft. Both born in Richmond, Utah.

31. Howard Milo Egan, md. 1892, 77. Laura Hill of Richmond Chil: 78: Milo H. b. 14 Sept 1893, 79. Edna L. b. 22 Sept. 1895, 80. Wm. R. b. 24 Nov. 1897, 81. Russel b. 23 Nov. 1899. 82. Winnie I. b. 1 Sept. 1901, 83. Hoarce D. b. 22 Mar. 1903, 84. Lee L. b. 13 Jan. 1906, 85. Arnold F. b. 13 Mar. 1908 All born in Richmond Utah

32. Mary Elizabeth Egan, md. 1893, 86. Walter J. Hill of Richmond. Chil: Leonard W. b. 22 Sept 1895, Coila L. b. 18 May 1898, Mary G. b. 7 Sept 1905, d. 1906. Born in Richmond Utah.

33. William Ira Egan, md. 1897, 87. Mary Chatterton of Richmond. Chil: 88. Phebe L. b. 20 Nov. 1898, 89. William b.

1900, d. 1900 90 Mary P. b. 10 Mar. 1903, md. (2nd wife)
91. Mary M. Gunter **Chil**: (2nd wife) 92. Loren b. 16 Feb.
1910, 93. Alva b. 1912. All born in Richmond, Utah.

34. John Ransom Egan, md. 1897, 94 Annie C. Smith b. 1877.
Chil: 95. Annie V. b. 9 July 1898, 96 Carlos R. b. 12 Oct.
1899, 97. Hoarce R. b. 27 Jan. 1901, 98. Flossie L. b. 14 Sept.
1902, 99. David D. b. 6 Oct 1904, 100. Howard V. b. Feb.
1906, 101 Amanda C. b. 3 June 1909. All born in Richmond, Utah.

35. Linnie June Egan, md. 1897, 102 Riley Bair of Richmond
Chil: Howard Bair b. 25 June 1898, Gertrude b. 24 Aug. 1899,
Ivan L. b. 24 Aug 1901, Maurice L. b 17 Aug. 1903, Doris
b. 17 Aug. 1903, Riley R. b. 3 April 1905. Walter A. b.
14 March 1907, Richard E. b. 12 Dec. 1910. Elmo E. b.
2 Feb. 1913, Glen G. b. 24 Feb. 1915. All born in Richmond
except Maurice L. in Rexburg, Idaho.

36. Charles Erastus Egan, md. 1911, 103 Paula Krupa of Ger-
many.

37. George Ernest Egan, md. 1902, 104. Minnie Hope of Richmond. **Chil**: 105. Nada I. b. 12 Feb. 1904, 106. Edith E. b.
8 March 1905, 107 Delbert E. b. 14 Apr. 1907. 108 Alta L.
L. b. 1 Feb. 1910, 109 Millie b. May 1913. All born in
Richmond, Utah.

38. Hoarce Walter Egan, md. 1912, 110. Anna B. Tengberg
Chil: 111. Myrtle A. b. 20 Nov. 1912 in Preston Idaho. 112.
Inis B. b. 19 Aug 1914 in Tremonton, Utah.

39. James Alva Egan, md. 1911, 113. Zina G. Christensen
Chil: 114 Merlin A. b. 29 Sept. 1912, 115 Thelda Z. b. 8 May
1914. Children born in Richmond.

40. Inis Percilla Egan, md. 1907, 116. N. E. Maben of Richmond.
Chil: Inis V. Maben b. 23 Jan 1910 in Richmond, Utah.
*In addition to those given above of this branch, (the
children of No. 17 Nos. 29 to 40 Inclusive), there were five
grand children married and ten great grand children born
but no details were given.

SECOND BRANCH; FAMILY OF NO. 18 THEIR MARRIAGES AND CHILDREN.

42 Tamson Minnie Egan, md. 1888, 117. William Marshall b. in
Bountiful.. **Chil**: William E. Marshall b. 2 Apr. 1889, Darell
b. 24 July 1891, Minnie L. b. 8 Dec. 1896. First two born in
Bountiful last Randolph.

43. Erastus Howard Egan, md. 118. Alice Moss of Bountiful
Chil: Erastus: 119 Howard E. b. 19 June 1890, 120 Christie
b. 21 Aug. 1891, 121. Clifford J. b. 25 Jan. 1897, 122. Minnie

R. b. 6 Mar 1900, 123. Ethel W. b. 1902. All born in Prospect, Idaho, except 1st born in Bountiful.

45. Horace Fredrick Egan, md. 1891, 124. Eveline E. Benson Chil: 125. Horace Fred. Jr. b. 23 Sept 1892, 126. John Perry b. 23 Mar. 1894, 127. Minnie E. b. Feb. 1896, 128. May b. 9 Nov. 1898, d. yg. 129. Loyd B. b. 5 July 1900, 130. Neva b. 24 Mar. 1909, 131. Rodney, b. 1913. First born in Bountiful, next three in Skelton, Bingham Co. Idaho, next in Willow Creek, last two in Salt Lake City.

46. John Leroy Egan, md. 1896, 132. Millie Benson Chil: 133. Elsie b. 26 July 1897, 134. Leroy B. b. 9 Dec. 1899, 135. Carlos B. b. 25 Sept. 1901, 136. Alta b. 7 Apr. 1903, 137. Mabel b. 6 Feb. 1905, 138. Ezra B. b. 14 Jan. 1907, 139. Lucille b. 14 Nov. 1909, 140. Wren B. b. 1 Aug. 1911, 141. John B. b. Apr. 1913, 142. Lyle B. b. 3 June 1915. First five born in Bountiful, last five in Byron, Wyo.

48. Willard Richard Egan, md. 1901, 143. Lelis Sessions. Chil: 144. Vera S. b. 21 Jan. 1902, 145. Minnie b. 29 May 1903, 146. Linnie b. 29 May 1903. All born in Bountiful, Utah.

50. Ira Irvin Egan, md. 1898, 147. Margaret R. Colvin Chil: 148. Ira O. b. 30 Nov. 1899, 149. Rozelle b. 12 Aug. 1902, 150. Lorin R. b. 25 Aug. 1904, 151. Wanda b. 25 Sept. 1906, 152. David M. b. 26 Sept. 1908. First three born in Eden, Utah last two born in Byron, Wyo.

51. Linnie June Egan, md. 1900, 153. Robert A. Moss Chil: Emma L. b. 18 Feb. 1907, Robert D. b. 10 Dec. 1908. Born in Salt Lake City.

52. Mary Adelade Egan, md. 1901, 154. Oscar J. Evans Chil: McClellan J. Evans b. 10 Sept. 1902, Oral J. b. 4 June 1905, Iris b. 10 Sept. 1907, Oscar E. b. 9 Apr. 1909, Alta M. b. 6 Apr. 1910, Durell E. b. 20 Nov. 1911, Baby b. 14 Apr. 1914. All born in Randolph, Wyo.

53. Charles Merit Egan, md. 1906, 155. Clara R. Hatch Chil: 156. Mary E. b. 3 Aug. 1907, 157. Charles S. b. 3 Jan. 1910, 158. Delbert H. b. 14 Sept. 1913. Born in Salt Lake City

54. David Egan, md. 1907, 159. Elizabeth Easton Chil: 160. Harold E. b. 26 July 1908, 161. David E. b. 9 Dec. 1909, 162. Florence b. 25 Feb. 1911, 163. Laura b. 4 Dec. 1912, 164. La Rue b. 30 July 1914, 165. Helen b. 23 Dec. 1915. First two born in Byron Wyo. Third in Centerfield the rest in Salt Lake City.

57. Ora May Egan, md.. 7 June 1911, John W. Simmons Chil: Glenn Winn b. 3 Mar. 1912, Raymond E. b. Feb. 1914. born in Byron, Wyoming.

58. Nellie Loretta Egan, md. 11 Sept 1912, Frank J. Sylvester Chil: Louise b. 28 July 1913 at Byron, Wyo.

FAMILY OF NO. 22 THEIR MARRIAGES AND CHILDREN

65. Effie Irene Egan, md. 1904, 166. Milo Andrus **Chil:** Emma
J. b. 1905, Clifford M. b. 1906, Zelda b. 22 Aug. 1912.

66. Emma Myrtle Egan, md. 1907, 167 John W. Pitcher **Chil:**
Stanley J. b. 25 June 1908, Ernest J. b. Feb. 1911, d. June
1911, Adrian b. 10 April. 1912, Vernon b. 12 May 1914.
Born at Smithfield, Utah.

68. Ira Erastus Egan, md. 1912, 168. Annie P. Rudd, **Chil:**
169. Gladio Myrtle b. 13 Nov. 1913 in Salt Lake City,

FAMILY OF NO. 27 THEIR MARRIAGES AND CHILDREN

72. Hyrum L. Egan, md. 1894, 170. Mary L. Kidd **Chil:** 171.
Howard H. b. 4 Feb. 1895, 172. Douglas R. b. Sept. 1896,
173. Mary E. b. 30 Nov. 1897, 174. Troy C. b. 18 Apr. 1899,
175. Edith M. b. 5 Mar 1901, 176 Leonard E b. 6 Sept 1903,
177. Lucy A. b. 6 Sept. 1904, 178. William A. b. 9 Apr. 1907.
First six born in Oakley, last two in Bason, Idaho.

73. Theresa E. Egan, md. 179. Joseph H. Dayley **Chil:** Clara
E. b. 19 Feb. 1893, Joseph M. b. 18 May 1894, James H. b.
14 Oct. 1896, Dewey L. b. 17 Sept. 1898, Emilly T. b. 8 Dec.
1900 Laura b. 17 Nov. 1901, Cora L. b. 6 Dec. 1904, Mary
B. b. 12 Jaan. 1908 Richard L. b. 5 Apr. 1910. Born in Bason,
Idaho.

75. Vida V. Egan, md. 1903, 180. Walter W. Kidd **Chil:** Hazel J.
b. 19 Sept. 1904, Garnet W. b. 20 Jan. 1905, Buel E. b. 14
Apr. 1907, Thurman, A. b. 30 Aug.. 1909 All born in Bason,
Idaho.

Descendants of male line of Howard Egan No. 11 including
     wives and children   **155**
Descendants on Female line of Howard Egan No. 11 including husbands and children none of 2nd generation   **85**

               240

DESCENDANTS OF NO. 4, NO 11's UNCLE.

4. William Egan, md. 1805, 181. Miss Watson **Chil:** 182. *Edward
b. about 1806, in Tullemore, Kings Co. Ireland.

182. Edward Egan, md. a. 1828, 183. Margaret Coffey **Chil:** 184.
*William b. a. 1829, 185. John b. 1831, 186. Margaret
b. a. 1833, 187. Ann b. a. 1835. born in Tullemore, Ireland.

184. William Egan, md. 1857, Maria Murphy, b. a. 1833 **Chil:**
188. Edward b. 9 Aug. 1858 in Tullemore, Kings Co. Ireland
and the last of this line. He is the man standing in the
doorway of old home page 10.

FAMILIES OF SISTERS AND BROTHER OF NO. 11 BROTHER'S CHILDREN.

6. Eliza Egan, md. 1830, 189. Henry Benallack **Chil:** George
b. 25 Dec. 1831, Henry J. b. 14 May 1833, Ann E. b. 9 Mar.
1835, John Howard b. 25 Jan. 1837 d. 1878 John G. b 14

Nov. 1838, Eliza b. 21 Mar 1841, d. 1890 Howard b. 5 May 1843, Maria b. 18 Feb. 18 Feb. 1846. Born in Montreal, Canada.

7. Mary Egan, md. 1833, 190. Adam Higgins b. 1802 Chil: Eliza b. 21 Feb. 1835, Annie b. 1 Mar. 1836 Thomas Wm. b. 1 Sept 1837, Howard Egan b. Nov 1838 Maria b. 1841. Adam b. 1843. Margaret b. 1845 John G. b 22 May 1846. Born in Montreal, Canada.

8. Catherine Egan, md. 1828 191 John Ransom Chil: Annie b. Apr. 1829, Mary b. 17. Oct. 1830, Jane b. 19 Mar. 1832, Eliza b. 19 Mar. 1832, Aaron F. b. 24 Oct 1833, John b. 25 Nov. 1835, Howard b. 5 Feb. 1838, Richard b. 1 Oct 1840. All born in Montreal, Canada.

FAMILY OF NO. 13 THEIR MARRIAGES AND CHILDREN

13. Richard Egan, md. 1841, 192. Maria Stuart Chil: 193. Francis Howard b. 10 Aug. 1843, 194 William J. b. 25 Mar. 1846, 195. Maria b. 22 May 1847, 196. * Richard b. 15 May 1848, 197. Eliza b. 9 July 1850, 198. *Robert b. 28 Oct. 1851, 199 * Henry A. b 20 Mar. 1855, 200. *Maria b. 22 Feb. 1857. All born in Montreal, Canada.

196 Richard Egan, md. 1870, 201 Charlotte Stuart Chil: 202. Henrietta b. 5 July 1871, 203 Maria b. 3 May 1873 204. 204 Beatrice M. b. 8 Apr. 1874, 205. Lilly E. b. 1 Jan 1876, 206. Charlotte F. b. 6 Apr. 1879, 207. Laura G. b. 24 Jan. 1881, 208. Richard W. b. 3 Nov. 1882. All born in Montreal, Canada.

198 Robert Egan, md. 1882, 209. Annie HcCuaig Chil: 210 Annie L. b. 17 May 1883, d. yg. William H. b. 3 Dec. 1884 212 Bertha M. b. 6 May 1887, 213. Malcolm R. b. 25 Dec. 1888. d. yg. 214 Eva M. b. 21 Aug. 1890, 215 Florence R. b. 28 Apr. 1892, d yg. 216. Alice E. b. 28 Apr. 1892, d. yg. 217. John S. b. 20 May 1894, 218. Violet A. b. 28 Mar. 1897. All born in Montreal Canada

199. Henry Adam Egan, md. 1882, 219. Elizabeth Ann Lumsden Chil: 220. Robert F. b. 23 Nov. 1883, 221. Mary H. b. 3 Mar 1886, 222. Lilly S. b. 21 Feb. 1888, 223. Henry A. b. 18 Nov. 1889, 224. James A. b. 15 June 1891, 225. Richard E. b. 31 Mar 1896. All born in. Montreal, Canada.

200 Maria Egan, md. 1877, 226. John Andrew Peard Chil: William H. b. 23 June 1878, Francis A. S. b. 12 Jan. 1881. Edith F. b. Mar. 1882, John T. b. 24 Nov. 1885 Walter P. b. Dec. 1887, John A. L. b. 16 June 2891. All born in Montreal, Canada.

(Serial numbers are applied to those bearing the Egan name and those whom they married only. Those marked with * married and their names appear the second time as head of family.)

*IRISH HISTORY

A little idea of Irish History may be gained by the following brief sketch, which should be read in connection with Genealogy before given:

It was first peopled in the 4th century after the Deluge according to tradition by Parthenius from Japheth stock in the 80th year of the age of Abraham B. C. 2100.

After 300 years in Erin the entire colony of 900 were cut off by a dreadful pestilence.

Nemidius, a distant relative of Partholan 39 years after arrived there 1761 B. C. with 1000 followers. In a short time Ireland was invaded by the Formorians, giants from Africa. They were fought successfully in many engagements, but in the great battle of Tory Island the army of Nemidius was totally destroyed. Those who survived fled, some to the north of Belgium to become the ancestors of the Firbolgs or Bogmen, some wandered to Greece to give parentage to the Tuatha De Danaan, and others escaped to the neighboring island of Britain, which it is said took its name from Briotan, the Nemedan leader who settled there.

The Firbolgs, kept in cruel bondage in Belgium seized the ships of their masters and landed in Ireland B. C. 1397 and in the desisive battle of Tara the Formorian forces were nearly annihilated.

The Firbolgs were in their turn disturbed of their prize 80 years after by the Tuatha De Danaans. Nauida, their king was immediately attacked by his Firbolg's kinsman under their Monarch, Eocha. The battle of Moytura was fierce and bloody, and after six days of the greatest slaughter that was ever heard of in Erin, the victory remained with the Tuatha De Danaans, and they remained in power 200 years.

The last conquerors of Pagan Ireland were called Gael or Gadian from one of their rulers, Gadelas who was bitten by a serpent, but healed by Moses when he was preparing to liberate Israel from Egypt. In gratitude Gadelas supplied Moses and the Children of Israel with provisions after their passage of the Red Sea.

For this they were driven out and settled Phonecia and afterwards in Spain under King Breogan. who had two sons Ith and Bile. The latter was the father of Milesius, who in turn became King of the Colony, called Galicia.

Milesius went back to Egypt and Pharoah gave him the chief command of the Royal Army. He was successful and Pharaoh gave him his daughter Scota in marriage and he returned to Spain.

A dreadful drouth caused King Milesius to send his uncle Ith to seek the most western island of Europe.. Ith set sail with his son Louy and a large force. They soon landed on the Irish coast, were attacked and in a sharp struggle Ith fell and they were forced to retire. Louy barley escaped with a few companions and embarked for home. In the mean time Milesius, after reigning 36 years died, the hero of 1000 battles.

The Milesians, on the return of the expedition, prepared themselves to avenge the death of Ith and conquor Ireland. A fleet of 60 vessels were equipped, and the entire colony embarked under 40 leaders, including the eight sons of Milesius, their Mother Scota and Louy the son of Ith.

"They arrived at Ireland B. C. 1120. Five of the brothers perished before landing. The remaining sons Heber, Hermon, and Amergin with all their attendants effected a landing at last near Sleive Mish Mountain in Kerry. They were attacked by Queen Eire. She was put to flight after loosing 1000 men. The Milesians loosing 300 besides Scota and many chiefs.

After the first advantage, plans were laid which resulted in a decisive battle on the plain of Telton, in Meath. A well contested and bloody battle was fought and the sovereignty of Ireland passed into the hands of the Milesians, and the other dynasties passed away.

Heber and Hermon divided the sovereignty of Ireland between them. The two brothers ruled but a year when Heber's wife influenced him to declare war against Hermon. The two armies met at Geashill near Tullemore, King's County. Hermon was finally victorious and from him through over 100 Monarchs of Ireland we trace our genealogy.

HOWARD EGAN'S TRAVEL
From the Missouri River to the Valley of the Salt Lake in 1849. - Kept by Peter Hanson.

*This paper only recently came into my hands and was too late for insertion in the proper place and we will not now try to reproduce it but only make some notes concerning it.

It seems this was Howard Egan's third trip to Salt Lake. The paper states that the winter was severe until March and that Howard had a hard time of it having to travel most of the time, making preparations for the trip. It states that the company began to gather on the 15th of April 1849, Peter Hanson and others went through Kanesville and on the ninth day arrived at St. Joseph, which was very stirring on account of the "Gold fever" raging there about going to California. Their loads were heavy and the wagons rolled on the hubs for a quarter of a mile through the mud.

Howard Egan sent some goods on a steamboat, by Orson Whitney, up the river, but the boat sunk and Orson, got some help and got out the most part of them. On the 3rd of May Howard Egan with his wife Nancy and child Helen joined the company got them together and made preparations for the journey crossing the Missouri on the 15th of May at Fort Kearny.

On the 16th day of May, the paper states, "Bro. Howard Egan called the company together for the purpose of organizing.

Howard Egan was chosen Captain of the company. Elijah Elmer Captain of the guard and herding. Captains of Tens were
also chosen and a clerk.

A list of the names, ages and equipment of those in the
company are given in detail, showing that there were 57 persons,
6 horses, 3 mules, 97 oxen, 21 cows, 3 young cattle, 21 fowls,
6 dogs, and 22 wagons. The following with their families:
Howard Egan, James Graham, Elijah Elmer, James H. Christ-
man, Phillip Klingensmith, Jackson Clothier, Nathaniel Jones,
Stephen Winchister and most of the rest without families.

They commenced their first long drive the 17th day of May
and on the 19th 3 more wagons joined them, this, however, was
before the account was taken of the company. On the 21st they
met 3 teams of the gold seekers going back home, and more on
the 23rd.

They passed and were passed by other companies and on the
29th got the report that 60 individuals had died with cholera between Independence and Grand Island. Wagons worth $125 were
sold for $15 to $20. Bacon 1 cent per lb. 2000 wagons were at
the crossing of the South Fork of the Platt River.

On the 4th of June a company of U. S. Dragoons passed by
going to Oregon. On the 9th they met Thomas Williams and
Levi Merrill coming from the valley and going to the states.
They had been robbed by the Crow Indians. They saw many
buffalos and killed some. They met Lorenzo Young and others
from the valley on the 12th, also returning gold seakers, one of
whom had been wounded in a row among themselves. On the
27th a list of deaths in Nelsons Company from Diarrhea is given.
On the 30th day they laid up to shoe oxen and Captain Egan rode
on to the ferry on the Platt, where there were many companies
crossing. Some of the troups going to Oregon were trying to
cross. More than half of them had deserted already and about
half of the rest were getting ready to leave.

Captain Egan's company got there July 3rd and it was a
great joy to meet the brethern of other companies ferrying across
Several horses were drowned and several wagons lost. Frederic
Jones was shot while trying to melt out a ball in his gun on the
4th and died on the 8th. On the 12th they reached Independence
Rock. Tires had run off and wheels broke down and many
other troubles had been met and overcome. A large number
of dead cattle were lying along the road. Sister Klingensmith
had a daughter born on the 17th. They camped on the Sweetwater on the 19th and a report was brought to them that the
deserting soldiers were calculating to rob this and Pomeroy's Co.
for provisions. They arrived at Green River on the 25th and
ferried over. Many cattle died with bloody flux.

Captain Egan went on with the mail July 25th. Nat. Jones
had a steer stolen but overtook the thief and took it from him.
Some deserters were taken by Mr. Bridger's men, from whom
they had stolen horses. On the 28th Mrs. N. Jones gave birth
to a boy who died and was buried at Black's Fork.

On the 3rd of Aug. Captain Egan returned with others from the Valley with wagons and ox teams, which gave the company much joy. This was on the Weber River and they commenced their assent up Pratt's Pass. Aug. 7th they went over the mountain and into the valley. "Great Joy" said Peter Hanson as his last words in the Diary.

It will be noticed that Howard Egan made but a short stay in Salt Lake with his family before he commenced his California trip as given on previous pages of this book, and this should have preceeded that trip if we had known of it in time.

EGAN FAMILY ORGANIZATION

A meeting was called for June 15, 1914 and a temporary organization effected and later the following "Circular Letter" was sent out which explains itself:

The desire has been frequently expressed that the Egan Family should be organized, but expressions do not accomplish anything without acting upon them. The wide scattered condition of the family and the difficulty of getting them together made it seem like being almost impossible until a simple easy plan was hit on to reach the desired results without very much trouble to any of them.

A local organization for Salt Lake City and preliminary organization of the whole family was effected June 15th, 1914, in Salt Lake City and only requires the approval of the membership to be final which we hope to obtain by the 100th anniversary of our honored Pioneer, Howard Egan's birth June 15th, 1915, when we hope to have a reunion of all his descendants that can possibly attend.

We are sending this circular letter to each head of family and a copy of the Articles and expect they will submit them to all in their locality, who are interested, and to return their reply to the Gen'l Sec'y H. Fred Egan Jr.   3 Girard Ave., Salt Lake City.

It will be observed that there is absolutely no membership fee and therefore every descendent and those that have married into the family are members without any consideration. There is, however, some duties connected with it whether performed or not. You will notice the objects in view as referred to in the preamble of the Articles of Agreement. We know not how much of those objects we shall be able to accomplish.

Howard R. Egan becomes the President of the organization and has had in contemplation for some time the publishing ot a book, our Father's Journal of 1847, as captain of the 9th, Ten of the chosen 144 to seek a new home for the Latter-day Saints with some of his Biography and genealogy of the family to the present time and has had the work typewritten for that purpose

ARTICLES OF AGREEMENT:
PERPETUAL ORGANIZATION OF THE EGAN FAMILY SOCIETY.

"Whereas the descendants of Howard Egan are desirous of associating themselves for the purpose of social relations, renewal of old family ties and affections, honoring the dead and the living, erecting a monument to the name of our honored pioneer, the head of the family, to do temple and genealogical work and they do hereby certify, declare, and agree as followed that is to say:

FIRST:

The name of the society shall be the Egan Family Society.

SECOND:

Salt Lake shall be the Societys' headquarters, with branches in every place where any of its members may live.

THIRD:

The organization shall be perpetual.

FOURTH:

The membership shall consist of every descendant of Howard Egan and those who have married any of them and their children, any others can only be received by consent of the majority of members.

FIFTH:

The business and social relations that it is agreed to enter into shall be as indicated in the preamble.

SIXTH:

The offcers of the society shall be, a president, vice-presidents, secretaries, and treasurers (general and local) and committee on temple work, and a committee on amusements.

The president shall be the oldest male descendant of Howard Egan in succession, whose duty shall be to preside, but he may appoint a chairman or substitute.

The vice-presidents shall be the oldest male descendant in each locality and each family whose duty shall be to preside over the local branch or family and in the absence of the president shall perform all his duties. It shall be the duty also of the branch and family vice-presidents to receive reports pertaining to the society and comunicate the same to the branch or family and forward reports of all matters pertaining to their branch or family to the general society headquarters.

The secretaries shall be nominated and elected at any meeting of the society or branch, where there is a vacancy of the office, by a majority vote present. The secretary elected in Salt Lake City shall be the general secretary of the society provided that such officer be approved by the branches and families, but shall hold such office until a successor shall be approved. The duty of the general secretary shall be to take the minutes and keep the records of all proceedings of the society. The corresponding secretaries shall be appointed by the secretaries as necessities may require from any willing workers of the society, whose duty shall be to communicate with branches, families, and members and any other correspondence necessary.

The treasurer shall be nominated in the same manner as the secretary, whose duty shall be to receive and care for the donations and disburse all funds by order of the president or vice-presidents according to the desire of those who shall contribute the same.

The committee on Temple work shall consist of three persons, to act for the society. One to act as chairman, one to receive, collect and handle the funds and account for same so all will know what has become of their contributions, and one to act as recorder of family genealogy, whose duty it is to become acquainted with gathering and recording genealogy, with accuracy and care, preparing for the work to be done, and recording the completed work as it progresses. They shall be chosen with care from those best acquainted with the work and approved and sustained by the members. The committee on socials, consisting of three or more, shall be appointed or elected permanently and from time to time as desirable, who shall have in charge the programs of the yearly meetings, the preparations for those gatherings, and other duties common to such officers.

No membership fee shall be required from any member but it shall be considered the duty of every member to contribute according to their means and desire to assist in the temple work, but the actual work will be accepted and credit given in preference to the means of having it done. Regular contributions, if but small is desirable all of which must be carefully accounted for and reports made as to what has been done."

According to the plan and instructions, local organizations were formed in the different places where members of the Egan Family reside, and the Articles of Agreement accepted, and June 15 the re-unions was held with an interested attendance, with a good program and the organization was made permanent and perpetual by unanimously adopting the Articles of Agreement on the hundreth anniversary of Major Howard Egan's birth.

THE END.